*Helping the Bereaved
College Student*

**David E. Balk, PhD,** is a professor in the Department of Health and Nutrition Sciences at Brooklyn College of the City University of New York where he directs Graduate Studies in Thanatology. He is a member of the Editorial Board for *Omega*, and an Associate Editor of *Death Studies*, for which he serves as the Book Review Editor. Dr. Balk is a member of ADEC and of the Mental Health Advisory Board for National Students of AMF. He has taught at Kansas State University, Oklahoma State University, and Brooklyn College. Faculty in the College of Human Ecology at Kansas State University recognized Dr. Balk in 1992 as Outstanding Teacher and in 1995 honored him with the college's Faculty Research Excellence Award; he was elected Faculty Senate President of Kansas State University in 1996. Students in the College of Human Environmental Sciences at Oklahoma State University recognized him in 2004 as Outstanding Undergraduate Academic Advisor in the college. The President of Brooklyn College in 2006 appointed Dr. Balk Chair of the Institutional Review Board.

# Helping the Bereaved College Student

David E. Balk, PhD

SPRINGER PUBLISHING COMPANY
NEW YORK

Springer Publishing Company, LLC
11 West 42nd Street
New York, NY 10036
www.springerpub.com

*Acquisitions Editor:* Sheri W. Sussman
*Senior Editor:* Rose Mary Piscitelli
*Composition:* Newgen Imaging

ISBN: 978-0-8261-0878-4
E-book ISBN: 978-0-8261-0879-1

11 12 13/ 5 4 3 2 1

The author and the publisher of this Work have made every effort to use sources believed to be reliable to provide information that is accurate and compatible with the standards generally accepted at the time of publication. The author and publisher shall not be liable for any special, consequential, or exemplary damages resulting, in whole or in part, from the readers' use of, or reliance on, the information contained in this book. The publisher has no responsibility for the persistence or accuracy of URLs for external or third-party Internet Web sites referred to in this publication and does not guarantee that any content on such Web sites is, or will remain, accurate or appropriate.

**Library of Congress Cataloging-in-Publication Data**
Balk, David E., 1943–
  Helping the bereaved college student / David E. Balk.
    p. ; cm.
  Includes bibliographical references and index.
  ISBN 978-0-8261-0878-4 — ISBN 978-0-8261-0879-1 (E-book)
  1. Bereavement. 2. College students—Psychology. 3. School mental health services.
4. Counseling in higher education.   I. Title.
  [DNLM: 1. Bereavement. 2. Mental Health Services. 3. Student Health
Services. 4. Students—psychology.   BF 575.G7]
  BF575.G7B35 2011
  155.9′37088378198—dc22                                                    2011009766

Special discounts on bulk quantities of our books are available to corporations, professional associations, pharmaceutical companies, health care organizations, and other qualifying groups.

If you are interested in a custom book, including chapters from more than one of our titles, we can provide that service as well.

**For details, please contact:**
Special Sales Department, Springer Publishing Company, LLC
11 West 42nd Street, 15th Floor, New York, NY 10036-8002
Phone: 877-687-7476 or 212-431-4370; Fax: 212-941-7842
Email: sales@springerpub.com

Printed in the United States of America by Gasch Printing

*In Loving Memory of*

*Cleburn Brown and Mary P. Brown*
*1914–1987*     *1918–2010*

*Arnold C. Balk, MD, and Mildred V. Balk*
*1911–1981*     *1914–2010*


*Dedicated to My Wife, Mary Ann Balk*

*My Daughter, Janet Renee Balk*

*And My Sisters,*
*Elaine A. Daugherty and Jeanne M. Boland*

# Contents

*Preface*  *xi*

PART I: PRELUDE TO A DISCUSSION OF HELPING
THE BEREAVED COLLEGE STUDENT

1. Ambushed by Someone's Death      *3*
   Further Reading      *7*

2. What Do We Know About College Students and the
   College Environment?      *9*
   The Dynamic and Diverse Realities of
     Undergraduate Students      *9*
   The Role of the Undergraduate Experience      *10*
   Markers of Individual Development      *14*
   A Digital Generation      *21*
   Help-Seeking Behavior and College Students      *24*
   Concluding Comments      *26*
   Further Reading      *29*

3. What Do We Know About Bereavement
   Following a Death?      *31*
   The Holistic Impact of Bereavement      *31*
   Trajectories of Bereavement      *35*
   Explanations Why Humans Grieve      *38*
   The Two Primary Explanations of Human Bereavement      *39*
   Major Thinking on Coping With Bereavement Since
     Freud and Bowlby      *42*
   Concluding Comments      *58*
   Further Reading      *60*

4. Bereavement Seen as a Stressful Event      *65*
   An Overview About Stress      *65*
   The General Adaptation Syndrome      *66*
   A Model Depicting Human Coping With Stress      *68*
   A Sociocultural Model About Dealing With Stress      *77*

Concluding Comments    *83*
Further Reading    *85*

5. Bereavement and Different Causes of Death    *87*
Causes of Death Reported by Bereaved
   College Students    *90*
Event-Related Factors of a Death Impacting Grief    *90*
Anticipated Deaths    *93*
Unexpected Deaths    *95*
Concluding Comments    *104*
Further Reading    *105*

**PART II: INTRODUCING THE BEREAVED COLLEGE STUDENT**

6. What Do We Know About Bereavement and
College Students?    *109*
The Prevalence of College Student Bereavement:
   Anecdotal Evidence    *110*
The Prevalence of College Student Bereavement:
   The First Round of Empirical Study    *110*
The Prevalence of College Student Bereavement:
   The Second Round of Empirical Study    *114*
Concluding Comments    *117*
Further Reading    *117*

7. Bereavement's Impact on a College Student    *119*
Bereavement Affects People Differently    *119*
The Holistic Impact of Bereavement in the
   Words of College Students    *122*
Family Dynamics and College Student Bereavement    *131*
Concurrent Life Stressors    *132*
Family Resources    *133*
The Family's Perception of the Event    *134*
Family Coping Tasks    *137*
Using a Genogram    *139*
Concluding Comments    *143*
Further Reading    *144*

8. What Bereaved College Students Need    *147*
Ideas From the Great Bereavement Scholars    *147*
The Value of the Holistic Framework    *149*
Some Ways of Helping the Bereaved    *149*
What Bereaved Persons Say They Find Helpful    *152*
Bereaved College Students: What Helped Them
   and What They Wish Were Available    *157*

Bereaved College Students: What Has Proven
   Difficult for Them    *159*
Bereaved College Students: What Has Surprised
   Students About Bereavement    *161*
Concluding Comments    *162*
Further Reading    *163*

**PART III: DOING SOMETHING CONSTRUCTIVE**

9. What Can Happen on Campus    *167*
   Changing the Campus    *168*
   The Mission of the College    *168*
   Student Grassroots Initiatives    *169*
   Faculty Actions    *173*
   Planned Interventions    *174*
   Policy Decisions    *184*
   Concluding Comments    *189*
   Further Reading    *191*

10. Self-Disclosure, Bereavement, and
   College Students    *193*
   Bereavement Research and the Prospects
     of Recovery    *193*
   Instrumental and Intuitive Grievers    *195*
   Jourard and Self-Disclosure    *197*
   Empathy    *198*
   The Role of Acceptance in Fostering Self-Disclosure    *200*
   Story About Myself    *201*
   An Opportunity to Engage in Self-Disclosure    *203*
   Concluding Comments    *204*
   Further Reading    *205*

11. Reflections About Recovery Following Bereavement    *207*
   A Modest Proposal    *207*
   Dislike in Some Circles for the Word *Recover*    *208*
   People Do Recover Following Bereavement    *209*
   Different Meanings of the Word *Recover*    *210*
   Indicators of Recovery From Bereavement Based in Research    *211*
   Concluding Comments    *215*
   Further Reading    *219*

12. Spirituality and College Student Bereavement    *221*
   Assumptive Worlds    *221*
   Meaning Making, Spirituality, and Religion    *225*
   Programs to Promote Spiritual Development in
     College Students    *229*

College Student Bereavement and Spirituality    *233*
Concluding Comments    *237*
Further Reading    *238*

## PART IV: CONCLUSION

**13.** Hope    *243*
The Crux of the Matter    *244*
Making College Student Bereavement Intelligible    *245*
Offering a Reasonable Basis for Campus
    Policies and Procedures    *246*
Providing Conceptual Scaffolding for Interventions    *247*
Some Suggested Next Steps    *247*
Bringing This Book to a Close    *249*
Further Reading    *250*

*Afterword: A Letter to Bereaved College Students*    *253*
*Index*    *259*

# Preface

This book encapsulates a good bit of my professional life: the reading and thinking and teaching I have done as an adult and my conversations with mentors, colleagues, and my wife and daughter. The book represents my efforts to construct a coherent whole of the various threads of my education and professional experiences: philosophy, theology, counseling psychology, program evaluation, thanatology, community mental health, and life in a university.

My appreciation for some contemporary scholars and some mid-20th century intellectuals will be evident. One figure from earlier times, Alexander Leighton, particularly has remained salient for me. I wish more persons remembered and used his ideas about human beings' responses to distress.

The genesis for this book has both a distant and an immediate source. The distant source is twofold: (a) my doctoral work at the University of Illinois, culminating in a dissertation on adolescent bereavement following sibling death; (b) an offer from Joan McNeil, a department colleague at Kansas State University, to survey students in her large undergraduate class about their experiences with death and bereavement. The dissertation allowed me to make my start in thanatology and become known in those early days to other scholars interested in human grieving (for instance, Dennis Klass, Stephen Fleming, and Nancy Hogan). The survey of college students catapulted me into doing research, both descriptive and experimental, about college student bereavement. I had not realized the prevalence of bereavement in the lives of college students. It is correct to say the students at Kansas State University introduced me to the topic that became the research focus of my career as a professor.

The immediate source of my writing the book is a question Jack Jordan asked me at a November 2009 meeting of the Family Bereavement Program at Arizona State University. During a break in the proceedings, Jack asked me, "Why don't you write a book on college student bereavement?" The prospect virtually floored me. It seemed so obvious, and it had never occurred to me. I thought for a second and then said something to the effect, "Yes, I can do that." I thought it would take me four months. It took a bit longer.

At first I thought the book was going to be written primarily for college students. As I began writing chapters and then worked on a prospectus for Springer Publishing Company, it was obvious I was writing for professionals who are in positions to help bereaved students. These persons are college counselors, student services personnel, and campus ministers, for instance. Sheri Sussman, Executive Editor at Springer Publishing Company who has worked with Charles Corr and me on two books we edited, helped me think through the focus for the book. She showed me that my original title, *The Bereaved College Student*, did not quite capture the book I wanted to write.

While I want campus professionals to read this book, I hope the book meets a need expressed by college students. Many students have told me they looked in vain for a book on college student bereavement. I hope that bereaved college students read this book and find it speaks to them.

Illene Noppe sent me an e-mail after looking at the prospectus and suggested I include a letter to the grief-stricken student. Thus, I wrote "A Letter to Bereaved College Students." Jack Jordan wrote me and suggested I include material on bereavement and the family. Thus, I wrote in Chapter 7 the section titled "Family Dynamics and College Student Bereavement." Thanks to the creative people in Brooklyn College's Creative Services Office for drawing Figure 7.1.

Thanks are due to individuals who generously read portions of the manuscript and gave me valuable feedback. These persons are Laura Rabin, Tamina Toray, Robin Paletti, Brook McClintic, Kathleen Axen, and Kenneth Axen. Jeffrey Berman did yeoman's work and read the entire manuscript in a very short turnaround time and gave me feedback on the work as a whole and on every chapter.

The first person I approached when asking for feedback is my best friend, Mary Ann Balk, who also is my wife. She looked long and hard at some of the chapters. She helped me see phrasing that needed to be reframed, and posed difficult questions to ponder regarding my assumptions.

I wish my mother had lived to see this book reach the light of day. She and I talked about the book during the early months of 2010, and I wrote to her more than once about the progress I was making. She hoped the book would do well. She also encouraged me to write a novel that would sell like hotcakes. I intend to assume the pseudonym Charles Dickens. Knowing my mother and our love for one another, I believe she would have been proud of me for this book. I wish she were still here. There are lots of things I want to share with her, and I find myself wanting to share with her often.

*David E. Balk, PhD*
Brooklyn, NY

# I

## *Prelude to a Discussion of Helping the Bereaved College Student*

This part of the book begins with the overall reality of bereavement, a condition that is endemic to being human and that a significant percentage of college students experiences. Few persons recognize that college student bereavement presents a matter of habitual concern on a campus. After the introductory chapter, I focus on contextual matters: the complex growth and development of students over the course of their undergraduate studies; frameworks that offer descriptions and explanations of human responses to the death of someone loved; and the varying impacts that causes of death have on human bereavement. Once these chapters are completed, readers will have a foundation for reading about college students who are bereaved.

# Ambushed by Someone's Death

Life isn't fair. Some persons learn this lesson early, some as early as childhood. Others lead blessed lives, protected from encounters with nasty and emotionally wrenching events for most of their lives. If they did not know before, college students who are grieving the death of a family member or friend have learned that bad things do happen to good people, that at times life is radically unfair.

The death of Nate's mother from brain cancer, the death of Helen's sister in a car accident, the death of Shakera's uncle from a robbery gone very bad taught each person that life is not fair. They learned that irrevocable loss doesn't wait until you are prepared to handle it. It just happens and says, "Deal with me."

Many college students faced with the death of someone they care for are thrown into a maelstrom of emotional and cognitive confusion that challenges core assumptions on what life is about and what it means to live in a moral world. Perhaps the issue has nothing to do with whether life is fair. Perhaps the universe in which we live is simply there, and things happen with no regard for the effects on our lives. Albert Camus, the French essayist who won the Nobel Prize for Literature, wrote that he assumed the universe is neither benign nor malicious, but simply is, and the human struggle is to find meaning in the face of absurdity.

Persons who have assumed that the world is fair have a very hard time with the meaning and purpose of existence when the life of someone they care for is snuffed out. Clearly one of the effects of bereavement is a challenge to the student's assumptive world,[1] a challenge profoundly impacting the formative developmental issues going on in the life of a traditional-aged college student (that is, someone between the ages of 18 and 23).

A researcher in the state of New York uncovered that loss is one of the experiences characteristic of many college students. The types of losses varied, covering such experiences as the breakup of a friendship, the loss of a lifelong dream, the loss of valued possessions, and loss of self-respect. More students mentioned the death of a loved one than any other loss (mentioned by 28.5% of the respondents); the end of a love relationship ranked second (mentioned by 24.3%).

Most persons do not realize the significant proportion of college students who are grappling with bereavement over the death of someone they care for. Numerous surveys on campuses in the United States as well as in Europe and in Australia have reported continually that between 22% and 30% of college students are in the first 12 months of grieving the death of a family member or friend. Conversations with deans of student life and with university counselors have reinforced this finding. In the early 1990s, the initial reaction to this prevalence finding was disbelief. The finding was rejected as a fluke. When repeated surveys produced the same results not only on one campus but on several, people began to take notice. Jon Wefald, the President of Kansas State University, was the first administrator I knew who accurately estimated that the prevalence rate is around 25%. He said he knew it because he had been involved in university issues too long not to know.

It is not simply that many administrators and faculty are unaware of the prevalence of college student bereavement. The bereaved college students themselves are not aware of how many other persons on campus are dealing with grief. One reason for this lack of student awareness must be the discomfort others feel when a person mentions his or her grief, so students keep the story to themselves. What a power for change is lying dormant on college campuses. What if bereaved students knew of each others' existence and decided to do something proactive?

Some programs have emerged here and there as bereaved students decided they would not continue to endure alone and silently. While a person's coping with bereavement ultimately centers on the individual, as one college student grieving her father's death told me, "Why do I have to do this alone?"

It is clear that college students who are not bereaved have some intellectual grasp of the factors facing college students who are grieving. It is also clear that the great majority of persons, whether developing adolescents or mature adults, become very uncomfortable when in the presence of someone who is grieving and either figuratively or literally leave the room as quickly as possible. One strategy is simply to change the subject or ignore what the other person has said, but only after a truly noticeable and awkward silence.

Who among us has had the emotionally disjointed experience of sharing something very personal with another person only to have that person change the subject? Bereaved college students learn early that others do not want to hear about their loss, and if they don't curb such sharing they discover they will lose their friends. Outsiders to grief have no patience for how long bereavement lasts nor do they have courage in the face of the intensity of someone's grief. Consider this story told me by a student I will name Sarah.

> Sarah was in the middle of her junior year when her younger brother was killed in a car accident. It was now 10 months later, and Sarah had just landed a job at a popular bar near the campus. It was her first day at the job, and she was helping set up for the influx of customers around 5 PM.
>
> She was working with two male college students she had met at her job. They were getting to know one another as they set up the place. "What are you studying?" "Do you live in the dorms or off campus?" "Where are you from?" "Do you have any brothers or sisters?"
>
> When asked that last question, Sarah said "I had a younger brother Jimmy. He died in a car wreck about 10 months ago." And the two young men simply left the room.

What we know is that few persons who have dealt with bereavement fear being around someone who is grieving; in fact, I have not met one in my research with bereaved high school and college students.[2] We also know that undergraduates have some knowledge of how bereavement affects people, such as the emotional and interpersonal impact, the duration of grief, and efforts to cope with bereavement.

Why would bright college students with some awareness of the demands placed on grieving peers avoid talking with them? Three explanations come to mind.

1. They don't see they have any responsibility to respond. They recognize the other person is in pain, but that does not mean they should interact with that person. Interaction leads to commitment, and those entanglements are to be avoided. An analogy is offered by the common avoidance of many persons when faced with homeless individuals seeking spare change. Thus, one answer for lack of responsiveness to college students who are grieving is "I have no responsibility here, and I do not want to get involved."

2. Another explanation is that the bereaved individual's intense pain overwhelms some persons, and they become confused and disorganized. They would like to respond, but in effect they become socially paralyzed, unable to respond.

3. A third explanation is that some persons are aware of the individual's grief, but they don't know how to share their awareness. They don't understand how to share in words what they know about the person's grief. They may say something they consider inept, such as, "I know how you feel."

A matter of concern for me is that there are persons who feel a mission to help persons who are bereaved without understanding the intensity and duration of grief or not accepting that approaches to grieving differ. They know very little about the person's story, but they intend to fix the problem; they want to eliminate the other person's pain. They, in short, want to be this person's friend in the worst way. Actually, the compassion that often motivates these well-intentioned healers is a resource worth cultivating. A start in such an effort will be educating about the prevalence of college student bereavement, about the impact bereavement has on college students, and about the various models that have emerged to explain the process of grieving.

Not all is bleak. On every campus, there are undergraduates with social and emotional maturity. These individuals will respond positively to learning how to interact beneficially with grieving peers. An education program to train these persons is feasible and well within the resources of a college or university.

Finally, there is the 22–30% of the student body in the first year of bereavement. Some will welcome the opportunities offered by support groups. These groups can be run by licensed counselors, by interested faculty, by trained nonbereaved students, or by bereaved students themselves. Such outreach to bereaved students provides one example of how a university can offer something of value to students whose grief endangers their continued presence and success on campus.

This book is about the phenomenon of college student bereavement over the death of a family member or friend. In the following chapters, I look at what we know about bereavement, what we know about college students, what we know about bereavement in the lives of college students, what bereaved college students need, what colleges can do, and the place of self-disclosure when bereaved. Other topics include what recovery from bereavement means and the interplay between bereavement and spirituality.

All other books and journal articles I have written are filled with textual citations to sources. This book is different. The only citations in any chapters are for the few direct quotes I have used. At the end of each chapter you will find references pertinent to the information I have presented.

## NOTES

1. Simply put, a person's assumptive world encompasses what the person takes for granted about reality. In Chapter 12, I discuss the place of assumptive worlds for coping with bereavement.
2. Kathleen Axen, Professor of Health and Nutrition Sciences at Brooklyn College and a colleague in my academic department, mentioned she knows women grieving the death of a child who avoid being with other women who are grieving the same kind of loss.

## FURTHER READING

Balk, D. E. (1997). Death, bereavement, and college students: A descriptive analysis. *Mortality, 2,* 207–220.

Balk, D. E. (2008). Grieving: 22 to 30 percent of all college students. In H. L. Servaty-Seib & D. J. Taub (Eds.), *Assisting bereaved college students. New Directions for Student Services,* Number 121 (pp. 5–14). San Francisco, CA: Jossey-Bass.

Barnett, M. A., Thompson, M. A., & Pfeiffer, J. R. (1985). Perceived competence to help and the arousal of empathy. *Journal of Social Psychology, 125,* 679–680.

Camus, A. (1955). *The myth of Sisyphus and other essays* (J. O'Brien, Trans.). New York: Vintage Books.

Camus, A. (1963). *Notebooks* (J. O'Brien, Trans.). New York: Knopf.

Janoff-Bulman, R. (1993). *Shattered assumptions: Towards a new psychology of trauma.* New York: The Free Press.

Kauffman, J. (Ed.). (2001). *Loss of the assumptive world: A theory of traumatic loss.* New York: Routledge.

LaGrand, L. E. (1986). *Coping with separation and loss as a young adult: Theoretical and practical realities.* Springfield, IL: Charles C. Thomas.

Servaty-Seib, H. L., & Taub, D. J. (Eds.). (2008, Spring). *Assisting bereaved college students. New Directions for Student Services.* Number 121.

Vickio, C. J., Cavanaugh, J. C., & Attig, T. W. (1990). Perceptions of grief among university students. *Death Studies, 14,* 231–240.

# 2

## What Do We Know About College Students and the College Environment?

### THE DYNAMIC AND DIVERSE REALITIES OF UNDERGRADUATE STUDENTS

College students comprise one of the most studied groups of persons in the world and are convenient research participants for the innumerable investigations directed by university faculty and graduate students. To offer but a small set of examples, on my campus alone in the past few years, there have been research studies examining college students' compulsive shopping, Asian American college students' use of the Internet for managing depression, sex differences in dating preferences, and the influence of subliminal messages about atheism on thoughts about religion.

College students in the United States represent the diversity of cultures, religious beliefs, nationalities, races, ethnic identities, and ages. It is no longer a cause for notice that a significant proportion of college students are female, nor does it seem out of place for there to be mixed-racial couples on the campus. With federal support in the form of Pell Grants and with the vigorous pursuit that colleges engage in to attract students with high academic potential, college is no longer the domain primarily for the affluent or for males from the majority culture. The social changes that marked the United States in the latter half of the 20th century—civil rights and gender equality—have dramatically found a lasting presence on college campuses.

I noted that college students come from many age groups, and thus we have in simplified terms traditional and nontraditional students. The traditional students are individuals between the ages of 18 and 23. While recognizing that a notable portion of students are in the nontraditional group, I have restricted my comments to the traditional-age group.

This age group comprises the last phase of adolescent development, namely, later adolescence. Significant developmental changes are expected of 18- to 23-year-olds. These young men and women have negotiated with varying degrees of success the normative tasks anticipated of early and middle adolescents. By this time, we expect the later adolescent has dealt with forming an emotional identity separate from his (or her) parents and has gained greater insight into her (or his) personal identity. By later adolescence, we expect young adults will accomplish three major developmental tasks: (a) determining a career choice; (b) entering into lasting adult friendships; and (c) forming an autonomous self. Young men and women choose many venues, such as the armed forces, the world of work, and college, within which to accomplish these later adolescent development tasks.

## THE ROLE OF THE UNDERGRADUATE EXPERIENCE

What do we know about the role of the undergraduate experience on the development of college students? In at least four overarching ways, the undergraduate experience offers college students opportunities to grow and develop. These four ways are (a) living away from home and the supervision of parents, (b) interacting with faculty and with peers from varied backgrounds, (c) becoming intellectually stimulated, and (d) becoming more aware of diversity. There are puzzling gender differences in the impacts of the undergraduate experience on college students.

### Puzzling Gender Differences

Gender differences have surprisingly been found in students' responses to these four overarching ways that college impacts student development. For instance, there seems a distinct, positive link between the distance of females' homes from college and the females' growth in confidence and well-being; males' sense of well-being and confidence is not linked to geographical distance from parents. One supposition is that Western socialization has already prompted and encouraged males even before they go to college to separate emotionally from parents.

Female undergraduates' sense of well-being and academic confidence have been found much more than males' to be contingent on constructive faculty feedback. On the whole, females who challenge a faculty member's ideas in a class lecture show increases in stress, whereas males who do the same show a decrease. Perhaps the stress outcomes have also to do with how the faculty members respond to challenges from females and from males. Female undergraduates who are not taken seriously by their professors, for instance, exhibit downturns in academic ambitions and even in their physical well-being; males do not.

Evidence overwhelmingly supports the conclusion that students learn more when they are engaged in their studies. Studying pays off for both males and females. No one I have read or talked with believes otherwise. However, it is discomforting to learn from research that males profit more than do females from academic engagement, particularly in terms of academic confidence, attributions of success, motivations and aspirations to achieve, and thinking critically. The results encompass a host of examples: duration of time spent on studying, working on class assignments, reading over notes before class, and preparing for class, in general.

At every institution of higher education where I have taught, pluralism and diversity are valued. Cultural diversity was more difficult to come by at Kansas State University and at Oklahoma State University than at Brooklyn College, New York: You don't have to promote cultural diversity at Brooklyn College; you simply wade through it. However, the core belief at each institution was the same: Engaging students' encounters with cultural diversity is liberalizing, maturing, and beneficial. Research indicates that men benefit more than women from such encounters; that is, they become more motivated favorably about the values of cultural diversity and show more gains than do women in such fundamental college objectives as critical thinking skills, core beliefs, and academic achievement.

I for one am at a loss to understand these gender differences. Many of my undergraduate and graduate students have been females, with academic performances that range from superior to mediocre. The best students I have ever taught—at Kansas State University, at Oklahoma State University, and at Brooklyn College—are all females. (Note: I have been privileged to teach some gifted male students as well in each institution.) If the research findings about gender differences on effects of college on student development are correct, then the issue speaks to socialization before students get to college; the issue also speaks to practical interventions on college campuses to counter the insidious effects of gender discrimination. I am loath to accept that the differences reported are due to a fundamental disparity due to gender. You know those old and tired arguments about women not being able to do math or science or be great artists or even to be political leaders.

## Goals of an Undergraduate Education

The two critical goals of an undergraduate education are (a) fostering the students' development so that individuals become self-directed, autonomous, productive, and well-educated and (b) enabling individuals to become engaged in activities beyond their own private interests. Successful undergraduate colleges have a clear vision regarding academic requirements and guide students toward mastery of a major field of study and proficiency in language skills, breadth of understanding, connecting ideas, and applying knowledge to the world outside the college. Colleges intend to expand the horizons of undergraduates by exposing them to a major program of study and to a general education in which dogmas and prejudices are confronted and by preparing them for participating in society as educated adults.

Colleges help students build a sense of meaning and of purpose by offering intentional programs (primarily programs of study in various majors and in general education) and in a legion of infrastructure features that address students holistically. Examples of these infrastructure features include academic advising, student counseling, and recreational facilities. Building student engagement in college life is the major mechanism whereby colleges most impact students to build a sense of meaning and of purpose. Unless students become engaged, the college has marginal influence on them. Knowing this contingency has led to reflections on how colleges foster student engagement.

## Fostering Student Engagement

Colleges that notably impact student engagement are marked by four characteristics, such as an explicit vision on the values and mission of the place, a sense of community, a quality curriculum, and cocurricular (previously called "extracurricular") commitments. These four characteristics shape student engagement and promote holistic development of the student.

## Vision

A college's vision of itself remains but empty phrases until connected to a strategic plan that ties values and purpose into a blueprint with markers for attainment of goals. The college's strategic plan is mostly unknown to many students and faculty, but it provides the organizational schema for creating a culture that fosters student engagement.

## Sense of Community

Belonging to a definite human group is one feature of community, is an essential part of what humans strive to achieve, and is clearly a primary means of engaging students. Feeling included and feeling that one matters lead to greater engagement and participation. A college's sense of community takes in all the relationships and interactions that develop on the campus and the engagement of the college with individuals, groups, and organizations beyond the campus. Community service off-campus is one of the primary indicators of colleges that successfully promote students to grow cognitively, emotionally, interpersonally, and spiritually.

This sense of community on a college campus works itself out in a hierarchy of organizational purposes that starts with providing a safe environment, moves into offering a host of opportunities for becoming involved, and converges into an eventual seamless experience of belonging and commitment. One can see parallels between this organizational hierarchy for actualizing successful learning environments and Maslow's hierarchy of needs for actualizing psychological fulfillment.

## Curriculum

A quality curriculum taught by expert faculty is what most of us think about when we consider the chief indicator of a good college. Curriculum programs that influence students engage them cognitively and affectively. The student becomes more adept with such higher critical thinking skills as applying information, analyzing complex data, synthesizing coherent accounts of what otherwise remain disconnected ideas, and evaluating the merit and worth of ideas and programs. In addition, students become more open to receiving disparate points of view and building their own core set of beliefs and standards whereby to form judgments. The best college curricula challenge students to become active learners, to connect seemingly disparate points of view, and to consider knowledge in light of their personal experiences. The best college courses challenge students, and most students acknowledge they expect to be challenged in college courses and they despise watered down versions of college material.

*Cocurriculum*

What once was called extracurricular and is now termed cocurricular is another of the fundamental ways good colleges engage students and promote their development. A college's cocurriculum includes both activities and places. Cocurriculum activities include, for instance, student organizations on campus, informal study sessions, athletic events, and activity affecting the community beyond the campus. Cocurriculum places include the very architecture of the campus and such specifics as classrooms, faculty members' offices, the library, the gyms, the student union, and on some campus chapels and other places of prayer and worship.

## MARKERS OF INDIVIDUAL DEVELOPMENT

We now turn to six markers of individual development of traditional-age college students during their undergraduate years. These makers are (a) identity formation, (b) intellectual growth, (c) moral reasoning, (d) career choice, (e) faith conciousness, and (f) interpersonal relationships.

### Identity Formation

The central developmental task for adolescents is identity formation. It is not as though persons are blank slates or mindless bodies prior to entering puberty. However, the dramatic changes that occur physically, cognitively, emotionally, and socially during the adolescent years have led to a paradigm that identity formation is the salient overarching issue for persons in this stage of the life span.

Erik Erikson is the major thinker who has influenced scholars and clinicians since the early 1950s about adolescent identity formation. He proposed, actually, that growth in personal identity is a lifelong journey, centered on crises and corollary commitments endemic to each part of the life span. The sense of crisis during adolescence fixes on the process of self-discovery, with the ultimate stake being either the formation of a clear identity or the malformation of a vague sense of self (that is, a confused identity).

The pitfalls facing an adolescent in the crisis of self-discovery are twofold. First, by selecting too quickly, the adolescent may settle on a path approved by others rather than one the adolescent has personally chosen. Erikson called this pitfall "identity foreclosure," a choice ruling out exploring options and excluding experiences necessary to make a personal commitment to the self the adolescent wants to become.

The second pitfall is called "identity confusion" (sometimes called "identity diffusion"). Persons who develop this form of self-identity actually avoid making decisions; they drift through life without lasting commitments to anyone or to any values. Adolescents in identity confusion are usually self-centered, emotionally immature, rootless, and lacking any lasting friendships.

Erikson said the adolescent's journey to identity must include a phase of "psychological moratorium," that is, an extended time allowing the adolescent to experiment with possible roles without the pressure to fulfill excessive obligations. This moratorium is healthy and adaptive, and in the eyes of many scholars marks one of the essential characteristics of the undergraduate years. By offering a psychological moratorium, college enables an adolescent to explore options and gain the basis for a fulfilled identity, in many places called an "achieved identity."[1]

The desired end results of a moratorium are (a) a sense of purpose and (b) a sense of continuity in one's life. Erikson called this continuity "fidelity," that is, faithfulness to the person of one's past, one's present, and one's future. Fidelity to one's sense of self is particularly threatened during adolescence because of the physical, cognitive, emotional, and social changes the person experiences. Add in the death of a friend or family member during adolescence, and one can see the potential threat to identity formation; however, my experience and my research as well as the work of other researchers have indicated that the great majority of bereaved adolescents weather these blows from bereavement and emerge more mature than their nonaffected peers.

## Intellectual Growth

Do college students grow intellectually? Longitudinal studies of students on many campuses uncovered evidence demonstrating intellectual growth attributable to the undergraduate years. This growth was found in writing skills, thinking critically, engaging in reflexive judgment, and handling conceptual complexity.

### Using Writing Skills

College seniors do considerably better on tests of writing than do freshmen. Analyses indicate that these results cannot be explained as the results of differing academic aptitude or due to simple maturation over time. These results have been uncovered in studies stretching back to the 1970s, including the present day.

## Thinking Critically

Critical thinking involves the higher order cognitive skills of interpreting, evaluating, and synthesizing information. It also involves basing judgments on evidence rather than on personal preference. In addition, critical thinking involves making judgments about the logic and substance of arguments for or against a position. A mark of mature critical thinking is the knack to present reliably and thoroughly the viewpoints of persons with whom one disagrees, and not caricaturing those ideas in order to make it easy to rebut obvious mistakes.

Numerous studies conducted at several colleges have demonstrated gains in critical thinking during the college years. The pattern of significant results all showed the same mold: Statistically significant gains in critical thinking, not only among 18- to 23-year-olds but also among adults who returned to college as nontraditional students.

## Engaging in Reflective Judgment

An influential model of college students' intellectual growth suggests that students perceive knowledge and learning in one of three divergent ways: They adopt a dualist, relativist, or committed relativist position. Dualists are interested in facts, do not consider that shades of meaning exist, believe that facts are true or false, and understand answers to be correct or incorrect. Rather than a changing, evolving body of understanding, knowledge is seen as stable, unchanging, and true for dualists. Connections between disparate ideas are difficult for dualists to comprehend, and synthesizing information to form theories is beyond their scope. A semester or two at college is usually sufficient to shake dualists' confidence and get them searching. They emerge eventually as relativists.

Relativists have reached a more advanced stage of intellectual development than dualism. Relativists engage in a more critical, skeptical approach to claims about truth and to claims based on tradition or on authority. They look for evidence. They appreciate that several sides can exist to a story and that alternative points of view compete for allegiance. They appreciate that some ideas explain reality better than other ideas, and that all ideas are open to revision. Because all ideas are open to revision, choosing which ideas to endorse becomes a problem for relativists. They see no basis for choosing one position over another. They are convinced that relativism is correct, and they can show the subtlety of arguments for and against a position, but make no commitment to a position other than relativism.

The tipping point out of relativism and into committed relativism would appear to be a variety of challenges from peers and teachers, perhaps even from family members. There is a slippery smugness to relativism, and others begin to challenge the student to express what she (or he) believes to be the case, not just to tell all the various positions one can hold on an issue. Thus, social interaction plays a role in moving a person toward developing his (or her) core set of beliefs and personal evaluation of issues. The relativist moves into a committed relativist stance.

Committed relativists have achieved a level of intellectual growth beyond that of relativism or dualism. In addition to being able to reason abstractly and to compare competing points of view, committed relativists make evaluations based on their reasoning. Unlike dualists who consider facts to be right or wrong, committed relativists see the ambiguity in knowledge, the need to remain open to new information, and the strength of persuasive arguments. Unlike relativists who accept that alternate views of reality are normative but choose none as more persuasive than others, committed relativists weigh evidence and choose a position. The pluralism in competing claims does not overwhelm committed relativists, but rather they winnow claims, evaluating their persuasive power and forming personal decisions about what is the truth. Committed relativists take stands, though remaining open to new evidence that may require reevaluating what they have endorsed. Committed relativists recognize that intellectual inquiry requires taking risks, and that these risks expose one to change.

Several studies have demonstrated growth from dualism to committed relativism in the undergraduate years. These gains are found particularly in reasoning about issues that possess no correct, verifiable answers. These are the sorts of problems one encounters as part of human existence (for instance, poverty, abortion, evil, and suffering, and the existence of God). Gains in reflective judgment do not seem attributable to academic aptitude or to growing older (sometimes called maturation) but rather to the continued exposure to the challenges provided in formal education at the undergraduate level.

### Handling Conceptual Complexity

An overarching standard for assessing cognitive growth is the extent to which an individual can produce plausible criteria for ordering and judging distinctions between ideas, can engage in nuanced evaluations of subtle associations between ideas and between phenomena (for instance, biochemistry and efforts in stem cell research or between political science and local government initiatives), and can combine these disparate ideas into a meaningful whole. Evidence from several researchers indicates that college enables undergraduates to handle conceptual complexity more proficiently as they proceed through their studies.

## Moral Reasoning

The majority of adolescents and adults use conventional moral reasoning principles. In other words, they comply with and uphold societal rules and expectations. They reason it is correct to uphold these rules and expectations because of what is in the best interest of society. In effect, the moral development of the majority of adolescents and adults has culminated in an acceptance of the social order. An example of such a person is an American soldier who accepts orders to deploy to the wars in the Middle East because it is his or her duty to the country.

Only a minority of persons use postconventional moral reasoning principles. Postconventional moral reasoning states that one should act to ensure the greatest good for the greatest number; another postconventional set of core beliefs is that behavior should conform to universal ethical standards. A postconventional person would question following social rules that conflict with the principles of human rights. An example of postconventional reasoning is the rationale of civil rights workers who used nonviolent protest during the 1950s and 1960s to stop racial segregation in the United States. An example of postconventional reasoning is the decision of a young Kansas State University student to report her male supervisor, a professor with tenure, for sexual harassment despite the refusal of several of her peers, who had also been victimized by this man, to join her because they feared reprisals.

There has been controversy over the research into moral reasoning. Carol Gilligan said the template being used discriminated against females who exercise interpersonal principles of care and compassion to guide ethical decision making, whereas males draw on principles of justice. Gilligan argued that the feminine voice in moral reasoning, that is, the interpersonal component, was being excluded from all examinations of growth in moral development. While Gilligan's writings have resonated positively with many persons, independent analyses of over 150 research studies into the moral reasoning of adolescents and adults found males and females used both interpersonal and justice principles, although moral reasoning decisions of adults born prior to the 1970s were more likely to be gender specific than were the decisions of persons born from the 1970s on. Clearly, such generalizations contain limits; for instance, persons raised in tightly conservative religious traditions are more likely to hold gender-specific views than are persons raised in secular societies.

Evidence from a multitude of studies confirms that an increase in use of postconventional moral reasoning occurs during the undergraduate years. While many of these studies have not been designed to identify changes over time and have not included control groups of young men and women who are not in college, use of postconventional principles correlated positively with the amount of formal education, confirming the influence of college on moral reasoning.

## Career Choice

A body of scholarship consistently demonstrates that upper-division undergraduates engage in significantly more critical thinking about careers than do first- or second-year students. This thinking involves formulating career plans, obtaining accurate knowledge about a career, and making clear career choices. Feeling the pressure of impending graduation seems to spur many students to develop their career development skills. It is unnerving to be a senior in college and still be unsettled on a career choice. However, there are late bloomers who just take longer to settle on something to sink their teeth into.

In some researchers' findings, the single most useful predictor of a student's career choice at the end of college remains the initial choice made when the student entered college. This evidence implies that little change occurs about career choice during a student's years in college. Such research is counterintuitive to many of us; we know from experience that some students have a clear fix on a career from the first day of college, others experiment with options before choosing, and others enter college unsure of what to do but gain guidance from mentors and from their studies. Longitudinal studies about how college affects students have underscored since the 1970s that faculty play an important role in students' career decisions. I remember the student who was clueless about his future but, who to his and many others' great surprise, became fascinated by Greece and went on to become a professor of religious studies. There is also the unusual minority of students who relish the learning that college represents—they relish learning for its own sake—and who do not take courses to fit career options. They may even have already selected a career that is not contingent on a college education, such as vehicle restoration or motorcycle repair, but value the difference being educated offers.

## Faith Consciousness

A mark of development is the quality of the person's exploration of and commitment to find what ultimately matters. Such exploration and commitment may lead to active involvement in a religious tradition, but it also includes persons whose views are agnostic or atheistic; consider, for instance, the pluralism presented by known dignitaries such as Mother Theresa, a fervent Catholic; Charles Darwin, a confirmed agnostic; and Albert Camus, a committed atheist. While not pretending to read these historical figures' private thoughts and beliefs, I think it is clear that these dignitaries had made profound choices about engaging in the world contingent on their acceptance of what it meant to act on one's faith about what ultimately matters.

Thus, faith consciousness—the development of one's understanding of what ultimately matters—encompasses but is not limited to religion or religious beliefs. In today's parlance, one can be spiritual without being religious; one's beliefs may include religion, but they do not necessarily.

Faith consciousness develops in stages and occurs because human beings inherently search for meaning. The stage of faith that is said to characterize most 18- to 23-year-olds is called "individuative reflective." People reach this stage of faith consciousness only when they engage in two important actions related to self-identity. One, they examine what they have been told to believe and make conscious, personal choices, rather than accept unexamined commitments. The second important change in self-understanding that makes it possible to move into the stage of individuative-reflective faith is to examine the roles and responsibilities that have been imposed and make personal choices about which roles and responsibilities to assume.

The obstacle facing persons in a foreclosed identity from moving into individuative-reflective faith is self-evident: Only with difficulty do persons with foreclosed identities question authority. Note that it is not necessary that the person casts aside what she (or he) has been told to believe, although rejection of traditional beliefs may occur. What is necessary is that the person examines what she (or he) has been told and decides what to accept on the basis of being personally persuaded. The person may well decide to accept the beliefs she (or he) has been told to accept, but she (or he) now does so with more nuanced understanding. There is interplay here with movement toward committed relativism and toward an achieved identity as persons move into individuative-reflective faith.

I have found no evidence that entering into individuative-reflective faith is more likely for traditional-age college students than for young men and women who are not in college. The college experience provides numerous glimpses of alternative beliefs, roles, and responsibilities. It provides the milieu for exploring and choosing, for moving from foreclosed identities or diffuse identities into moratorium and then into fulfilled or achieved identities. The necessary triggers are examining, evaluating, and restructuring one's beliefs and values and one's roles and responsibilities. Thinking, exploring persons need not be in college to engage in such fundamental actions.

## Interpersonal Relationships

Once undergraduates experience the freedom from parental controls that college affords, some find the temptations intoxicating. For many of these students, intoxication literally becomes a way of life extending through every weekend. Some evidence suggests that peers strongly influence college students to engage in problem drinking as well as drug use. It has surprised researchers that college students seem more influenced by peer opinions than had been expected given the noticeable growth in identity formation, critical thinking, and moral reasoning that occurs during the undergraduate years.

Actually, there are concerns over the research that produced these pessimistic findings about the negative effects of peers on college students. These studies seldom control for effects of emotional maturation, typically include small or very small samples, and rarely involve students from many institutions. We know that over the course of their undergraduate years most college students become more interested in a select group of friends and may spend most of their time with one close friend. What is typical of college students as they mature is to become more competent at and desirous of entering into and maintaining friendships with one or at best a few individuals.

## A DIGITAL GENERATION

The current cohort of traditional-age college students is portrayed in many quarters as technologically savvy, sophisticated in accessing information online, and digitally connected to peers and to the global environment. Educators are warned that giving lectures and assigning print material are passé and will be opposed by this digital generation, called also the "Net Generation," "digital natives," and "Millennials." However, recent empirical studies have challenged these virtually rhapsodic portraits of the digital generation. I will present the various views that have been given, beginning with general comparisons between the digital natives and others who are called digital immigrants.

Digital natives, persons born since 1982, have not known a time without computers, the Internet, and web access to the world. Digital immigrants grew up without the all-pervasive presence of computers, the Internet, and the like. There are estimates that by their 21st birthday digital natives have played 10,000 hours of video games, watched 20,000 hours of television, spent at least 10,000 hours using cell phones, and consumed at most 5,000 hours reading printed works. While listening to music and reading a course assignment, digital natives send and receive instant messages and surf the Internet. They remain in touch with their peers by means of Facebook and text messages, and failure to engage with peers digitally results in social isolation.

Some critics argue that these multitasking digital natives demonstrate at best surface understanding of what they learn and are unwilling to expend the time and effort to master nuances. Neurologists assert that the brains of these youth are being rewired by the constant activity with digital tools, and one worrisome trait seen in many digital natives is a short attention span. Digital natives are used to getting instant results. The quip is that the digital generation dislikes instant gratification because it takes too long.

Having reflected on what digital natives bring to college, some educators have championed a radical change in how colleges structure and deliver curriculum. Engaging students in learning does appear a prime interest, but there is an underlying theme that (a) a sea change has occurred in how learning takes place and (b) refusal to adapt will relegate colleges to obsolescence. The calls for making these radical changes are grounded in the belief that the new generation of college students has wide and deep experience using digital technologies and has, as a result of extensive digital exposure, learning styles radically different from how digital immigrants learn. In fact, the assertion goes so far as to claim the cognitive capabilities of the Net Generation differ qualitatively from the capabilities of other learners. A vocal group of educational commentators says we must adapt to the demands of digital natives. "Yield to the pressure of the Millennial Generation" seems an accurate summation of what we are told is needed to make colleges current and vital.

Persons skeptical about the importance of digital natives for college education have a different view than the advocates for radical change. The skeptics portray the Net Generation as self-absorbed and pampered. Millennials are said to have been reinforced since they began school to think their opinions matter, regardless of the content. They respond poorly to criticism. They are used to winning awards even if they have done mediocre work. They will learn only what is required. This portrait of digital natives is not flattering, and I doubt it applies to each person in this group. In terms of implications for the growth and development of individuals in this group and their entry into adulthood, the portrait raises serious concerns.

Persons raising questions about the digital generation agree that its members engage in multitasking. But their multitasking interferes with being well-informed. As these late adolescents enter college, they do not come with skills in critical thinking. Rather than mold college education to meet the demands of the Net Generation, the skeptics argue it is the job of faculty members to shape how these digital natives learn.

Empirical studies in Australia, the United Kingdom, Canada, South Africa, and the United States have independently come to similar conclusions. These studies indicate that

- Students respond to the culture of the individual classroom and will work to meet the educational objectives of the professor.
- Students will refrain from texting in classrooms when told that behavior is not acceptable; however, there are some stories of students being miffed at being told to desist from texting and being rude to the professor when told to stop.
- Digital natives' expertise in information technology (IT) is actually limited for the most part to traditional tools: email, instant messaging, Facebook, and YouTube, for instance.
- Students in technical majors, such as engineering, make more intensive use of IT and are more adept with using these tools than their counterparts in majors such as social work.
- A gap in IT use and sophistication separates digital natives in terms of socioeconomic status, gender, and racial/ethnic identity: In short, in this country, lower income adolescents, females, and Hispanic and African American adolescents manifest less sophistication and know-how regarding IT.
- Digital natives have engaged throughout their education in collaborative learning, and they look forward to teacher-formulated classroom experiences using group work with peers.
- The notion that the digital natives are constantly connected is hotly debated. Some youth seem practically if not actually addicted to constant texting, but they are said to be outliers of the Net Generation, not typical of this cohort of young adults.

It would be foolish to overlook the potential for learning in college presented by IT. There are so many riches available that take us beyond the traditional model of a professor lecturing to students. Yet, there is fundamental value in professors who provide coherent, engaging conceptual frameworks. I use a variety of approaches in my courses: lectures, small group work, lots of reading and writing, and projects. Access to Internet resources makes eminent sense to me. For instance, when teaching about the rise of crisis intervention following the Cocoanut Grove Restaurant fire, students can be encouraged to access Web sites that vividly present that horrific event in American history. I can't imagine digital natives not going to Google to find out on their own about persons and topics covered in courses. As an example, I present in my courses the accomplishments of Alexander Leighton; typically, students will come to subsequent classes having found out more about Leighton by accessing Web sites such as http://www.hsph.harvard.edu/now-archive/20070831/leighton.html and http://tps.sagepub.com/content/43/1/45

We know that many students enjoy computer games. Developing games for integral use in college curricula is an insight many educators have put into practice in fields as widely varied as business, history, psychology, and theater. Using games to understand the impact of bereavement on college students merits consideration, and I will offer some ideas in Chapter 9, but I realize developing quality products using IT is beyond my skills.

To my frame of mind, what matters most for college students are cognitive and affective development. Colleges do a good job assisting students to become more emotionally mature, to move beyond dualism and beyond relativism, to gain both broad and deep knowledge, and to become ready to take their place in the work force. Digital natives face developmental transitions of forming an autonomous identity, choosing a career path, and developing interpersonal maturity. Finding ways whereby IT will promote such growth seems both prudent and smart. But thinking somehow that digital natives set the agenda in college strikes me as a mistake of the worst kind, akin to what I found extremely distasteful during my college years when some professors in the 1970s, in their desire to be relevant and accepted, came into classrooms and started the lesson by asking, "So, what do you want to do today?"

## HELP-SEEKING BEHAVIOR AND COLLEGE STUDENTS

Colleges establish various programs to assist students with academic, residential, financial, legal, physical health, and mental health issues, as primary examples. A rule of thumb is that a student likely to seek help is female and comfortable with self-disclosures; she has had positive experiences with seeking help, and trusts that seeking help will turn out positive. Students are more willing to seek help for academic problems than for other types of issues. College students are more willing to use student health services than mental health services. Perhaps because of the focus of their major, students in psychology are more positive about seeking professional help with counseling issues than are other students.

On the whole, men in college underutilize programs and services offered by student affairs offices and mental health counseling. The main explanation is that seeking help is shameful for males, something in conflict with a mainstream view of masculinity emphasizing autonomy and control. There is a stigma attached to seeking help, a sense of weakness. Programs designed to help males succeed in college, whether the issues be academic, financial, physical health, or mental health, are perceived to be essentially nurturing and feminine, and thus repudiated by most males. It is argued that these programs need to appreciate the press for young college males to conform to visions of masculinity that abhor appearing out of control or vulnerable. A tension is to create places males see as safe and yet that offer challenges for growth and development.

Reframing "seeking help" as "problem solving" has proven successful with some college men. As an example, I'll relate this story of a male student (let's call him Jacob) who came to see me the very week I wrote this part of Chapter 2. Jacob came to enquire about my department's baccalaureate programs in health. He made it clear that he had no clear direction in his life and was wondering what kinds of jobs emerge for someone with a bachelor's degree in health. While I told Jacob that some persons pursue careers in health care management or health education and others go on to graduate school in such areas as medicine and nursing and occupational therapy, he said he didn't want to go to graduate school and just wasn't sure what he wanted to do or how to go about talking with employers. I strongly urged him to get an appointment with a student services program that helps students land internships, develop competitive resumes, and learn to present themselves to people who hire. I emphasized they could help him. Jacob said he does not feel comfortable asking for help. I said, "Think of it as problem solving. You are taking direct action to solve a problem you recognize." Jacob said that way of looking at things put it in a better light. In the spirit of full honesty, I must say I do not know whether Jacob did or will seek out this student services program. It seems obvious to me they can assist him. He may not feel need enough to seek them out, regardless the reframing I offered.

Members of cultural and ethnic minorities are even less likely to seek help than are Whites. For Asian American students, there is a profound shame cast on the individual and on the student's family for seeking help with mental health issues. The fact that Asian American students utilize Internet programs aimed at helping with issues such as depression may suggest a way that these students overcome shame when seeking help.

African American students are less likely than Whites to use counseling services on campus. One obstacle is a mistrust of White counselors, as well as cultural attitudes toward mental health concerns. One finding is that positive attitudes toward mental health counseling increase in direct relation to the number of college credits African American students earn.

## CONCLUDING COMMENTS

The focus of this chapter is on what we know about college students. Obviously, there are aspects of the college undergraduate experiences not touched on. Sexuality, for instance, has not been examined. This chapter describes many of the central trappings of the stage on which the main concern of this book, bereavement in a college student's life, plays out.

A college's ecology in many ways presents options unlike what a young adult has known before. There is considerable freedom, but that freedom is embedded in the expectation that success comes to persons who manage their time, stay focused, and complete tasks. Classes meet perhaps two or three times a week, not every school day. The demands are to read a lot and to write (in some schools a lot). Persons who have done well in high school but have not learned how to study meet some very rude awakenings in college courses.

How do undergraduate students spend their time? Students taking a full load of credits during a semester spend on average each week about 48 hours engaged in academics; 50–56 hours a week sleeping; at least 20 hours a week at a job; around 10 hours a week socializing with friends and 9 hours at least watching television or movies, playing computer games, or being online. Reading outside of textbooks (for instance, reading the newspaper or novels) is rare: Less than 25% of undergraduates spend even 3 hours a week in leisure reading. Less than 20% talk with a faculty member outside of class even for 30 minutes a week. The new cohort of digital natives spends considerably more time accessing the Internet, sending and receiving text messages, and using other IT tools than more recent generations of college students.

Significant changes for college undergraduates occur as aggregate outcomes. That is, these changes are not due to any single experience but rather to a series of connected experiences that extend over time. When asked what is most memorable about their undergraduate years, graduating seniors seldom mention a class they took or a professor they knew, though there are a few students who do mention such things.[2] The students typically mention experiences with peers or taking advantage of the diverse intellectual, cultural, and social life of the campus. Some note that college life introduced them to persons from other cultures and walks of life and woke them up to a greater range of values than they had known existed prior to coming to college. Some mention projects in places far removed from the campus, such as working in rural parts of developing countries on housing or water purification or nutrition or medical care.

My choice was to examine what has been learned about the role of the college experience on young adults and to look at issues of identity formation as they mature. It is widely accepted that campus cultures that promote student engagement foster holistic development of students. There is puzzling research that males profit more from the undergraduate experience than do females.

College has a definite influence on certain aspects of development in the lives of 18- to 23-year-old undergraduate students: identity formation, intellectual growth, moral reasoning, career choice, faith consciousness, and interpersonal relationships. In effect, in this chapter I offered an overview of certain salient features about college students as prelude to examining what we know about bereavement in the lives of a significant proportion of these young adults.

Several obstacles restrict college students from seeking help. Gender is significantly associated, with females being much more inclined than males to seek help for a variety of issues, including academic, physical health, and mental health. For males and for Asian Americans and African Americans, stigma attaches to help-seeking behavior.

By now, I hope there are questions percolating about the relationship of the material in this chapter to the overall focus of this book. I don't believe any researcher has yet examined any of these questions.

1. Do bereaved college students perceive the campus as a safe place where they feel included, where they matter, and where they are engaged?
2. Do colleges recognize the approximately 25% of students in the first year of bereavement and reach out to them as community members who matter?

3. Do colleges think they have any obligations or roles to play in these issues?
4. Do colleges recognize that bereavement will dampen engagement in studies, and do colleges make any responsive gestures to address this issue?

Various individual markers characterize the undergraduate experiences. We don't know how bereavement in a student's life plays out in these markers. In particular,

1. How does bereavement in a student's life play out in the person's identity formation?
2. How does bereavement in a student's life play out in the person's moral reasoning?
3. How does bereavement in a student's life play out in the person's career decision making?
4. How does bereavement in a student's life play out in the person's faith consciousness?
5. How does bereavement in a student's life play out in the person's interpersonal relationships?
6. In what ways do bereaved college students seek assistance, and what types of assistance do they request?

An agenda with pregnant implications for practitioners (counselors, teachers, social workers, for instance) beckons researchers interested in the development of college students touched by a friend's or family member's death. Hopefully, the questions raised in this last segment of the chapter will lead to collaborative work between researchers and bereaved students.

## NOTES

1. In her response to this chapter, Robin Paletti said she wondered whether the notion of a psychological moratorium as essential to healthy adolescent development is an ethnocentrically bound construct that is neither valued nor promoted in some ethnic groups.
2. In his response to this chapter, Jeffrey Berman wrote to me that faculty who connect with students' personal lives, core beliefs, and experiences often have lasting impacts on college students.

## FURTHER READING

Balk, D. E. (1995). *Adolescent development: Early through late adolescence.* Pacific Grove, CA: Brooks/Cole.

Bloom, B. S., Madaus, G. F., & Hastings, J. T. (1981). *Evaluation to improve learning.* New York: McGraw-Hill.

Boyer, E. L. (1987). *College: The undergraduate experience in America.* New York: Harper & Row.

Braskamp, L., Trautvetter, L. C., & Ward, K. (2008). Putting students first: Promoting lives of purpose and meaning. *About Campus, 13,* 26–32.

Brown, C., & Czerniewicz, L. (2010). Debunking the "digital native": Beyond digital apartheid, towards digital democracy. *Journal of Computer Assisted Learning, 26,* 357–369.

Carlson, S. (2005). The Net Generation in the classroom. *Chronicle of Higher Education, 52*(7), A34–A37.

Crawford, M. B. (2009). *Shop class as soul craft: An inquiry into the value of work.* New York: Penguin Press.

Erikson, E. H. (1961), Youth: Fidelity and diversity. In E. H. Erikson (Ed.), *Youth: Change and challenge* (pp. 1–23). New York: Basic Books.

Erikson, E. H. (1968). *Identity: Youth and crisis.* New York: Norton.

Fowler, J. W. (1980). *Stages of faith: The psychology of human development and the quest for meaning.* San Francisco, CA: Harper & Row.

Gilligan, C. (1982). *In a different voice: Psychological theory and women's development.* Cambridge, MA: Harvard University Press.

Goode, J. (2010). Mind the gap: The digital dimension of college access. *The Journal of Higher Education, 81,* 583–618.

Kellom, G. E. (Ed.). (2004). *Developing effective programs and services for college men. New Directions for Student Services* (107). San Francisco, CA: Jossey-Bass.

Kohlberg, L. (1980). *The meaning and measurement of moral development.* Worcester, MA: Clark University Press.

Leighton, A. H. (1959). *My name is Legion: Foundations for a theory of man in relation to culture.* New York: Basic Books.

Light, R. J. (2001). *Making the most of college: Students speak their minds.* Cambridge, MA: Harvard University Press.

Margaryan, A., Littlejohn, A., & Vojt, G. (2011). Are digital natives a myth or reality? University students' use of digital technologies. *Computers & Education, 56,* 429–440.

Maslow, A. H. (1968). *Toward a psychology of being.* New York: Van Nostrand.

Moore, W. S. (2002). Understanding learning in a postmodern world: Reconsidering the Perry scheme of ethical and intellectual development. In B. K. Hofer & P. R. Pintrich (Eds.), *Personal epistemology: The psychology of beliefs about knowledge and knowing* (pp. 17–36). Mahwah, NJ: Lawrence Erlbaum.

Oblinger, D. G. (2004). The next generation of educational attainment. *Journal of Interactive Media in Education, 8,* 1–18.

Pascarella, E. T., & Terenzini, P. T. (1991). *How college affects students: Findings and insights from twenty years of research.* San Francisco, CA: Jossey-Bass.

Pascarella, E. T., & Terenzini, P. T. (2005). *How college affects students: Volume 2. A third decade of research.* San Francisco, CA: Jossey-Bass.

Perry, W. G. (1970). *Forms of intellectual and ethical development during the college years.* New York: Holt, Rinehart, & Winston.

Richtel, M. (November 21, 2010). Growing up digital, wired for distraction. *The New York Times,* CLX (55,231), pp. 1, 26–27.

Safer, M. (May 23, 2008). The "Millennials" are coming. *60 Minutes.* Retrieved November 29, 2010, from http://www.cbsnews.com/stories/2007/11/08/60minutes/main3475200.shtml

Sax, L. J. (2009). Gender matters: The variable effect of gender on the student experience. *About Campus, 14,* 2–10.

Small, J. L. (2009). Faith dialogues foster identity development. *About Campus, 13,* 12–18.

Strange, C. C., & Banning, J. H. (2001). *Educating by design: Creating campus learning environments that work.* San Francisco, CA: Jossey-Bass.

Verhasselt, H. (2008). *An examination of group differences in college students' preferences for seeking academic help.* Unpublished doctoral dissertation, University of Houston, Houston.

Vogel, D. L., Wade, N. G., & Ascheman, P. L. (2009). Measuring perceptions of stigmatization by others for seeking psychological help: Reliability and validity of a new stigma scale with college students. *Journal of Counseling Psychology, 56,* 301–308.

Walker, L. J. (1989). A longitudinal study of moral reasoning. *Child Development, 60,* 157–166.

Warren, T. M. (2010). *Attachment security, distress disclosure, and attitudes toward seeking psychological help among racially diverse college freshmen.* Unpublished doctoral dissertation, Fordham University, New York.

Worden, J. W. (1996). *Children and grief: When a parent dies.* New York: Guilford.

# What Do We Know About Bereavement Following a Death?

Jill, reflecting on the death of her brother from an accident and her reactions to his dying, said to me,

> I didn't understand, and I kept saying it wouldn't happen to me. My brother wouldn't die. I wouldn't have to go through it. I still wish it hadn't happened, but I still realize that it's happened. I'm still shocked that he died, yet I realize that it has happened. I don't call what I felt "numb." When he died, I felt empty. I like that word better than "numb." Because it wasn't like I could do anything. I just felt like that something was missing, something important. I didn't understand what had happened. Everything came too quick. I didn't understand why. That was the big question. "Why?" Everything was just too fast. I guess I will always feel confused because not everything is answered. I could ask a million questions and not get answers. I didn't want to do anything. I felt the loss, and I was never in the mood to go out. I was scared because everyone wasn't there. I was angry that the accident happened. I wasn't blaming anybody. If I blamed anybody, it would be God; but I wasn't saying, "Why did you?"

## THE HOLISTIC IMPACT OF BEREAVEMENT

The hospice movement has adopted a whole person approach, sometimes called a holistic approach, to understand the impact of dying and of bereavement on people. With their holistic approach, hospice organizes its services to treat the whole person by understanding that dying and bereavement affect persons in at least six fundamental dimensions of existence. This whole person approach strikes me right in many ways: practically, philosophically, theologically, and personally. I have adopted the holistic approach as an overarching framework to understand human bereavement over the death of a loved one.

Using the holistic approach, we can examine bereavement's pervasive effect in six dimensions of being human. Bereavement impacts us physically, emotionally, cognitively, behaviorally, interpersonally, and spiritually. While there are distinctions between these holistic dimensions, as you examine a bereaved person's case story, you will find interplay between them. In several places in the book, I look at stories of bereaved persons from the vantage point of this holistic approach, and I point out links to other points of view, in particular existential phenomenology and what is called the acute grief syndrome. For starters, here are some illustrative examples of each dimension in the holistic approach.

## Physical Impacts

Examples of the physical impacts of bereavement are numerous. There is incontrovertible evidence that the immune system is compromised due to the distress of bereavement, thereby leaving persons vulnerable to opportunistic diseases they would have otherwise successfully blocked. Bereavement leaves persons easily fatigued. It can lead to chills and diarrhea. Problems with sleeping are common. Readers of this book who have been bereaved undoubtedly can provide examples of how bereavement affected them physically. In fact, this same observation about personal examples applies to each of the six holistic dimensions of existence that bereavement touches.

## Emotional Impacts

A cascade of emotions engulfs bereaved persons. Among these emotions are guilt, anger, anxiety, fear, dread, confusion, self-doubt, and sadness. People feel guilty for being alive when their loved one is dead; they may blame themselves for not preventing the death or for being complicit in the death. They may be mad as hell at the person for having died and left them. Anger and guilt can both interplay when the death was a suicide. They may be anxious and fearful over their future when money becomes scarce because the major source of income has died, or they may be anxious and fearful over their health when a close relative dies of breast or prostate cancer. They may be confused about the circumstances of the death and about how to continue with life as normal. They may dread interactions with people. They may feel incapable of accomplishing things that matter to them, and thus in their helplessness show insidious self-doubt. Throughout it all, there is an enduring sadness, a legacy that seems present from then on, even if muted and camouflaged. Some bereaved persons talk of feeling depressed, but bereavement seldom induces people to feel utterly worthless, a significant aspect of clinical depression. In fact, persons who have been clinically depressed at some point in their lives and who at another point become bereaved can distinguish very clearly that depression and bereavement are not the same.

## Cognitive Impacts

Difficulty concentrating or remembering are common cognitive impacts of bereavement. A person can read a whole page in a book and realize she (he) has no clue what the author wrote because her mind was elsewhere. Intrusive thoughts and images of the person who died, perhaps of how the person died, flood the bereaved person. Intrusive thoughts and images during bereavement are the mirror image of an adolescent's infatuation with someone; in both cases it seems nigh impossible to stop thinking about the other person, but during bereavement the intrusive thoughts primarily bring pain and distress, and inability to stop the thoughts and images can be scary. When a person can think about the individual who died without becoming upset, there is evidence that the grief is lessening. Auditory and visual hallucinations are reported by a significant minority of bereaved individuals; they either see or hear the person who died in familiar settings, such as standing in the kitchen doing the dishes or walking across the campus.

Cognitive impacts of bereavement can jeopardize a student's academic record and career dreams should grades plummet. In addition, research demonstrates that not uncommonly in the first semester in which a student is dealing with bereavement "grades go into the toilet" as one person put it. Many students in their first semester after a death would benefit from a reprieve from the academic rigors of school, but they push ahead and not uncommonly suffer the consequences. I have not found any student who has said that his (her) school had instituted any policies to provide a leave of absence given the student's circumstances. Some universities allow students to petition for retroactive withdrawal from one or more semesters when documented evidence supports that extraordinary life circumstances imperiled course work. Kansas State University and Brooklyn College have such a policy.

## Behavioral Impacts

Crying is common as is restless agitation. Some people start smoking tobacco or drinking alcohol to excess. Some engage in sexual promiscuity or driving with no regard for safety. Keeping to a schedule and remaining organized is challenging to say the least. Grievers will scan crowds of people to find the face of the dead person. Praying and reading scripture remain familiar activities for believers in religion, unless the death has undermined faith in God and religious teachings. Grieving individuals may lash out at other people with a rage that leaves everyone, including the bereaved, baffled; such irrational outbursts may prompt grievers to wonder if they are going insane.

## Interpersonal Impacts

Bereaved individuals learn very quickly that outsiders to their grief have little comprehension of the duration and intensity of grief; prior to being bereaved, they too would have underestimated grief's strong hold. Bereaved individuals learn that others typically become uncomfortable when they are present, and they learn that conversations about their bereavement are unwelcome after but a short period of time following the death. To keep their friends, they learn to muffle their grief. Many bereaved persons find being with other persons difficult, and they may select social isolation. It is difficult to be in the midst of persons who are upbeat and having a good time when you are miserable.

## Spiritual Impacts

Spirituality manifests itself in several ways: a search for meaning, interconnectedness to others, a sense of wonder at the majesty of nature, and in many persons an experience of the sacred. Some people prefer to refer to an existential rather than a spiritual dimension.

How does bereavement manifest itself in the spiritual dimension of a person? One impact is that hope is hard to come by. The future holds no promise. A woman I was counseling following the death of her husband said she knew she was healing when she began to feel hopeful once again.

Another spiritual impact is on a person's sense of meaning and purpose. What is the point of human existence when a good person can be taken away without any apparent reluctance? How can everything continue as though the death did not happen? How can a benevolent, powerful God allow such heartbreak? How can a benevolent, powerful God not answer prayers to spare the life of someone loved and needed? Why care for anything, even for oneself and certainly not for God, when life seems meaningless, absurd? Bereaved persons may find their faith and hope deeply tested. It is unlikely that, as they search for answers and meaning, the bereaved will come back to the assumptions they had about existence before the death. They may come to a deeper faith, greater empathy, more courage. They will not be the same person, and will understand what it means to be human in a way that nongrievers do not.

Another example of the spiritual impact of bereavement is that it leads people to reorganize their fundamental understandings of (a) who they are, (b) their relationship with the world, and (c) their interactions with other persons. Thus, bereavement affects people in three fundamental aspects of existence: self-identity, assumptions about reality, and interpersonal relationships. It is likely that a bereaved person, particularly someone already in the midst of major developmental transitions such as a college undergraduate, will emerge from bereavement with alterations in her (or his) understanding of—and relationship to—self, the world, and other persons.

## TRAJECTORIES OF BEREAVEMENT

"How long am I going to feel this way?" is a common question bereaved persons ask. They are finding out in ongoing, daily experience that bereavement lasts longer and is more intense than they had anticipated. Prior to being bereaved, college students uniformly admit they would have underestimated the duration and force of bereavement.

There is evidence that bereavement follows a U-shaped curve for many persons, that is, great intensity at the start, a gradual lessening, an unexpected resurgence of distress that does not last as long as the first bout, and then a decline of intensity that becomes the new normal. The image often used to describe this pattern to bereavement is of a roller coaster of emotions. Persons whose grief has abated are greatly unsettled when the feelings they thought were over return to engulf them. Here is a point for counselors to remember as a preventive intervention: Let bereaved persons know about the roller coaster of emotions that many individuals experience; give them some advance warning.

Bereavement falls into one of three trajectories or paths.[1] The three paths are (a) a resiliency trajectory, (b) a recovery trajectory, and (c) an enduring grief trajectory. I will take up each in turn. First, we will look at what has been uncovered about the resiliency trajectory.

Of great surprise to many scholars, the plurality of grieving persons whose bereavement trajectories have been studied follow a path that shows initial difficulty with intense sadness but fairly quick resiliency and low symptoms of grief; by quick is meant a return to normal functioning within a couple of weeks following the death. In some studies, the persons in this trajectory form a majority of bereaved individuals. The proportions of bereaved persons in this trajectory range from nearly 50% in some studies to nearly 60% in others. These persons find happiness and solace when thinking about or talking about the person who died. For them the grief process produces comfort. This path following bereavement has been named the *resilient* trajectory.

Consider the case of Joanne, a 22-year-old college senior I knew at Oklahoma State University, whose father died suddenly of a heart attack. Her father's death bothered her, but it presented no challenge to her assumptive world. She believed firmly in her Mormon faith. She continued with her classes, did well in her courses, graduated on time, and found a job related to her college major. She had a very secure bond with her mother, whom she saw often and whom she had introduced me to at a college function several months before her father's death. A few weeks into her bereavement, Joanne approached me on behalf of her mother, who wondered if there were any books I could recommend for her to read. I suggested Attig's *How We Grieve*, and a few months later Joanne told me that her mother had found the book very helpful. When she graduated, Joanne came to my office and gave to me a treasure that she said had proven enormously helpful to her, *The Book of Mormon*.

Another trajectory that many scholars have long assumed was the more typical path is found in 40–44% of persons. This trajectory involves sadness, anxiety, guilt, confusion, and other intense symptoms that last for several months, even beyond a year following the death, eventually leveling off to a noticeably improved situation. This path was for years assumed to be the expected course of grief. It has been called the *recovery* trajectory.

Roberto was a 19-year-old college sophomore I met at Brooklyn College, and he provides an example of someone in the recovery trajectory. His family had moved to New York City from Puerto Rico when he was a baby. Roberto was a devout Roman Catholic who was grieving the death of his grandfather due to an illness. The death had occurred not quite 9 months ago. Several aspects of his bereavement indicated that it either distressed him moderately or, in some cases, quite a bit. For example, Roberto said he was having some trouble staying asleep, he got irritable and angry quite a bit since the death, and he frequently had intrusive thoughts about his grandfather's death. He experienced trouble concentrating and acknowledged he had yet to deal with a lot of feelings about the death. He was managing his course work, though problem concentrating got in the way, and he had a 30-hour-a-week job to boot. On top of his grandfather's death, in the past year Roberto had experienced the end of a close friendship and the death of his dog.

A third trajectory is one of unremitting distress, which accounts for the experience of approximately 15% of grieving persons. For these persons, their acute grief never lessens. They may well experience clinical depression in response to the death, and their grief symptoms remain intense. Only professional intervention seems able to assist persons in this trajectory. This complicated bereavement path has been called the *enduring grief* trajectory.

Increased attention has been paid in the past several years to the difficulties accompanying the phenomenon of enduring grief. Various terms have been proposed for this phenomenon; "traumatic grief," "pathological grief," "complicated grief," and "complicated mourning" are some of the more common terms. More recently the term "prolonged grief disorder" was introduced, and efforts are underway to include prolonged grief disorder as a diagnostic category in the forthcoming fifth edition of the *Diagnostic and Statistical Manual of Mental Disorders*.

There is a significant correlation between complicated bereavement, depression, and anxiety. Physiological indicators distinguish bereaved individuals who are coping with depression and/or anxiety from bereaved individuals whose bereavement is considered normal. Consensus has built that psychological indicators of complicated grief include the severity and duration of intrusive thoughts and images, spasms of acute emotions, excessive loneliness and isolation, extreme avoidance of reminders of the deceased, and enduring sleep disturbances.

James provides an example of a college student whose bereavement was in an enduring grief trajectory. I met him at Brooklyn College when he came to talk to me about my research on bereavement and to tell me a bit about himself. He was a 20-year-old sophomore. His girl friend had died in a car accident about 8 months ago. He was finding it very difficult to keep his mind on his studies, and it seemed he might fail several of his courses because he had simply stopped going to class. He was constantly longing for his girl friend, and he expressed an overwhelming sense of bitterness at life's unfairness. He shared a story he had written in response to a photograph he had seen of a man sitting alone, staring out a window of a skyscraper. James wrote,

> I see a man who is in despair. He is looking for something that is miss-ing. It is possible the reason he is sitting by a window ledge is because he is having suicidal thoughts. There must have been a devastating occurrence in his life. He might have ended a relationship that meant a lot to him. Or maybe someone in his inner circle has had some kind of life changing or traumatic experience. Somebody obviously died, and this person meant a lot to the man. It is possible that he is jeal-ous of birds, birds who have freedom and can get away from things while he cannot. He is trying to find himself in solitude. Sometimes certain people deal with difficult times by distancing themselves from the larger society and sit and contemplate what it is that is bothering them. He cannot picture life going on without the deceased. Life is just not worth living for him if that person is not with him. This man needs help with coping with his losses, and it appears he doesn't realize him-self that he needs to let go and deal with himself.

I saw James only that one time. I had made a list of counseling resources available to students in need, a list given as a matter of course to any person who participates in my bereavement research, and I gave him a copy. I invited him to come back and see me any time, and strongly encouraged him to see a counselor who could help him with his loss. He thanked me and left.

## EXPLANATIONS WHY HUMANS GRIEVE

Three core elements must be present for bereavement to occur. First, some-one or something must be highly valued. Second, whatever is highly val-ued must be taken away irrevocably. Third, a human being is left behind to bear the loss, in other words to be bereaved.[2]

What we value can be tangible (for instance, a house or parcel of land that has been in the family for generations) or it can be intangible (for instance, one's reputation or hopes for a career). In this book, I am addressing bereavement due to the death of a family member or friend. Relationships with persons we care for combine both tangible and intan-gible elements. What matters is that the person is gone forever, and that places us in a state of loss (what we call bereavement), eliciting complex reactions (what we call grief), and finding expression in a myriad of ways (what we call mourning).

# THE TWO PRIMARY EXPLANATIONS OF HUMAN BEREAVEMENT

There are two influential explanations for our grief following the death of someone we care for. These explanations come from Sigmund Freud, whose name every educated person knows, and from John Bowlby, whose name is less well known than Freud's but who is very well known to early childhood educators and to child development psychologists. I estimate that most writing on bereavement in the 20th and 21st centuries has been commentary either on Freud's or on Bowlby's ideas.

## Freud

Freud's ideas about responses to bereavement are found principally in a short manuscript he wrote in 1915 and published 2 years later. His intent was to learn more about clinical depression by comparing it to grief, two situations that Freud realized bore striking similarities but were actually very different: Freud noted that clinical depression is a pathological condition that calls for professional intervention, whereas grief, despite its intensity and duration and apparent features of clinical depression, is a normal human response to irrevocable loss, is not a form of psychological pathology, and does not require professional intervention.

Freud was no stranger to bereavement, grief, and mourning. His personal correspondence makes clear the devastating impact that the deaths of his daughter and grandson had on Freud. It is possible that his examination of what it takes to recover from grief amounted to reflections on his own experiences with bereavement. He would not have agreed to accept for treatment a person who was bereaved; he considered bereavement a deep human misfortune that heals over time, a normal response to the death of someone loved, and not a pathological condition requiring professional intervention.

In Freud's explanation, the difficulty of recovering from bereavement is the refusal to accept that the person has died and the refusal to relinquish emotional ties to the person. For Freud, recovery from bereavement involves a painful, distressing struggle to accept the reality of the situation, and to come to terms with all the reminders of the person: photos, music, fragrances, letters, memories, TV shows, favorite places, and so on.

Freud said that bereaved persons recover when they do three things:

1. They confront all the reminders of the person, including the distress such reminders elicit, so that eventually these reminders lose their emotional poignancy.
2. They let go of their emotional connection to the person.
3. They form a mental representation that does not trigger emotional distress when they think of the one who died.

Bereavement scholars know the first two points in Freud's ideas about what recovery from bereavement requires. Many clinicians following Freud have stressed the need to confront the pain of one's bereavement and to detach from the person who died. I have seen few discussions by scholars about the need to form a mental representation whereby one can remember the person but without the emotional pangs of bereavement. An exception is the work of Silverman, Nickman, and Worden in their longitudinal research into children bereaved over a parent's death.[3]

## Bowlby

John Bowlby, a British psychiatrist, turned to ethology (the study of animals in their natural settings) to explain bereavement in the lives of human beings. He noted that survival of mammalian young depended upon attachment bonds between infants and caregivers. Brief reflection shows what he meant: Mammalian infants are in great need of protection and caregiving in order to survive; in contrast, consider the utter lack of any attachments between reptile young and their parents.

Bowlby argued that attachments are an evolutionary survival mechanism for mammals.[4] Bowlby said attachment bonds between caregivers and infants permit the infant to develop and thrive. In response to how they are treated when young and in need of care, protection, and nurturing, infants form attachment schemas (expectations of interpersonal relationships) that greatly influence their interpersonal relations throughout their life spans. These attachment schemas do get modified as the person interacts with the environment, and not until the end of adolescence do the schemas become relatively impervious to further change.

There are highly respected research studies that have shown attachments fall into two broad categories: secure attachments and insecure attachments. Each of these attachment styles exists on a continuum. Insecure attachments can take a variety of forms such as insecure avoidant and insecure ambivalent. People with secure attachments (a) trust that when they are in need, others will respond, (b) are comfortable with emotional and personal intimacy, and (c) have a history of positive interpersonal relationships. People with insecure-avoidant attachment styles show discomfort with emotional and interpersonal intimacy. Persons with insecure-ambivalent attachment styles fear personal rejection and have a history of relationships marked by overdependence, difficulty separating personal feelings from the other person's feelings, and difficulty establishing and maintaining personal boundaries.

Bowlby came to attachment theory as a means to explain the responses of British children removed from their parents during the height of Nazi bombing of English cities. The British government took children in urban areas away from their families and moved them to the interior of the country to live in the care of strangers. You can see this strategy depicted in the film *The Lion, The Witch, and the Wardrobe*. Upon being reunited with parents, children's responses distinctly differed as a function of the type of attachment formed with the parents prior to the migration to the interior of the country.

It is because humans become attached to others that bereavement enters the picture. Without emotional bonds that link us to someone else and lead us to care about that person's welfare, we would not grieve the death of that person. Thus, Bowlby proposed a mechanism to explain the presence of bereavement in humans: We grieve because we are attached to someone who has been taken irreparably from us. There is growing interest to examine the influence that types of attachment, secure and insecure, have on bereavement outcomes for persons when attachment bonds are sundered irreparably.

Bowlby and persons closely allied with him (in particular, another British psychiatrist, Colin Murray Parkes) have described the unfolding of grief when someone is bereaved. They propose that grief occurs in the following sequence of phases. Initially, the bereaved person feels numb, and this first phase is typically short lived, at most lasting a few weeks. Then the person enters the phase of yearning for and searching for the person who died, and this second phase can manifest itself in such behaviors as scanning a crowd of faces for the person who died, expecting that a sound heard in the house was made by the person who died, dreaming about the person, and mistaking someone else for the person who has died. The second phase lasts until the person realizes that the search is futile; typically, the second phase lasts a few months or more. The third phase, disorganization and despair, begins when the bereaved person understands that the searching in phase two is futile; the third phase can last a year or more, and during it the person feels no zest for living, no purpose in life, no hope in a worthwhile future; he or she likely functions in daily tasks such as completing work or school demands, but does so as if going through the motions; the person's heart is not in it. Eventually, the bereaved person moves out of disorganization and despair, and takes an interest in life again. The person enters the fourth phase of recovery from bereavement, termed reorganization. He or she finds renewed joy in personal attachments, and may initiate new pursuits such as taking up a musical instrument, becoming intimate with someone, joining a martial arts dojo, learning to paint, reading great books, or studying film making.

These four phases comprise what Bowlby considered the natural responses of human beings to normal bereavement over the death of someone with whom one is attached. While descriptive of changing experiences over time, the four phases strike many persons as a passive depiction of waiting out bereavement rather than an active process of grieving.

## MAJOR THINKING ON COPING WITH BEREAVEMENT SINCE FREUD AND BOWLBY

### Erich Lindemann

In the early 1940s, a Boston psychiatrist who taught at Harvard University and practiced at Massachusetts General Hospital faced a daunting task. He and his multidisciplinary team of psychiatrists, clinical psychologists, and social workers were working with friends and family members of 492 persons who had perished in a fire at a Boston nightclub called the Cocoanut Grove. Lindemann turned to Freud's writings for direction on what to do, and he initiated interventions to get persons to confront their distress and emotionally let go of the person who died. Lindemann reported that bereaved persons showed noticeable signs of improvement when they engaged in this grief work. He also said it was important for bereaved persons to speak openly about their grief, a requirement that men found difficult according to Lindemann.

You may have noted a change from what Freud wrote about bereavement. Freud wrote that it would never occur to him that a bereaved person needed professional help. Further, what Lindemann said about the need to talk openly about one's grief is a matter of controversy. It would be a mistake, I believe, to prescribe that bereavement recovery comes only to persons who talk about their experience. While true for some, perhaps for many individuals, it is equally true that some persons turn inward to deal with distress; it is true that some persons engage in physical activity (for instance, sports or gardening or working on cars), don't engage in introspection, and don't talk with others about their misfortune. Because research on life crises has revealed that interpersonal relationships form a crucial means of coping, I find it plausible that bereaved persons benefit from being able to share their thoughts and feelings with someone they trust. I am hesitant to assert that all persons must talk about their grief in order to recover from bereavement.

Lindemann identified a group of symptoms that were present in all of the people his psychiatric team served. He referred to these symptoms as an acute grief syndrome, and this discovery has been a lasting contribution to our understanding of bereavement. The acute grief syndrome contains these features:

1. Sensations of somatic distress that occur in waves lasting from 20 to 60 minutes, receding, and then returning—for instance, tightness in the throat, choking and shortness of breath, continual sighing, empty feelings in one's stomach, intense headaches, constant exhaustion and fatigue.
2. A sense of unreality—something has to be wrong since everything in the world seems normal even though an irreparable loss has occurred.
3. Increased emotional distance from other persons.
4. Intense preoccupation with images of the person who died.
5. Feelings of guilt—for instance, searching for something that occurred prior to the death that indicated personal negligence as the cause of death.
6. Irritability, anger, lack of warmth toward others, even outbursts of hostility that both surprise the bereaved person and lead to questions of losing sanity.
7. Loss of patterns of conduct, manifested in several ways: agitated restlessness, aimlessness, inability to remain focused, difficulty making decisions, lack of initiative, and going through the motions, with no zest for living.

## J. William Worden

J. William Worden, an American clinical psychologist, has developed a prominent model that explains coping with grief in terms of four tasks to be accomplished, which accomplished probably explains the appeal of his model to Americans who appreciate a pragmatic focus on how to deal with a problem.

In the first edition of his book, Worden's four tasks were to

1. accept the reality of the loss
2. work through to the pain of grief
3. adjust to an environment in which the deceased is missing
4. withdraw emotional energy and reinvest it in another relationship

A Kansas State University undergraduate student whose husband died in a car accident told me she absolutely refused to accept Task 4: "If that is what recovery from bereavement means, then the hell with it," was her statement when she read Worden's task-based model.

Because of fairly persuasive empirical and conceptual challenges from Dennis Klass, a researcher who has studied bereaved parents for more than 25 years, and from Phyllis Silverman, a researcher who has studied bereaved spouses and children for at least as long as Klass has studied parents, Worden revised the fourth task in the second edition of his book.[5] Klass showed that many, if not all, of the parents he had come to know had accomplished Tasks 1 through 3 but remained emotionally attached to the child who had died. Worden revised the task to read, "To emotionally relocate the deceased and move on with life." Worden retained this rephrased notion of the fourth task in the 2002 edition of his book. The rephrasing, while still very close to Freud's overall idea of letting go, suggests the possibility of maintaining a continuing attachment to the one who died.

In the past couple of years Worden has revisited his fourth task and rephrased it to state explicitly the normality of an ongoing connection with the one who died. His most recent statement of Task 4 is "to find an enduring connection with the deceased in the midst of embarking on a new life." One senses that, for Worden, the prospect of an ongoing attachment, what is called in many circles a continuing bond with the deceased, has become a description of normality, rather than a description of what occurs as some persons cope with and recover from bereavement. We will discuss continuing bonds later in this chapter.[6]

While there is not a sense that the tasks must be completed in a specified order, Worden does admit that there is a pattern to the tasks as he has defined them. One aspect that critics like about Worden's approach over their criticism of the phase models of grieving (think of Bowlby's four phases) is that tasks to accomplish make grieving a proactive process.

Working on these tasks provides a renewed sense of control, a sense of autonomy. The tasks give direction to grief counselors in planning and assessing their sessions with bereaved clients.

## Continuing Bonds

Perhaps no construct has so quickly captured the imagination of bereavement researchers and clinicians as has that of *continuing bonds.* This idea emerged from the careful research observations of Dennis Klass and his multiyear work with bereaved parents, of Phyllis Silverman and her longitudinal studies of bereaved children, of Nancy Hogan and her research with bereaved adolescent siblings, and of Steven Nickman and his research with individuals involved in adoption.

At its base, the notion of *continuing bonds* challenges the idea that recovery from bereavement requires severing emotional ties with the person who has died. What many bereaved individuals have reported is that they have an ongoing connection with the deceased. At times this continuing bond reveals itself in what other persons have called paranormal experiences, and what some would simply consider hallucinations or delusions. Because there had been such a solid discrediting of ongoing attachments with the deceased—primarily discredited by bereavement clinicians and researchers as a manifestation of pathology—it was not until bereaved parents began sharing their experiences with each other that open acknowledgment of an ongoing attachment was recognized. Continuing bonds provided a needed corrective to the judgment that only emotional withdrawal from the deceased marks normal grieving.

There has been a significant swing from characterizing ongoing attachments to the deceased as a sign of pathology to prescribing them as what is expected of people when bereaved. There has been a bandwagon acceptance of continuing bonds as normative for everyone. Much as the damage that has been done by imposing the Kübler-Ross idea of stages of dying onto terminally ill or bereaved individuals, stipulating that grievers should have an ongoing attachment to the dead person is a grave danger.[7]

Clearly, not all persons report an ongoing attachment to the person who died. In a study of attachment and bereaved college students, the students with the most acute and enduring grief reported feeling a closer attachment to the person who had died than did bereaved students with markedly diminished grief; it also seemed that the closer in time to the death, the closer the attachment reported by the bereaved students.

Empirical evidence indicates that secure attachments prior to a death can lead to bereavement resolution marked by ongoing attachment after the death. In cases of insecure attachment bonds prior to the death, letting go or detaching from the deceased would be in the best interest of the griever. The book *Liberating Losses* provides articulate expression that, indeed, not all deaths produce bereavements with ongoing attachments. As the authors of that book illustrate, some husbands were oppressive and abusive, leaving their wives with an exhilarating sense of freedom when the men died.

A serious issue for recovery from bereavement is that letting go is often difficult for persons with ambivalent attachments to someone who died. Laura Rabin, associate professor of psychology and director of Brooklyn College's Mental Health Counseling Master's Program, pointed out that in ambivalent relationships, death leaves many feelings unresolved and also leaves the bereaved wrestling alone with the emotional turmoil aroused by the relationship.

## The Dual-Process Model of Coping With Loss

A recent addition to thinking about coping with loss is the dual-process model. This new model is a significant advance in thinking about the psychology of separation and loss. It arises from extensive clinical experience and research studies with bereaved persons, primarily widows. The model, developed by British psychologist Margaret Stroebe and Dutch psychologist Henk Schut, who are part of a team of researchers at the University of Utrecht, is called the dual-process model of coping with loss.

Stroebe and Schut have proposed a refinement to the grief work hypothesis. They maintain that work with bereaved persons indicates two distinct processes, not merely a confrontation with distress, enable bereaved persons to adapt to their loss. They acknowledge that the grief work hypothesis is correct in pointing out the importance of focusing at times on the distress of one's losses. However, it is also important to attend to other aspects of life. Stroebe and Schut proposed that recovery from bereavement requires a loss orientation (the grief work notion) and a restoration orientation (life goes on). Bereaved persons oscillate between these orientations as they deal with their bereavement. See Figure 3.1 for an illustration of the oscillation process Stroebe and Schut have proposed. This oscillation is normal; it is what people do naturally. The dual-process model offers a necessary correction to bereavement counseling that emphasized only the grief work hypothesis. Telling a bereaved person only to focus on the distress that their bereavement causes them is not only incorrect but also misguided.

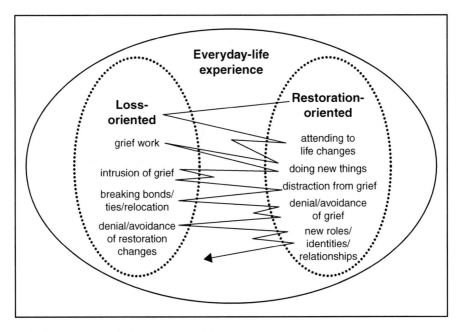

**FIGURE 3.1**   The dual-process model.

## Intuitive and Instrumental Grieving

Most persons I know assume males and females respond quite differently to bereavement. There is a catch to such thinking. Are there trustworthy clinical or research data to support this assertion about gender differences in bereavement responses? The great preponderance of participants in bereavement research and in bereavement interventions are female. Much of what we know, therefore, about responses to bereavement is based on what women report and how females cope. Women typically seek vocal expression of their grief, whereas men seem much less inclined to talk about their feelings. Men seem much more inclined to become introspective and to do things rather than talk about what they are experiencing. I have wondered whether the males who take part in bereavement research and in bereavement interventions are so unlike males who don't take part that we actually have no trustworthy empirical data on gender differences, but rather understandings based on anecdotal evidence.

There is an expectation in several circles (see Lindemann's influence here as a major example) that the appropriate approach to grieving is affective and vocal. Bereaved persons who do not respond affectively and do not talk about their experience are considered to be doing it wrong. They are assumed not to be grieving or at least to be grieving incorrectly.

A seminal contribution to bereavement scholarship has not only attacked this assumption but has actually proposed an alternative point of view that has captured many persons' attention. This alternative point of view distinguishes between two approaches to grieving: intuitive grieving and instrumental grieving.

Intuitive and instrumental approaches to grieving manifest in each of the holistic dimensions of human existence, and they have subconscious origins. Intuitive grieving primarily involves affect and talking, whereas instrumental grieving primarily involves thinking and action. As examples, an intuitive griever would look for someone to share what she feels, and an instrumental griever would look for something to do (for instance, develop a memorial for the person who died) and would think about how to deal with the loss. While there are males who do fit the intuitive approach and females who fit the instrumental, it is more likely—given socialization patterns on gender role development—for males' response tendencies to be instrumental and for females' response tendencies to be intuitive.

There are bereaved persons whose outward manifestations do not match their response tendencies to grieving; thus, some intuitive grievers adopt stoicism and curb their feelings, and some instrumental grievers become disorganized and display their emotions (for instance, by crying). Comparisons of intuitive and instrumental approaches to grieving are presented in Table 3.1.

The idea about intuitive and instrumental approaches to grieving has profound implications for helping bereaved college students. We will consider the idea when discussing interventions and when discussing the issue of self-disclosure and college student bereavement.

## Disenfranchised Grief

Kenneth Doka, a prolific writer and seminal thinker about issues of death, dying, and bereavement, coined the phrase *disenfranchised grief*. What in the world could this mean? According to the online version of the *Oxford English Dictionary*, the verb *disenfranchise* means "to deprive of the right to vote" and "to deprive of a right or privilege" (http://www.askoxford.com/).

Disenfranchised grief brings in the role of society and gets beyond considering grief solely as a matter for individuals. The idea is twofold:

**TABLE 3.1**  Intuitive and Instrumental Grieving Compared

| Intuitive | Instrumental |
|---|---|
| Bereavement experienced affectively | Bereavement experienced cognitively |
| Outwardly express grief | Focus on mastering one's situation |
| Share with others one's feelings | General reluctance to discuss feelings |
| Primary strategy is to experience the distress that bereavement produces | Primary strategy is to problem solve and conceptualize |
| Secondary strategy is to care for others and fulfill responsibilities | Secondary strategy allows for expressing feelings in private |
| Prolonged periods of Lindemann's acute grief syndrome | Intermittent, brief periods of cognitive confusion |

(a) some relationships are deemed illegitimate or improper or marginal or unimportant and (b) bereavement experienced at the loss of such relationships won't be accepted by mainstream society. Examples would include relationships between homosexual partners, divorced couples, or long-term clandestine lovers in extramarital affairs. Other examples include grief over a miscarried or aborted fetus,[8] grief experiences of prisoners over the death of someone loved, and grief following a pet's death.

In short, disenfranchised grief denotes that reactions to some losses are not socially approved or sanctioned. Society disenfranchises bereavement in such cases because the loss is not recognized and/or social norms do not provide a role for grieving such a loss. As stated earlier, such losses would be associated with relationships that are considered marginal, illicit, or unapproved. In effect, sorrow felt over such losses must be kept hidden, the bereaved is deprived of the right to grieve, and thereby is a victim of disenfranchisement. Societal norms for what is acceptable lead to recognized losses and to approved grieving roles. The societal rules or norms that apply for recognized losses can, in turn, disenfranchise reactions to other losses. At times, these societal rules are culturally bound, as for instance is the case when a Muscogee Creek Indian is not permitted leave time from work to be with his extended family when an uncle dies. In other cases, the lack of a grieving role can also extend to the lack of social support, as would be the case for a man bereaved over the death of an extramarital lover, grief over the death of one's former spouse, or grief over early pregnancy losses.

A concern is that disenfranchised grief can lead to serious complications because the person must mask the impact of bereavement. Shakespeare captured well this notion when he wrote in *Macbeth*, "Give sorrow words. The grief that does not speak whispers the o'er-fraught heart, and bids it break." The isolation that disenfranchisement produces leads to increased feelings of anger, guilt, and depression because social outlets for expression, communication, and support are absent.

I believe another aspect of disenfranchisement comes from grief being dismissed or ignored. The example of grief over a pet's death contains this notion of a loss dismissed as unimportant. We know of other examples. The ignoring of bereaved siblings when a child dies in the family is one I learned when I was doing my dissertation on sibling death during adolescence. The example of importance for this book is the ignoring of bereavement in the college student body.

There are various ways that disenfranchised grief characterizes college student bereavement. Consider, for instance, the reaction of "so what?" that many unaffected outsiders on the campus have when learning that up to 30% of college students are in the first year of bereavement. Consider as well the reaction of people who underestimate the duration and intensity of grief reactions and say in effect to a bereaved peer, "Aren't you over that yet? It's been 3 months." Consider the basic fact that grieving college students comprise a hidden population. Consider that in many cases the student's grief is over the death of someone unknown to others on the campus, such as is the case of a student whose grief is for a mother or father and whose home town is far from campus. Consider the problems for an instrumental griever whose approach to grieving is questioned by persons on campus. Finally, consider the issue facing students who are grieving the types of relationships considered illicit or marginal, such as the death of a homosexual partner or the loss of a fetus due to miscarriage.

## Restoration of Meaning

Another significant contribution to our thinking about bereavement has come from the constructivist camp in psychology. Thinkers in this camp emphasize the fundamental assault that bereavement can impose on one's assumptions about reality.

Current models of coping with life crises make establishing the personal significance of the situation one of the central tasks in coping. For instance, a college student faced with the death of her father needs to recognize the reality of this rupture to the family and come to terms with the permanence of the loss. Establishing the personal significance of a life crisis is an ongoing task to which the person will return as life events change. Consider again the student dealing with her father's death. She may slowly (or quickly) learn that major events in her life will take place without her father's presence. When her sorority hosts parents for Parents' Day, when she graduates from college, when she gets married, when she gives birth, when she goes to a family reunion, when her family celebrates the new year, she may have to face again the fact that her father's death has changed her life. In short, there is a "regrief phenomenon" that people report to be common when developmental milestones and idiosyncratic reminders of the absence occur. A developmental milestone could be graduating from college, and an idiosyncratic reminder could come as a whiff of cologne that brings to mind the person who died.

Attention to the importance of meaning making in the midst of crises has emerged as psychologists, philosophers, sociologists, and psychiatrists have examined the issues actually occurring as persons cope. One of the early proponents of the importance of meaning making when in crisis was Viktor Frankl, the Austrian psychiatrist whom the Nazis imprisoned in various concentration camps. For Frankl, maintaining hope was at the heart of successful coping; hope gave the prisoner meaning, something to look forward to after the war. Frankl noted that when a prisoner lost hope, the person quickly died.

An intricate theory of personality has been constructed around the central importance of meaning making. George Kelly proposed a theory of personality that he called "personal construct theory." Kelly maintained that the core tendency of the human person is to predict and control events. We develop constructs about reality in order to increase our accuracy in predicting and controlling events. The constructs we develop enable us to consign meaning to experiences. The construct either fits our experience (what would be called "assimilation" by psychologists such as Piaget) or we must form new constructs or somehow adjust how we already understand reality (what would be called "accommodation").

Let us imagine that a college student's constructs about reality are that the world is a fair and benevolent place and that God will not allow harm to come to someone who is good. Subsequently, that student's sister contracts a disease that causes great pain and eventually kills her. Making meaning out of this experience begins as the student attempts to fit her sister's illness and death into the construct about a benevolent and fair world in which God protects the good.

For some persons, such assimilating would be possible because the experience does not signify that the world has a grudge against them, and it does not mean that trusting God is a mistake. These individuals accept on faith that there is a plan for good, even though it is unclear to them how the death they grieve fits into that plan. For other persons, their constructs about the world and about God would be sorely tested, and they would have to form new constructs that allowed for prediction and control of experience in the face of ambiguity.

This move toward meaning making is what some experts consider at the heart of dealing with bereavement. The chief proponent is Robert Neimeyer, a professor of psychology at the University of Memphis. Neimeyer says that meaning making—what he calls "meaning reconstruction"—is an active process involving three activities: (a) sense making, (b) benefit finding, and (c) identity change. We will take up each in turn, and then look at some of the challenges to the idea that meaning making is at the core of coping when bereaved.

## Sense Making

Neimeyer notes that difficult life experiences that fail to make sense are the ones that most challenge personal equanimity. They plant seeds of self-doubt and stir up mental and emotional turmoil. To regain a sense of predictability and control, the natural step is to find a reason for what happened.

In cases of bereavement, people look for information about how the death happened, and look for answers to why it happened, for answers how the death is going to impact life from now on, and perhaps for answers why this burden came to them. Thus, sense making is a three-fold process for Neimeyer:

1. the grieving person questions her (his) bereavement
2. the grieving person looks for meaning in the loss
3. the grieving person makes sense of the bereavement

In the third step, if making sense of the bereavement leads the griever to determine that the meaning corresponds to assumptions about reality, then the griever fits the experience into overall constructs about existence. If, however, assumptions about existence fly in the face of the experience the griever has had, then making sense requires the griever to construct a new sense of reality. Persons who search for meaning but find none are the most distressed grievers.

Some persons have asked, "Why can't some grieving persons find meaning?" I will identify some of the cases of persons left bereft of meaning when they search for it following a death, and perhaps inferring the difficulties involved will be apparent. Think of the parents of a child who is kidnapped, tortured, and killed by a serial killer. Think of parents whose apparently perfectly healthy infant dies in his (her) sleep. Think of the college student whose best friend is killed in a drive-by shooting. In each case, is it difficult to imagine the assault on beliefs in a moral order and a just world? What purpose could such a wanton death serve?

## Benefit Finding

Coping theorists talk about "reframing" or "positive reappraisal." One form such benefit finding takes is becoming more attuned to letting other persons know they are loved. The notion that benefit finding comes quickly is dispelled by Neimeyer who notes that some benefits emerge only over time as the person matures, gains experiences, reflects on life, becomes more educated, and interacts with others.

A coping skill noted among persons dealing with life crises is pursuing alternative rewards. Such an example of benefit finding can be seen in the investment that some persons make in assisting individuals to manage similar events, for instance, the persons who start support groups for bereaved college students.

## Identity Change

Reconstructing meaning in the face of bereavement, the prototypical life crisis, in effect means constructing oneself anew. Responding to loss in adaptive ways can result in transformation or personal growth. Such growth does not mean anguish is eliminated. The person matures, gains a deeper perspective on the tragedy embedded in human existence, and becomes attuned to the suffering of others.

In constructivist theories of meaning making, it is the distress inherent in the bereavement that impels the person to attempt to make sense of a significant loss. The hypothesis proposed is that without distress there would be no need to make sense out of the loss. There is the prospect, however, that too much distress immobilizes efforts or energy to search for what will make sense of the situation. There is also the possibility that some persons by temperament simply are not reflective and do not engage in sense making. Perhaps these persons are more likely to be, for instance, kinesthetic rather than self-reflective, and to become physically active when dealing with an event challenging their coping skills and presenting a threat to their well-being.

Making sense of a crisis seems to be more helpful when accomplished early in the process of coping. In fact, Neimeyer has concluded that benefit finding fortifies adjustment as the person's coping continues over time. However, decreases in distress are not the earmarks of personal growth or identity change for bereaved persons. They learn how better to deal with the tragic side of life, but such growth does not eradicate the distress inherent to bereavement.

Empirical studies have uncovered the unexpected finding that some bereaved persons who do not engage in a process of meaning making perform well on all measures of functioning (for instance, school work, job performance, personal relationships, spirituality). The concern that these persons are at risk for delayed grief reactions has been dispelled by Bonanno, whose extensive longitudinal research has uncovered no evidence that delayed grief occurs.

I noted earlier that there are some persons plagued because they cannot find any meaning in their loss, and this failure to make meaning out of the event has left them worse off than bereaved individuals for whom loss does not inspire them to search for meaning. The fact that some persons apparently would have been better off had they not needed to find meaning but looked for it and it eluded them underscores the constructivist ideas. The very fact of such painful outcomes to bereavement highlights that meaning making is central for these persons; they cannot find meaning and desperately want to, and if they could they would be able to deal with their loss.

However, the fact that meaning making is not central to the experience of some bereaved persons could be seen (but I think mistakenly) to challenge the constructivists' assertion. A plausible explanation leads us back to the ideas of George Kelly about personal constructs about reality. The reason some persons experience no need to reconstruct meaning out of a loss or even to look for meaning is that the experience of this loss is in accord with their constructs about reality. What happened does not challenge their assumptions about the world. Consider the case of the student whose brother dies in a high-speed car crash; she grieves his death, but she doesn't find the death out of synch with her expectations about this world: Physics indicates persons in vehicles that crash at high rates of speed are likely going to be hurt, even killed.

## George Bonanno

George Bonanno is a bereavement researcher at Columbia University who has challenged assumptions about bereavement that were held for most of the 20th century. For one thing, his research led him to posit the three trajectories of bereavement presented earlier. Data indicating that more people respond resiliently to bereavement rather than struggle to achieve equilibrium have made researchers and clinicians rethink the assumption that severe, debilitating distress is the norm when people are bereaved. For another thing, Bonanno approached bereavement as a stressful event, not as a phenomenon guided by intrapsychic processes or a reaction to sundered attachment bonds. He has expressed severe skepticism that the grief work theory accurately depicts what people need to do when bereaved. Further, he has asserted that research into human psychology emphasizes that confronting the distress that bereavement causes could increase the power of that distress. He has taken to task the idea of delayed grief, and wonders how such an idea ever obtained such a strong following when it has no empirical evidence to support it. Bonanno agrees strongly with the oscillation ideas put forward in the dual-process model and is a leading voice for examining the resiliency of humans in the face of adversity.

Bonanno gathered longitudinal data on bereaved individuals and focused on positive emotions, particularly genuine laughter. He reported that persons who cope better with bereavement spontaneously show genuine smiles or even laugh at times when talking about the person whose death they grieve. Bonanno noted that one of the benefits that such humor produces is setting other people at ease. When discussions of bereavement are interspersed genuinely with moments of laughter and are not marked by uninterrupted gloom and doom, they lead to more satisfying conversations and the likelihood of persons wanting to be together.

## Elisabeth Kübler-Ross

Elisabeth Kübler-Ross was a psychiatrist who was born in Europe and moved to the United States and started working at the University of Chicago. In 1969, Kübler-Ross published a book that captured the imagination of many persons in the United States. In her book she told of her work with persons who were aware they were dying. Of central importance to Kübler-Ross was to get the medical profession to treat dying individuals as living human persons who were dying, not as diseases. This value has been emphatically adopted by hospice.

Kübler-Ross wrote that she interviewed many dying patients and determined that acceptance of dying required passing through five distinct stages. These five stages are described in the following sections.

### Denial
This stage is the initial response to being told one has a terminal disease. Kübler-Ross sees denial as a useful defense mechanism to help a person deal with the news. However, denial is quickly replaced by limited acceptance.

### Anger
The second stage, best expressed by the outcry of "Why me!," is one of rage and resentment at knowing one's life is coming to an end.

### Bargaining
The third stage involves irrational attempts to strike a deal that will postpone one's impending death. People make promises to God such as, "If you let me off the hook, I'll devote my life to working for the poor."

### Depression
The fourth stage has two aspects to it. On the one hand, there is a reactive depression due to losses that come about because of one's illness. For instance, a woman may become depressed when her hair falls out due to chemotherapy or become depressed when her breast is removed in a mastectomy. A man may become depressed when surgery for prostate cancer leaves him impotent. In addition, there is an anticipatory depression that occurs as a person begins preparing for imminent losses such as not seeing grandchildren or being separated forever from loved ones.

### Acceptance
This fifth stage involves foregoing efforts to survive and is characterized by "a degree of quiet expectation (rather than) a resigned and hopeless 'giving up'" (Kübler-Ross, 1969, pp. 112–113).

It is remarkable how widely known Kübler-Ross's five stages are and how much they have been applied to situations other than dying from a terminal illness. For instance, there are articles and dissertations applying Kübler-Ross to reactions to divorce, to unemployment, to retirement from professional sports, and to parent death and sibling death. Somehow, very quickly, the five stages of dying became the five stages of grief, and Kübler-Ross endorsed this application of her ideas.

Concerns over these applications of Kübler-Ross's ideas stem from two sources. One, there is concern that the five stages have become a normative prescription, and if a person is not following the sequence then the person is not dying or grieving properly. As a doctoral student in a field placement, I vividly recall sitting in a cancer specialist's office and hearing her talking on the phone to a woman who had read Kübler-Ross's book.[9] The woman was worried that her husband who had terminal cancer wasn't angry and if he didn't get angry he would never reach the bargaining stage. The doctor gently told the woman not to take Kübler-Ross so literally.

Another concern is that despite efforts to demonstrate empirically the progression through the five stages, no evidence has emerged. These efforts have taken the notion of stages seriously and applied the criteria that must be present for a stage theory to work: The stages must be qualitatively different; they must be irreversible; they must occur in an invariant sequence; and they must be universal. Two examples of stages of development that have strong empirical evidence are the cognitive stages of development proposed by Piaget and the overall stages of human development from infancy, childhood, adolescence, adulthood, and old age. To apply just one of the criteria that must be present for a stage theory to be accepted, let us look at "irreversibility." This criterion means that once a person moves from one stage to the next, there is no return to the former stage. Thus, once a person enters puberty and becomes an adolescent there is no return to childhood.

The issues I have presented about Kübler-Ross's description of the psychosocial response to awareness of dying and loss have not an inkling of importance to bereaved persons who find that the five stages give them a means to understand what they are experiencing. Rather than remaining overwhelmed by not comprehending what is going on, the person finds that he or she can name his/her experiences. Consider these statements, typical of what students have told me about their bereavement. "I know what it means to be angry. And I was really angry when my dad died." "I just couldn't comprehend my sister had died. I was in denial." "I just felt so blue and sad. I was depressed."

One thing is certain about people who respond positively, even enthusiastically, to Kübler-Ross about stages of grieving: They are not impressed by university professors' discussions of why her model is not really a stage theory. "So what?" they seem to say. "I don't care if I moved back and forth. I just know that the names of the stages gave me a way to understand what I was experiencing." And then they say something to the effect of "Go stuff your skepticism." Or "What do your theories have to do with what I know I experienced?" Perhaps we have here a down-to-earth example of a gap separating scholars from real life.

I don't find the Kübler-Ross model the best choice for understanding what bereavement brings and for explaining how persons grieve. My academic colleagues and I are likely to dismiss her model as a faithful description of human responses to loss. Perhaps we have forgotten to honor her accomplishment as a pioneer whose work took place in the face of ridicule and serious obstacles from her medical colleagues. It is certainly an irony that the central value in her work, namely, to treat dying patients as living persons rather than as diseases, has been truncated in some quarters to treating persons according to what stage the person represents. The same irony applies to dealing with bereaved persons. Imposing Kübler-Ross's stages on people keeps us from a personal encounter with a person who is grieving. We focus on what stage is manifest, rather than on being present to the person.

## CONCLUDING COMMENTS

In this chapter, I have commented on the holistic impact bereavement has on us physically, emotionally, cognitively, behaviorally, interpersonally, and spiritually. I described three different bereavement trajectories: a resilient trajectory, a recovery trajectory, and an enduring grief trajectory. I have presented the two main explanatory models that guide thinking about bereavement: Freud's notion of grief work and Bowlby's notion of sundered attachment bonds. Clinical direction was found in Freud's idea of grief work and manifested itself chiefly in the influential writings of Erich Lindemann and of J. William Worden: Lindemann strongly endorsed the practice that bereaved persons confront the distress of their grief, and he identified the acute grief syndrome; Worden provided a conceptual model based on tasks to accomplish as the core of dealing with bereavement.

The prominent contributions since Lindemann and Worden for understanding what coping with bereavement entails have come in the form of (a) two direct challenges to the grief work assertion and (b) the constructivist paradigm that the core of coping with bereavement involves restoring meaning to one's assumptive world. The notion of continuing bonds has challenged the assertion that emotional withdrawal from the person who died is both central to, and necessary for, bereavement recovery. The dual-process model has noted that in the normal course of living, bereaved persons do more than connect continually with the distress that bereavement causes; at times they engage in what it means to be alive. They move back and forth between this loss orientation and this restoration orientation. The idea of intuitive and instrumental grieving postulated that adapting to bereavement occurs in two distinct patterns: a matter of affect and interpersonal sharing for some grievers, and a matter of introspection and physical activity for other grievers; there are no clear cut lines such that persons only use one pattern, although one pattern likely predominates. Some losses are dismissed as of no importance or seriousness; some losses are considered improper. Some grievers are thereby disenfranchised. The constructivist view of bereavement puts all its chips on the human species' penchant for meaning making, and identifies three core activities for the restoration of meaning when bereaved over someone's death: (a) sense making, (b) benefit finding, and (c) identity change. The ideas of George Bonanno have challenged traditional bereavement theory and assumptions, and he has argued that the common human response to bereavement is one of resilience, not enduring distress; he has championed research into the role that positive emotions play in bereavement recovery.

The most popular understanding of grief is Kübler-Ross's idea of five stages of loss. The names of the stages provide people a means to construe meaning out of what is chaos. There is a gulf separating bereavement scholars, who typically dismiss the five stages as a simplistic depiction of what is much more complicated, from persons who have never studied bereavement but who have experienced loss and are looking for a way to make sense out of their wrenching situation. There are, unfortunately, clinicians and other professionals who (a) think their job is to identify what stage of loss a bereaved person presents but forget to be present attentively to the griever in their midst or who (b) think their job is to scoff at the use of Kübler-Ross and in the process cut out from the person the conceptual scaffolding helping them understand their bereavement.

## NOTES

1. These trajectories were identified by George Bonanno, whose research is a topic for later in this chapter. Bonanno discovered the trajectories by examining longitudinal data of bereaved adults. Some readers to earlier drafts of this chapter expressed skepticism that bereavement forms only three trajectories.
2. Laura Rabin, an associate professor of psychology at Brooklyn College and director of the Mental Health Counseling Master's Program, introduced an important qualification. She noted that usually what is lost is highly valued, but the bereaved may have an ambivalent attitude toward the person who died, and such ambivalence can produce complicated bereavement reactions.

3. Recovery from bereavement is hard work and takes a long time according to Freud. His ideas were given the catchy phrase "grief work," but commentators seldom mentioned the task of forming a mental representation as part of completing grief work. It strikes me that with the advances in magnetic resonance imaging (MRI) it would be a very useful and practical project to determine whether brain activity in bereaved persons shows a shift from responses in the amygdala to brain areas where more rational thought occurs. In effect, one could do a longitudinal study following bereaved persons over time, use MRI technology, show pictures of the person who died, conduct functional MRI (fMRI) scans, and see whether changes occur in areas of the brain that are stimulated when the person views the pictures. Why would such a study have any practical value? If there are these shifts in brain activity, there would be empirical credence to Freud's ideas on what bereavement recovery entails. Persuasive fMRI evidence would provide solid evidence whether engaging in grief work is fundamental to bereavement recovery.
4. Bowlby admired Charles Darwin, and even wrote a lengthy biography of Darwin. In fact, he explained Darwin's debilitating physical symptoms that emerged in his adult years to be the consequences of delayed grief to his mother's death when Darwin was a young boy. Few scholars accept this explanation, and the competing explanations refer to three factors: (a) Darwin had been infected with parasites while on the 5-year voyage of the Beagle; (b) Darwin had ingested arsenic as a remedy for ills to such an extent that his body was eventually adversely affected; (c) Darwin developed severe psychophysiological symptoms in anticipation of the volatile reactions that would greet his theory of natural selection. Current thinking accepts the third factor as most likely.
5. Longitudinal evidence from the bereaved children he, Silverman, and Nickman studied offered further persuasion that he reconsider the fourth task of his model.
6. Worden's 2009 edition of his book rephrases Task 2 to read, "To process the pain of grief."
7. Kübler-Ross is discussed later in this chapter.
8. Jeffrey Berman noted that many students in his writing classes, both males and females, wrote about grieving abortions.
9. When she got the phone call, I got up to leave the office, but the physician told me she wanted me to stay.

## FURTHER READING

Attig, T. (1995). *How we grieve: Relearning the world*. New York: Oxford University Press.

Balk, D. E. (1996). Attachment and the reactions of bereaved college students: A longitudinal study. In D. Klass, P. R. Silverman, & S. Nickman (Eds.),

*Continuing bonds: New understandings of grief* (pp. 311–328). Washington, DC: Taylor & Francis.

Bonanno, G. A. (2009). *The other side of sadness: What the new science of bereavement tells us about life after loss.* New York: Basic Books.

Bonanno, G. A., Boerner, K., & Wortman, C. B. (2008). Trajectories of grieving. In M. S. Stroebe, R. O. Hansson, H. Schut, & W. Stroebe (Eds.), *Handbook of bereavement research and practice: Advances in theory and intervention* (pp. 287–307). Washington, DC: American Psychological Association.

Bowlby, J. (1961). Processes of mourning. *The International Journal of Psycho-Analysis, 42,* 317–340.

Bowlby, J. (1969–1980). *Attachment and loss.* [Vol. 1, *Attachment;* Vol. 2, *Separation: Anxiety and anger;* Vol. 3, *Loss: Sadness and depression.*] New York: Basic Books.

Bowlby, J. (1991). *Charles Darwin: A new life.* New York: W. W. Norton.

Colp, R. (1977). *To be an invalid: The illness of Charles Darwin.* Chicago, IL: University of Chicago Press.

Crosby, J. F., Gage, B. A., & Raymond, M. C. (1983). The grief resolution process in divorce. *Journal of Divorce, 7,* 3–18.

Doka, K. J. (Ed.). (2002). *Disenfranchised grief: New directions, challenges, and strategies for practice.* Champaign, IL: Research Press.

Doka, K. J., & Martin, T. L. (2010). *Grieving beyond gender: Understanding the ways men and women mourn.* New York: Routledge.

Eldredge, N. (2005). *Darwin: Discovering the tree of life.* New York: W. W. Norton.

Elison, J., & McGonigle, C. (2003). *Liberating losses: When death brings relief.* Cambridge, MA: Perseus.

Folkman, S. F. (2001). Revised coping theory and the process of bereavement. In M. S. Stroebe, R. O. Hansson, W. Stroebe, & H. Schut (Eds.), *Handbook of bereavement research: Consequences, coping, and care* (pp. 563–584). Washington, DC: American Psychological Association.

Frankl, V. E. (1959). *Man's search for meaning.* New York: Pocket Books.

Freud, S. (1957). Mourning and melancholia. In J. Strachey (Ed. & Trans.), *The standard edition of the complete psychological works of Sigmund Freud* (Vol. 14, pp. 243–258). London: Hogarth Press. (Original work published 1917)

Gillies, J., & Neimeyer, R. A. (2006). Loss, grief, and the search for significance: Toward a model of meaning reconstruction in bereavement. *Journal of Constructivist Psychology, 19,* 31–65.

Hogan, N., & DeSantis, L. (1992). Adolescent sibling bereavement: An ongoing attachment. *Qualitative Health Research, 2*(2), 159–177.

Horowitz, M. J., Siegel, B., Holen, A., Bonanno, G. A., Milbrath, C., & Stinson, C. H. (1997). Diagnostic criteria for complicated grief disorder. *The American Journal of Psychiatry, 154*(7), 904–910.

Jacobs, S. (1993). *Pathologic grief: Maladaptation to loss.* Washington, DC: American Psychiatric Press.

Kelly, G. A. (1955). *The psychology of personal constructs* (Vol. 1). New York: Norton.

Klass, D. (1997). The deceased child in the psychic and social worlds of bereaved parents during the resolution of grief. *Death Studies, 21*(2), 147–175.

Klass, D., Silverman, P. R., & Nickman, S. L. (Eds.) (1996). *Continuing bonds: New understandings of grief.* Philadelphia, PA: Taylor & Francis.

Kübler-Ross, E. (1969). *On death and dying.* New York: Macmillan.

Kübler-Ross, E., & Kessler, D. (2007). *On grief and grieving: Finding the meaning of grief through the five stages of loss.* New York: Scribner's.

Lehman, D. R., Wortman, C. B., & Williams, A. F. (1987). Long-term effects of losing a spouse or child in a motor vehicle crash. *Journal of Personality and Social Psychology, 52*(1), 218–231.

Lindemann, E. (1944). The symptomatology and management of acute grief. *American Journal of Psychiatry, 101,* 141–148.

Moos, R. H., & Schaefer, J. A. (1986). Life transitions and crises: A conceptual overview. *Coping with life crises: An integrated approach* (pp. 3–28). New York: Plenum.

Mulholland, K. A. (2001). *Experiencing and working with incongruence: Adaptation after parent death in adolescence.* Unpublished doctoral dissertation, University of Wisconsin at Madison.

Neimeyer, R. A. (Ed.). (2001). *Meaning reconstruction and the experience of loss.* Washington, DC: American Psychological Association.

Nickman, S. L. (1996). Retroactive loss in adopted persons. In D. Klass, P. R. Silverman, & S. L. Nickman (Eds.), *Continuing bonds: New understandings of grief* (pp. 257–272). Philadelphia, PA: Taylor & Francis.

Oltjenbruns, K. A. (2001). Developmental context of childhood: Grief and regrief phenomena. In M. S. Stroebe, R. O. Hansson, H. Schut, & W. Stroebe (Eds.), *Handbook of bereavement research: Consequences, coping, and care* (pp. 169–197). Washington, DC: American Psychological Association.

Prigerson, H. G., & Jacobs, S. C. (2001). Traumatic grief as a distinct disorder: A rationale, consensus criteria, and a preliminary empirical test. In M. S. Stroebe, R. O. Hansson, W. Stroebe, & H. Schut (Eds.), *Handbook of bereavement research: Consequences, coping, and care* (pp. 613–645). Washington, DC: American Psychological Association.

Prigerson, H. G., Maciejewski, P. K., Reynolds, C. F., Bierhals, A. J., Newsom, J. T., Fasiczka, A., et al. (1995). Inventory of Complicated Grief: A scale to measure maladaptive symptoms of loss. *Psychiatry Research, 59*(1–2), 65–79.

Prigerson, H. G., Vanderwerker, L. C., & Maciejewski, P. K. (2008). A case for inclusion of prolonged grief disorder in DSM-V. In M. S. Stroebe, R. O. Hansson, W. Stroebe, & H. Schut (Eds.), *Handbook of bereavement research and practice: Advances in theory and intervention.* (pp. 165–186). Washington, DC: American Psychological Association.

Rindt, S. E. M. (2002). *Sudden sibling loss: Reflections of women on their experience during adolescence.* Unpublished doctoral dissertation, Alliant International University, San Diego, CA.

Rosenblatt, P. C. (1983). *Bitter, bitter tears: Nineteenth-century diarists and twentieth-century grief theories.* Minneapolis, MN: University of Minnesota Press.

Salazar, M. J. (1992). *Retirement adjustment of professional athletes.* Unpublished doctoral dissertation, Widener University, Institute for Clinical Graduate Study, Chester, PA.

Servaty-Seib, H. L., & Taub, D. J. (2008, Spring). *Assisting bereaved college students. New Directions for Student Services,* Number 121. San Francisco, CA: Jossey-Bass.

Silver, R. C., & Wortman, C. B. (1980). Coping with undesirable life events. In J. Gardner & M. E. P. Seligman (Eds.), *Human helplessness: Theory and applications* (pp. 279–340). New York: Academic Press.

Silverman, P. R. (1987). The impact of parental death on college-age women. *The Psychiatric Clinics of North America, 10*(3), 387–404.

Silverman, P. R., Nickman, S., & Worden, J. W. (1992). Detachment revisited: The child's reconstruction of a dead parent. *The American Journal of Orthopsychiatry, 62*(4), 494–503.

Stroebe, M., & Schut, H. (1999). The dual process model of coping with bereavement: Rationale and description. *Death Studies, 23*(3), 197–224.

Stroebe, M., Schut, H., & Boerner, K. (2010). Continuing bonds in adaptation to bereavement: Toward theoretical integration. *Clinical Psychology Review, 30*(2), 259–268.

Stroebe, M. S., & Stroebe, W. (1989). Who participates in bereavement research? A review and empirical study. *Omega, 20,* 1–29.

Stroebe, W., & Stroebe, M. S. (1987). *Bereavement and health: The psychological and physical consequences of partner loss.* New York: Cambridge University Press.

Tyson-Rawson, K. J. (1993). *College women and bereavement: Late adolescence and father death.* Unpublished doctoral dissertation, Kansas State University, Manhattan, KS.

Walker, A. C. (2008). Grieving in the Muscogee Creek tribe. *Death Studies, 32*(2), 123–141.

Winegardner, D., Simonetti, J. L., & Nykodym, N. (1984). Unemployment: The living death? *Journal of Employment Counseling, 21*(4), 149–155.

Worden, J. W. (1982). *Grief counseling and grief therapy: A handbook for the mental health practitioner.* New York: Springer Publishing Company.

Worden, J. W. (1992). *Grief counseling and grief therapy: A handbook for the mental health practitioner* (2nd ed.). New York: Springer Publishing Company.

Worden, J. W. (2002). *Grief counseling and grief therapy: A handbook for the mental health practitioner* (3rd ed.). New York: Springer Publishing Company.

Worden, J. W. (2009). *Grief counseling and grief therapy: A handbook for the mental health practitioner* (4th ed.). New York: Springer Publishing Company.

Wortman, C. B., & Silver, R. C. (1989). The myths of coping with loss. *Journal of Consulting and Clinical Psychology, 57*(3), 349–357.

# 4

## *Bereavement Seen as a Stressful Event*

Until recently most writing about bereavement amounted to footnotes to Freud and Bowlby. In recent years, some scholars have begun to question what these men taught. We encountered some of those questions in the previous chapter: Questions about withdrawing emotional connections to the deceased as a necessary step in bereavement resolution have emerged with the extremely popular notion of continuing bonds; an oscillation between confronting the distress of one's bereavement and engaging in the world has been proposed as a more accurate portrayal of how bereaved people really function. In addition, some scholars have asserted that no studies have been conducted to establish the veracity of the grief work theory, and others have questioned whether grief work actually works.

Taking a different tack at understanding bereavement, a group of scholars interested in human responses to stress has proposed that bereavement be examined as a distressing event requiring adaptation. A considerable body of literature has examined human coping with stressful life events. In this chapter, I have synthesized this information, and then offered opportunities for readers to examine if thinking of bereavement in terms of stress matches their experiences.

## AN OVERVIEW ABOUT STRESS

In the most general sense, stress refers to hardship or some sort of adversity with which a person must cope. Obviously stress affects other living beings and is not unique to humans. There is even the notion that inanimate objects are subject to stress, as in the case of the amount of weight a steel girder can bear before it cracks. In this book, we are focused on stress and humans, and in particular on the notion that bereavement should be considered a stressful life event.

We know that stress can have environmental, psychological, or biochemical origins as well as possessing combinations of these various sources. As an example, environmental stress could come from being exposed to extreme cold temperatures or from being trapped in a burning building or being in a firefight during combat. Sorting out where sources of stress begin and end is complicated. For instance, when a person feels psychological stress over a nasty argument with a friend, there is also an element of environmental stress involved since the source of the stress is not only internal but also external to the person. When a person is mourning the death of a family member, such stress involves all three sources: the psychological component we call grief, the environmental component that the death presents, and the biochemical component whereby bereavement affects a person's immune system and other physiological reactions. In short, stress involves internal or external demands requiring a person to respond. So, we are going to start with this notion: Stress refers to internal or external hardship or adversity that requires a person to respond adaptively, that is, to cope with the demands and manage them.

## THE GENERAL ADAPTATION SYNDROME

I am going to move now to examining a model called the General Adaptation Syndrome that has been proposed to explain what stress requires in terms of coping or adaptation. The model was developed by Hans Selye, a Canadian researcher who examined the effects of stress on biological organisms, and, in particular, on the human body.

According to the General Adaptation Syndrome, the human body's reaction to unremitting and extreme stress occurs in three chief phases:

1. The first phase is one of **alarm and mobilization of resources**. For example, consider the response of the immune system when it detects that an infection has invaded the body. The immune system has evolved to distinguish microorganisms such as viruses or parasitic worms that don't belong in the body. When the immune system detects "non-self" substances, it produces antibodies to eliminate the infection.

2. The second phase is the **stage of resistance**. According to Selye, during this phase the maximum biological effort is made to defend

against the identified danger. Thus, in the example of an infection, white blood cells rush to the source of the infection.
3. The third phase is **exhaustion and disintegration**. If the threat is not overcome in the second phase, eventually bodily resources will be depleted, and the body will lose its ability to resist. This outcome is what happens to many persons who are infected with HIV and do not receive antiretroviral drug treatment: Despite massive efforts of the body to overcome the infection, eventually the virus overwhelms the immune system and leads to death.

Psychological decompensation, which can occur after a person experiences extreme hardship or adversity, seems to follow a course similar to what Selye noted for biological systems. There is first the **alarm and mobilization of resources**. For example, consider your first reaction when walking in the forest and confronting a full-grown bear. Imagine your reaction upon learning that you have lost your entire life savings because of a very bad investment decision. For many individuals, the reactions to either of these events would include feelings of anxiety and fear.

The second phase, the **stage of resistance**, means the person begins examining options for coping with the threat. In the example of seeing the bear, some people would react by running, while others would remain still; in either case, there would be a rush of adrenalin from the alarm and mobilization phase saying "fight or flee." In the example of having lost one's life savings, one coping response may be to locate a lawyer who could help recoup the losses because of criminal activity on the part of investors who squandered your money.

The third phase, **exhaustion and disintegration**, sets in if a person's resources are depleted in efforts to overcome the threat. What occurs psychologically with persons who reach this stage can involve a break with reality, including hallucinations and delusions, and other manifestations of psychological disorganization. Persons overwhelmed with financial ruin may become so distraught and depressed that they take their own lives. Running from the bear could just as well lead to death if the bear decides to chase the person down and attack.

Let's consider a less extreme example of psychological exhaustion, one well-known to some college students: studying a subject that makes no sense to the person or even one that the student fears. Statistics encompasses both dreaded aspects for many students I know; the material confuses them, and they fear they will not learn it. They enter the classroom already with a sense of alarm. The professor gently mentions that she knows there are probably persons in the course who fear they will not do well, but she advises them that by studying 2–3 hours every day, even when the material makes no sense, at some point a light will go on and they will say, "Of course." However, if they do not spend time studying, the professor warns that their predictions of doing poorly will come true.

Rather than give in to their fears, the students set aside time to study the material, but it just doesn't make any sense to them no matter how hard they work on it. Thinking about statistics exhausts them, and they just cannot seem to get it despite studying. Eventually, many simply do give up and feel defeated. There are, however, subsets of the students who entered the classroom with dread, but who trusted the professor's advice to study 2–3 hours every day. They feel overwhelmed and confused, but keep plugging away. And all of a sudden, something clicks and they say, "Of course." From that point on, they no longer feel exhausted when thinking about the material but actually feel energized. Thus, there is a model of the human response to stress built on the work of Hans Selye, who studied the reactions of biological organisms to stress. This model is called the General Adaptation Syndrome, and it depicts a progressively worsening condition if resources cannot repair the problem attacking the organism. The General Adaptation Syndrome has been applied to psychological responses to stress and offers a general framework for understanding a deteriorating sequence of events should coping prove inadequate.

## A MODEL DEPICTING HUMAN COPING WITH STRESS

The mainstream models in psychology that examine stress and coping are fundamentally cognitive. In other words, they take as their starting point the assumption that human beings plan, analyze, evaluate, and make decisions based on information, rather than respond solely to stimuli. A characteristic example of this approach is seen in the model developed by Rudolf Moos and Jeanne Schaefer to explain what is required to cope with a life crisis.

For Moos and Schaefer, human beings are able to analyze life situations and respond adaptively by using their minds. The model they have developed is also based on the expectation that people will take action to resolve adversity. The model states that a significant component of coping involves appraisal of the stress, that is, sizing up what is causing the problem or challenge the person is facing. The model is also based on the notion that there are structural features to life crises—crises present a threat to well-being, crises defy a person's normal coping abilities, and crises contain within themselves the prospects for growth as well as dissolution depending upon how a person handles the situation. Life crises are sometimes called dangerous opportunities, a sign that the person is living in interesting times.

## Three Life Components

Three life components come to bear on how effectively a person will deal with a stressful event or situation. These three components are

1.  Background and personal factors such as a person's age, gender, previous experience dealing with stress, developmental maturity, cultural and ethnic background, religious beliefs, education level, approach to dealing with challenges, and socioeconomic status. As an example, consider the growing acceptance that some persons are intuitive grievers and others instrumental. Intuitive grievers prefer talking about their experiences and their feelings, whereas instrumental grievers prefer taking action and remaining private. While persons may combine aspects of both instrumental and intuitive grieving, the thinking is that one form dominates. I imagine (though I am guessing) that Oprah Winfrey is primarily an intuitive griever, and I have long thought Paul Newman was an example of an instrumental griever. Jacqueline Kennedy's public image suggested an instrumental griever; I am hard-pressed to identify a well-known male who strikes me as an intuitive griever, but I suspect readers will know of some. My father, who described himself as not being a demonstrative person, was an instrumental griever, and my mother, who liked to share experiences with friends, I would describe as an intuitive griever.

2.  Event-related factors such as the extent to which the event was anticipated or unexpected, who the situation most threatens, and the overall extent of impact the event will have. Event-related factors clearly impinge on bereavement, grief, and mourning. Did the person die in an accident and thus without warning, or did the person die from a lingering illness? How will the death affect different persons in the family, such as the children should a parent have been the one to die? How will the death impact both short- and long-term plans and dreams? For example, will a parent's death create financial hardship and force an adolescent to take a job to help support other family members? Will the death make going to college less

likely? Alternatively, perhaps the payout from a life insurance policy opens up possibilities never before considered.

3. Physical and social environmental factors such as family relations and communication, community sources of support, and the overall presence or lack of an infrastructure within society to help persons facing various forms of stress. Some families have a tradition of open, meaningful communication and thus matters are dealt with and confusion removed during difficult times; other families have clear rules prohibiting any sharing of personal information or showing of emotions so that people need to go their own way when times get tough. Grief over the loss of a pet, death of a friend, or death of a celebrity may feel raw and real to an adolescent—but such grief may be dismissed as of no consequence and not permitted within the youth's family or larger community. Similarly, a student's grief may simply not be recognized and its salience not understood by individuals at the student's college or university.

## Tasks to Be Accomplished

The Moos and Schaefer model emphasizes *tasks to be accomplished* and *coping skills to employ*. A person dealing with stress has five adaptive tasks that must be met if the stress is to be well managed. It is crucial to understand that these tasks present on-going issues to which the person will return, rather than resolve and never have to face again. Examples will be used to illustrate what I mean.

*Task 1: Establish the meaning and personal significance of the stressful situation.* Resolving this task will change over time for the individual. The initial understanding of the significance of the stress may not be clear until time passes, or a person may take a while to allow his/her emotional understanding and intellectual analysis to mesh. As an example, consider a family in which a parent has died. How does a 5-year-old child understand the significance of this event as compared to how her 13-year-old sister understands it? How does the 38-year-old husband who has a steady job and a college education understand the death of his wife in comparison to a 35-year-old wife who has lost her husband but who had quit college years before to care for her family and now has few "marketable" skills? As time unfolds deeper implications may become apparent. For instance, the 5-year-old begins to learn that her father is not going to come back and the 13-year-old revisits, at her high school graduation, the fact that her father will not be there to celebrate with her. For the grieving husband and the grieving wife, issues of parenting become prominent as they think about the significance of the death of their spouse. As time unfolds, the bereaved husband may learn he has nurturing skills he had not recognized; the bereaved wife may finish her education and take on roles outside the home that would not have been imagined when her husband was alive.

*Task 2: Confront reality.* The person must deal with and respond to the requirements of the situation. Some of these realities will be immediate and, perhaps, time limited, whereas others will emerge slowly, over time. Should her husband die, a bereaved wife and mother will have to restructure certain roles in the family, and almost assuredly cope with a significant loss of income. The 13-year-old may find herself spending more time at home to watch her younger siblings because her mother has had to find work outside the home.

*Task 3: Sustain interpersonal relationships.* There is a necessity to keep open lines of communication. It is not uncommon for persons in the midst of feeling overwhelmed with stress to retreat from personal contact. Without sustaining interpersonal relationships, a person cannot get comfort and support, and the healthy distraction from troubles will be missing. There will be no possibility of gaining wisdom and advice if a person cuts off contact with others. It is well known that humans do better when emotionally involved with others. The danger found in many persons struggling with serious stress is to become isolated in their pain and confusion. For instance, as the stress piles up in a single-parent household headed by a woman whose husband has died, relationship between the mother and her children may become strained, adding to the overall problems people are facing because of their grief.

*Task 4: Preserve a reasonable emotional balance by managing upsetting feelings aroused by the situation.* This task includes both the expression of one's feelings and the realization of times when such expression is inappropriate. Sharing one's feelings with friends hopefully is acceptable, but impulsively disclosing one's grief to a complete stranger (for instance, the cashier at a convenience store) will likely not be appropriate. Common emotional reactions aroused by stressful events include fear, anxiety, anger, guilt, and confusion. Recent discussions of grieving emphasize the central place that emotions, often on an unconscious level, play in the resolution of bereavement.

*Task 5: Preserve a satisfactory self-concept and maintain a sense of self-efficacy.* Self-concept refers to a person's perception of himself (or herself) in relation to many perspectives, such as relations with others, ethics, vocation/career direction, emotional maturity, and sexual orientation. Self-efficacy refers to the person's belief that outcomes desired are within her (or his) ability to attain. Aspects included in this fifth task in the Moos and Schaefer model include self-confidence to explore new situations and new values. The person needs to feel that he/she can achieve outcomes that are desired. The person who succumbs to being helpless will be particularly vulnerable to not accomplishing this task. The importance of finding hope is mentioned by some persons as the essential response to manage a crisis.

It has not ceased to astonish me that some people who are bereaved report a loss of confidence and an increase in self-doubt. One form this self-doubt took for a Kansas State University college student following the death of her husband (a police officer killed in the line of duty) was feeling betrayed by what appeared to be compassion from a male friend but what turned out to be an effort at seduction; she said that she then began to doubt her judgment of other persons, an ability she had trusted implicitly before.

## Coping Skills

Moos and Schaefer present three sets of coping skills. You might think of them as strategies utilized to accomplish the five tasks described above.

1. *Coping Set One: Appraisal-focused coping.* The person who uses these skills is able (a) to determine the meaning of the stressful event; and (b) comprehend the threat that the stressful situation presents. Appraisal-focused coping involves the use of three specific skills:
   a. *Logical analysis and mental preparation.* This strategy involves breaking a seemingly overwhelming problem into workable components, anticipating consequences, and not getting overwhelmed. The person can mentally rehearse how to handle something related to the situation and draw on past experiences. As an example, the bereaved mother can think through how she is going to present herself at a job interview. The bereaved college student can plan how she will present her situation to the Dean of Student Life or what she will tell her roommates.
   b. *Cognitive redefinition.* People using this skill deal with the basic reality of the situation and readjust to find aspects that are favorable. Examples of what people do are to remind themselves that things could be worse, compare their situation to the plight of others, change their priorities, or focus on something positive that has emerged or will emerge from the adversity. A woman coping with her husband's death, for example, may remind herself that she had a good

marriage, but she may see that she now has a chance to pursue certain life goals that her husband obstructed. A woman I met at Brooklyn College, whose husband had so strenuously objected to his wife's becoming an attorney that she put aside these career goals, was now pursuing a law degree following her husband's death.

c.  *Cognitive avoidance or denial.* This skill involves an array of strategies aimed at denying, minimizing, or avoiding the situation. People will think of other things than what is troubling them or stay away from places that produce intrusive thoughts and images about the situation. There is a clear sense of the immediate value that cognitive avoidance or denial provides and growing evidence that as an intermittent strategy cognitive avoidance or denial helps people go on with living. The danger with these strategies, however, is to adopt them on a continual basis so that you do not confront the reality that the stressful situation presents. There is evidence from the dual process model of coping with loss that bereaved persons naturally spend some time staying away from the distress of their bereavement.

2.  *Coping Set Two: Problem-focused coping.* With this set of coping skills the person deals with the consequences of the situation and works to develop a more satisfying situation. Clearly, this set of coping skills enables a person to confront the reality of a stressful situation and its aftermath. Problem-focused coping has three specific skills:

a.  *Seek information and support.* The person will obtain information about the crisis and about alternate courses of action. The support may come from family members, friends, and other helpful persons in the community. One means of seeking information and support has been found in the growing popularity of support groups such as Parents Without Partners. Compassionate Friends is another influential support group for bereaved parents. The National Students of AMF Support Network is a student-led initiative on numerous college campuses to assist bereaved students. Typing in "locate a support group" at Google will produce many hits to consider.

b.  *Take problem-solving action.* These coping skills deal directly with actions to manage the situation. Examples include seeking a loan to cover unexpected financial obligations, putting together a plan to handle academic demands, and working out a strategy to find employment. Engaging successfully in problem-solving action builds a sense of competency and efficacy.

c. *Identify and pursue alternative rewards.* These coping skills encompass efforts to replace losses and find satisfaction in new endeavors and relationships. Sometimes these skills involve redirecting one's energies, for instance, the 13-year-old girl in the bereaved family plunges into school work or the mother becomes more active in her church. A college student may seek out a peer support group or spend time in community volunteer activities.

3. *Coping Set Three: Emotion-focused coping.* This set of skills helps the person to manage the feelings provoked by the situation and to maintain emotional balance. Emotion-focused coping involves the use of three specific skills:

a. *Regulate one's emotions.* These coping skills help the person maintain hope and control emotions when dealing with distress. Examples include tolerating the ambiguity of one's new situation, acting thoughtfully rather than impulsively, and maintaining composure in social events when expressing one's pain would be counterproductive. For example, let's take the case of a bereaved college student whose best friend has died. This student has been plunged into a situation totally new to her, but rather than giving into the temptation to turn her autonomy over to someone else (for instance, her parents), she steps back and says she is going to find out her options for dealing with her bereavement rather than let her panic control her.

b. *Express one's emotions.* These skills comprise a diverse array of responses that involve both expression of one's feelings and actions that reduce tension; some responses prove more productive in the long term than others. Examples include venting one's frustration, engaging in aerobic exercise, using jokes and other forms of humor, taking tranquilizers, smoking, drinking alcohol, writing poetry, singing, lashing out in anger, and crying. One bereaved college student whose mother died took up jogging with her roommate, joined the church choir, and occasionally spent extra time in the shower because then she could cry and others wouldn't see her. A second example is found in the response of David Fajgenbaum, the Georgetown University student who founded Students of AMF Support Network in collaboration with close friends (see www.studentsofamf.org/).

c. *Accept the situation.* These skills allow the person to come to terms with the situation and accept it for what it is. Examples are varied and include such actions as concluding that nothing can be done to change the situation, trying to avoid similar situations, concluding that there is an underlying tragic, even absurd, element to one's life, and thinking that the situation is God's will. A college student whose boyfriend died while driving under the influence has determined that she will never again enter a car with an intoxicated driver.

## An Exercise for Applying the Moos and Schaefer Model

I am going to offer a simple application of the various components of the Moos and Schaefer model. I have geared the exercise toward bereavement over the death of a family member or friend. The exercise assumes that the person completing it is willing to engage in self-disclosure. I hope the person has someone with whom to share the exercise when it is completed. A counselor could use the exercise after trust has been established and the student feels willing to explore aspects of his/her coping.

---

### An Exercise for Applying the Moos and Schaefer Model

Consider your current state of bereavement and reflect on answering these questions. If there is someone in your life who knows you and whom you trust, it will help to share this information with that person and ask for reactions, such as, does she or (he) see you as you have portrayed yourself?

- What background and personal factors influence how you cope with the death?
- What are the event-related factors that most characterize the death?
- What physical and socioenvironmental factors helped and which hindered dealing with the death?
- How well have you managed the adaptive tasks? Specifically,
  - □ Establishing the meaning and personal significance of the death
  - □ Confronting reality
  - □ Sustaining interpersonal relationships
  - □ Preserving a reasonable emotional balance by managing upsetting feelings aroused by the death
  - □ Preserving a satisfactory self-concept and maintaining as sense of self-efficacy.

■ How well are you using the sets of coping skills? Specifically,
  □ Logical analysis and mental preparation
  □ Cognitive redefinition
  □ Cognitive avoidance or denial
  □ Seeking information and support
  □ Taking problem-solving action
  □ Identifying and pursuing alternative rewards
  □ Regulating your emotions
  □ Expressing your emotions
  □ Accepting the situation.

Some students at Brooklyn College applied the Moos and Schaefer model to grieving the deaths of their grandfathers. They informed me that the exercise provided them with clarification. Here are some of the points they made.

### Background and Personal Factors

*Background and personal factors influencing how I cope with the death of my grandfather are religious, Christian, that we live hereafter in eternal heaven with God. This gives me strength and hope to grieve and heal.*

*My background and personal factors definitely influence how I cope with death. As a child growing up in a single mother home with extremely support-ive maternal grandparents, I was taught to believe in God, there is a Heaven, and that everything happens for a reason.*

### Event-Related Factors

*Event-related factors that most characterize the death of my grandfather were physical factors helping in dealing with death: Grandpa was old and his body was worn out. He did not want to suffer any more. He was at home at the time of death. I was not there at the time of his death.*

*Event-related factors that characterized my grandfather's death for me were that he seemed indestructible. When he started showing signs of his illness, it was difficult to watch.*

### Socioenvironmental Factors

*The physical and socioenvironmental factors that helped me to cope with my grandfather's illness and death were the love and support I got from my mother and sister.*

*We were kind of prepared because the last 6 months of his life he was not himself.*

### Adaptive Tasks

*I managed my adaptive tasks by considering what he would have wanted, and now what I selfishly wanted. I take comfort in knowing he is no longer suffering. He would not have wanted to be kept alive artificially, so he got what he wanted, drifting off in his own time, his own way.*

*(1) Establishing meaning and personal significance of the death: My grandfather's death was extremely significant because his death brought us as a family even closer. (2) Confronting reality: I realized a few weeks prior to his death that he was going to die really soon because we began making arrangements but indirectly. (3) Preserve a reasonable emotional balance by managing upsetting feelings aroused by the death: I will always be emotional when I speak about my grandfather's death because of the bond that we shared but, since his death I have tried to manage my emotions by thinking of good memories when he was alive. (4) Preserving a satisfactory self-concept and maintaining a sense of self-efficacy: I try to apply this in my life, but it is hard when you have such a bond with that individual.*

### Coping Skills

*With the use of the coping skills overall, I reflected on the fun side of the individual.*

*I keep pictures of grandpa and other family members visible in my house, and this seems to lower the stress while grieving. I also spoke at the funeral in honor of my grandfather. I think about the good times we had together throughout my life and this brings positive images to my mind rather than negative ones.*

## A SOCIOCULTURAL MODEL ABOUT DEALING WITH STRESS

In this section I present the extraordinary achievement of a multidisciplinary team of clinicians and researchers in the 1950s. The main figure behind this work was Alexander Leighton, a social psychiatrist with strong interests in anthropology and appreciation for the diversity of other cultures.

Leighton was the Director of the Program in Social Psychiatry at Cornell University. He gathered around him the talents of scholars and clinicians from such fields as social work, statistics, anthropology, clinical psychology, psychiatry, and epidemiology to examine the relation between psychiatric disorders and the sociocultural environment. At the core of Leighton's work was an interest in how persons, in the midst of a specific sociocultural environment, deal with stress.

Presenting material about Leighton's model is a natural progression for this book. We have moved from the broad model developed by Selye (the general adaptation syndrome) to the cognitive model of individual coping developed by Moos and Schaefer. Thus we have moved from the general to the individual, and now with Leighton we consider the influence of stress in the sociocultural environment on the development of adaptive and maladaptive outcomes.

The study that Alexander Leighton conducted occurred in a section of Nova Scotia. It is instructive to remember what life was like in the 1950s, when there were no cell phones, personal computers, the Internet, fax machines, microwave ovens, community counseling centers, or even a system of interstate highways linking the various parts of the United States and Canada. For instance, when someone became seriously incapacitated with a psychiatric problem, the options included expensive private help in an exclusive hospital or clinic, or less skilled help from state institutions called mental hospitals. What Leighton's research did was set the stage for the remarkable efforts that occurred during the 1960s to develop in the United States a comprehensive program of mental health services for the whole community.

Leighton found some communities in Nova Scotia whose differences were so stark as to provide a natural setting to test the impact of the sociocultural environment on the development of or resistance to psychiatric disturbances. He found some communities that were prospering and socially integrated and others that were failing and marked by social disintegration. A primary thesis of the research project was that social disintegration serves as a primary indicator of stress and that individuals in socially disintegrating communities are at risk for becoming overwhelmed with stress and developing psychiatric disorders. The study confirmed the thesis.

## Central Concepts in Leighton's Model

There are five core concepts in Leighton's sociocultural model. These concepts are (a) human personality, (b) the life arc, (c) the cross-section of the moment, (d) essential human sentiments, and (e) the essential psychical condition.

### Human Personality

Leighton uses the term *human personality* to designate the acting of a human being as a whole—the acting of a person considered a self-integrating, living unit. Human personality is the unfolding of human capacity and potential over the sequence of the individual's life. Leighton's views endorse and use holism.

### The Life Arc

Life-span human developmental psychology, with its emphasis on change and growth across the whole life span, owes a debt to Leighton. For Leighton, human personality is the unfolding of capacity over the temporal sequence of life, or over the *life arc*. Figure 4.1 depicts what Leighton meant by the life arc.

Remember, Leighton believed that human personality is the unfolding of capacity over time. The life arc is intended to illustrate this unfolding.

### Cross-Section of the Moment

The term *cross-section of the moment* is Leighton's term for what we would call a stressful event. Below I describe important aspects of the notion of cross-section of the moment.

1. While a cross-section of the moment can be a distinct event (for instance, the death of a friend in a car accident), a cross-section can also extend in time (for instance, the slow, steady decline of a family member with cystic fibrosis). Regardless of whether a distinct event or extended in time, every cross-section of the moment possesses duration of past, present, and future, what Leighton called *temporal thickness*. Bereaved college students eventually learn that their loss reaches out to them as they continue to live, for instance, when they reach milestones in life such as getting married, having children, or getting a promotion at work.

2. By *temporal thickness* Leighton meant that all significant life events are more than discrete happenings; rather, such events actually extend back in time, and also involve the present moment and stretch into

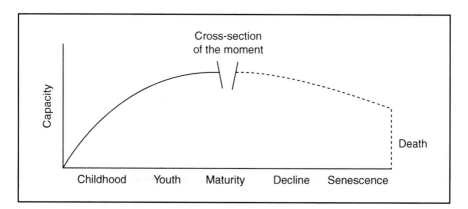

**FIGURE 4.1**  Leighton's life arc.

the future. In Figure 4.1, the solid line leading up to the cross-section of the moment represents the person's experiences up to this life event. The dotted line stretching away from the cross-section represents the person's expectations or anticipations of what the future holds, the outcome of coping with the moment, the resources developed as one copes, and the time required to adapt. To understand these aspects of the cross-section of the moment, consider the differences facing two family members hit with the sudden death of the mother. One family member is a 30-year-old husband/father and the other is a 4-year-old daughter.

While the death of his wife certainly catches the 30-year-old man by surprise, he has had 30 years of experience dealing with loss and responding to stress. He faces this present moment with dread about how he will take care of his child, grief over the loss of his closest friend, and anxiety about being alone for the rest of his adult life. His 4-year-old daughter has a very difficult time even comprehending the finality of death. Mommy is away but will be coming back. This young girl has a less clear sense of anticipating the future, because anticipating is much more circumscribed for a young child than for an adult. Her times without her mother had been always restored by her mother's return, until now. As she grows up, this girl will face many moments when she revisits the loss of her mother (for instance, at her high school graduation, going away to college, or getting married).

## The Essential Human Sentiments

Leighton proposed that striving to achieve certain human sentiments is basic to human existence. While he said that these sentiments vary from culture to culture and from individual to individual, he offered a basic set to consider. These sentiments include (a) to possess physical security, (b) to achieve sexual satisfaction, (c) to express hostility, (d) to express love, (e) to secure love, (f) to secure recognition, (g) to express creativity, (h) to be oriented in terms of one's place in society, (i) to secure and maintain membership in a human group, and (j) to belong to a moral order. I suggest another essential sentiment: to laugh.

The salience of sentiments changes as persons develop. Thus, the need for recognition will remain important but what will satisfy the need will change over time (the 5-year-old who gets a gold star from her kindergarten teacher—the same person 16 years later when she graduates *summa cum laude* from college—and the same person 10 years later when picked by her law firm to be a partner).

### The Essential Psychical Condition

Leighton considered all of human living to be an ongoing striving after, achieving, losing, and striving again for these essential human sentiments. The perpetual process of losing and recovering the essential human sentiments is our *essential psychical condition.*

The primary link for Leighton's model and this discussion of stress is found in the notion of being in a perpetual process of striving after essential human sentiments. In short, by definition stress involves being alive because of the ceaseless effort to attain sentiments essential to our well-being. Obstructions to achieving the essential human sentiments produce stress that can lead to distress if the obstacle is not overcome. As a primary example, consider the obstacles facing the 4-year-old girl now that her mother is dead: She certainly will find such sentiments as securing love hindered as well as wondering about her physical security. She may at times lash out in anger. She may respond in ways that suggest she wonders about there being any moral order. She will especially need consistent parenting comprised of nurturance and discipline to enable her to achieve the sentiments for which human strive.

## An Exercise to Apply the Leighton Model

I am going to offer a simple application of the various components of Leighton's sociocultural model. I have geared the exercise toward bereavement, which Leighton himself identified as an example of a cross-section of the moment presenting obstacles to achieving the essential human sentiments. As with the exercise using the Moos and Schaefer model, I assume that the person completing this exercise is willing to engage in self-disclosure. I hope the person has someone with whom to share the exercise when it is completed. A counselor could suggest the exercise at some point when trust has been established and the student feels willing to explore these aspects of responding to the death being grieved.

---

### An Exercise for Applying the Leighton Model

Consider your current state of bereavement and reflect on it when answering these questions. If there is someone in your life who knows you and whom you trust, it will help to share this information with that person and ask for that person's reactions, such as, does he (or she) view you as you have portrayed yourself?

- When did this cross-section of the moment occur in your life?
- Look at the list of essential human sentiments and assess how well you achieved each one prior to your loss and how well you are achieving each now. Specifically,
  - ☐ Possessing physical security
  - ☐ Achieving sexual satisfaction
  - ☐ Expressing hostility
  - ☐ Expressing love
  - ☐ Securing love
  - ☐ Securing recognition
  - ☐ Expressing creativity
  - ☐ Being oriented in terms of your place in society
  - ☐ Securing and maintaining membership in a human group
  - ☐ Belonging to a moral order
  - ☐ Genuinely laughing.
- What have been your anticipations of the future since the death occurred?
- How have your expectations of the future changed as you grieved your loss?
- Have any of the essential human sentiments become less important to you since the death? If so, which ones and why do you think each has lost its former salience for you?
- Have any of the essential human sentiments become more important to you since the death? If so, which ones and why do you think each has increased in salience for you?

The students at Brooklyn College who applied the Moos and Schaefer model to grieving the deaths of their grandfathers also completed the Leighton exercise. Below are some points they made.

### The Essential Human Sentiments

*(1) Possessing physical security: I just wanted to be alone. Achieving sexual satisfaction took a backburner for quite some time. (2) Expressing hostility: I did that a lot. I used that energy in a kickboxing class. Three times a week I let it all out on a punching bag. I was very angry, but I didn't want to talk about it. (3) Expressing love: Thank GOD for my mother and sister. That's who I shared my love with.*

*(4) Securing love: I know they loved me in return. (5) Securing recognition: It was well known that my grandfather practically raised my sister and me. There was jealousy in my family around that topic. We got the best of him all our lives. We were envied and recognized by our community for that which made us important.*

*My physical security was strong before and after the death. If it had occurred when I was an adolescent, however.... My sexual satisfaction was strong before the death and somewhat withdrawn during my mourning period. Prior to his death, I was unable to express hostility when my grandfather was alive because he was intolerant. After the death, I talked through these matters with my parents. I expressed love outwardly before his death, and I am able to do so now. I seem to be more expressive, according to my family, than I was before his death. Securing love both before and after are free flowing. Grandmother and our family have grown even closer. Recognition in helping the family gives me more self-esteem and allows me to be creative in ways to help the family memorialize my grandfather. An example is shadowboxing his war medals and finishing a hook rug he started the last 3 months he was alive. Grandma wants this rug in her bedroom, and I offered to complete it (in honor of my grandfather). I am oriented in my place in society and have a very positive attitude toward helping others grow and heal through times of crisis and grief. My faith in doctors, humanity, and the natural order of things allows me to accept death of an elder in the family with reverence and dignity.*

### Anticipation of the Future

*My anticipation for my future is to be successful helping others the way my grandfather did. He was not rich financially, but he had this huge heart that was always overflowing.*

### Change in the Essential Human Sentiments

*The human sentiment that has become more important to me has been securing/expressing love. It is important to me that people in my life know that I care and that I am there when they need me.*

*The essential human sentiments are more important to me now than before, as I now have people in my life to share it with, people to succeed for, and people to inspire. I have secured love, and that to me is at the core of it all. That allows me to do everything else with the full support of my loved ones.*

*Sentiments that have become more important to me since his death are the preservation of family history and the personal successes and accomplishments of our family elders being preserved.*

## CONCLUDING COMMENTS

The focus of this chapter has been to consider bereavement in terms of an event causing stress. Over the years considerable research has focused on understanding, both theoretically and practically, the role of stress in the lives of human beings. Bereavement over the death of a loved one is an example of a major stressful life event. I cannot imagine anyone being taken seriously if that person were to argue that bereavement does not create stress that challenges individuals to respond adaptively.

A beginning framework for thinking about the human response to stress is found in the General Adaptation Syndrome, with its three-phase notion of alarm and mobilization of resources, resistance, and, should resistance prove futile, exhaustion followed by disintegration.

Other than the overall clarity provided by the general description of how an organism responds when under stress, there is little specificity in the General Adaptation Syndrome to guide coping or to design interventions to assist people to cope.

The cognitive revolution that has overtaken psychology will be found at the center of models designed to explain human coping with adverse events. A chief example is the model of coping with life crises expounded by Rudolf Moos and Jeanne Schaefer. The model was applied to quite different but nonetheless stressful life events: coping with alcoholism, chronic and life-threatening illness, and bereavement. The take-home message was that certain structural features characterize human coping with stressful life events.

The Moos and Schaefer model proposes that for any life crisis a person faces, there are life components that fall into one of three categories: personal and background factors, event-related factors, and socioenvironmental factors. Whether consciously identified for what they are, certain adaptive tasks must be accomplished when coping with a crisis, and persons who cope well engage these tasks successfully. These tasks are to: (a) confront the requirements of the situation, (b) determine the personal significance of the situation, (c) maintain interpersonal relationships, (d) regulate emotional expression, and (e) preserve a satisfactory self-concept and belief in one's self-efficacy. Three domains of coping skills enable people to accomplish the adaptive tasks: problem-focused coping, emotion-focused coping, and appraisal-focused coping. When examining the rich detail of a person's coping with a life crisis, for instance, a college student's response following the death of her father, it becomes apparent that: (a) persons do not behave in a linear, step-like manner, (b) people move back and forth in using the adaptive tasks and coping skills; and (c) changes in one's life circumstances can reintroduce coping with the stressful event. As an example, consider the issues facing a college student whose mother died of breast cancer and who, 3 years later, discovers a lump in her own breast.

A richly nuanced understanding of human coping in the midst of human communities was then presented in this chapter. Leighton's sociocultural model integrates a dynamic model of human personality, which is presented as an ever-occurring project over time. Personality is seen to be the never-ending quest for achieving one's potential, by means of fulfilling essential human sentiments (such as receiving and giving love, securing one's place in an identifiable human group, and belonging to a moral order). Integrated, coherent communities facilitate persons to achieve their potential and fulfill their essential human sentiments, whereas communities in discord present obstacles to human growth and development. We are, as a matter of life, continually gaining, losing, and seeking again the essential human sentiments.

Leighton used bereavement as the example to illustrate how a stressful life event, which he called a cross-section of the moment, would stand in the way of gaining the essential human sentiments. He showed how persons in coherent communities fared much better when dealing with cross-sections of the moment than did persons in communities lacking integration. It is not much of a stretch of the imagination to engage in a thought experiment in which the stressful life event is bereavement, the persons at risk are college students, and the community is the college campus. The inference is manifest: how to enable the college as a community to assist bereaved college students achieve their potential and deal with their individual and varied cross-sections of the moment, all producing grief over the death of a family member or friend.

## FURTHER READING

Balk, D. E. (1996). Models for understanding adolescent coping with bereavement. *Death Studies, 20,* 367–387.

Balk, D. E. (2009). Adolescent development: The backstory to adolescent encounters with death and bereavement. In D. E. Balk & C. A. Corr (Eds.), *Adolescent encounters with death, bereavement, and coping* (pp. 3–20). New York: Springer Publishing.

Bonanno, G. A. (2009). *The other side of sadness: What the new science of bereavement tells us about life after loss.* New York: Basic Books.

Coleman, J. C., Butcher, J. N., & Carson, R. C. (1980). *Abnormal psychology and modern life* (6th ed.). Glenview, IL: Scott, Foresman and Company.

Doka, K. J., & Martin, T. L. (2010). *Grieving beyond gender: Understanding the ways men and women mourn.* New York: Routledge.

Frankl, V. (1962). *Man's search for meaning: An introduction to logotherapy.* Boston: Beacon Press.

Hughes, C. C., Tremblay, M.-A., Rapoport, R. N., & Leighton, A. H. (1960). *People of Cove and Woodlot: Communities from the viewpoint of social psychiatry.* New York: Basic Books.

Leighton, A. H. (1959). *My name is Legion: Foundations for a theory of man in relation to culture.* New York: Basic Books.

Leighton, D. C., Harding, J. S., Macklin, D. B., Macmillan, A. M., & Leighton, A. H. (1963). *The character of danger: Psychiatric symptoms in selected communities.* New York: Basic Books.

Moos, R. H., & Schaefer, J. A. (1986). Life transitions and crises: A conceptual overview. In R. H. Moos (Ed.), *Coping with life crises: An integrated approach* (pp. 3–28). New York: Plenum.

Selye, H. (1978). *The stress of life.* New York: McGraw-Hill. (Original work published 1958)

# Bereavement and Different Causes of Death

My father phoned me early in my doctoral studies and told me he had been diagnosed with squamous cell carcinoma, a cancer that can occur in many organs. It was in my dad's lungs. A hospice physician with whom I was doing a field placement in Champaign, Illinois, said when I told her about the diagnosis, "Oh, the smoker's disease." That comment fit; my dad smoked about a pack a day for many years.

While neither he nor I mentioned it directly, both my father and I had a tacit understanding that this cancer eventually would kill him. I saw my dad three or four times over the next 18 months. He looked fine for over a year and a half, and he and my mom came to visit Mary Ann, Janet, and me in Illinois a couple of times and even went to his high school class's 50th reunion in Michigan.

During late December 1980–early January 1981, my family and my older sister's family gathered at my folks' place in Phoenix for the holidays. My younger sister lives in New Zealand, and she and her two daughters had spent 3 weeks during the spring of 1980 with Dad and Mom; they were with him in May for his last birthday. He was still pretty well at that time.

Dad was much weaker by December and used an oxygen cylinder. He got tired easily. He was losing weight. Walking across the room could be an ordeal. He was not in a lot of pain, at least as far as he would say. His physician had warned that eventually the cancer would get so bad that the pain would become excruciating; the physician also warned there was nothing he could do when it reached that stage.

I had some of the best moments ever with my dad during this visit as he would sit in his favorite chair in the kitchen and I sat by him;

sometimes we talked and often just remained quiet. When Mary Ann, Janet, and I left my parents' home in early January to head back to Champaign-Urbana, it was with the utmost conviction that we would never see my dad again. I found that goodbye very difficult. Usually saying goodbye does not have finality attached to it.

Around 2 weeks later my dad died at home, in bed and in minimal pain, and cradled in my mother's arms. My mom and my older sister Elaine were with him at the end. Unlike what his physician had said was going to be the case, my dad did not die in excruciating pain. He died at peace and with loved ones at his side. If ever there could be a good death, my father's was one.

My mother and I considered ourselves blessed to be able to prepare for my father's death. We had 18 months. One afternoon during that last holiday, she and I were walking outdoors, and I asked her how it was for her knowing Dad was dying: "Would it be better if you did not know?" I asked her. She said without hesitation it was a blessing to know; she was glad she knew because it helped her to prepare.

Now, it is nearly 30 years later. For all that time after my dad's death Mom lived on her own in the house she and Dad bought in the early 1960s. Now she too has died, just a few months ago in April. She lived to be 95 and had become very frail. Her mind remained clear and her sense of humor ever present, but her body was failing her. She had entered an assisted living facility in Phoenix for the last few years of her life, and we would all visit her: Elaine and Roy from Denver, Jeanne and Chris from New Zealand, and I from Brooklyn (or Manhattan, KS, or Stillwater, OK). My daughter Janet Renee and her husband Tony came out one summer while Mom still lived in her house. Elaine's daughter, also called Jeanne, drove over from San Diego several times to be with her grandmother.

Mom said openly to me a couple of times in one of my last visits, "David, I am fading." We talked a few times about her dying. We also played a lot of cribbage and watched some baseball games or watched DVDs. When I visited with her in July and August of 2009, playing even one full game of cribbage exhausted her. None of us knew at the time that in the last months of her life she had developed pancreatic cancer.

She was rushed to the hospital in critical condition in March of 2010, and as was typical of her, she bounced back. But then, my sister Elaine phoned me a week or so later saying to hurry to Phoenix. I had been planning to come during Brooklyn College's spring break, but that was a week away and now no one knew how long Mom would last. My younger sister Jeanne had already flown in from New Zealand, and my older sister and her husband had been there about 2 weeks. Mom hung on for several days and talked with each of her children privately about things about them that really mattered to her. What she told me touched me deeply.[1] Hospice of the Valley entered the picture through my older sister's intervention and provided remarkable, exquisite care for Mom. She was never alone in any of her last days; Jeanne or Elaine spent the night with her, and always there was at least one person from the family with Mom during the day. The staff in the assisted living facility looked in on her regularly. The pain from pancreatic cancer that can become so unbearable never materialized, due in part to the pain management regimen the hospice nurse introduced and that Elaine, a registered nurse, administered with exquisite gentleness and care. Mom died in her sleep about 1 week after I got there. Hers, too, was a good death.

I consider it a blessing to have been able to prepare for my mom's death. I believe the rest of the family thinks the same. Given Mom's advanced age and all the debilitating conditions that mark the frail elderly, we knew and talked about getting prepared for her death. And then, we had several days to be with her as she indeed faded away.

My father's and my mother's deaths were anticipated. Considerable bereavement literature as well as clinical lore asserts that anticipated deaths prove less problematic for grievers than do sudden, unexpected deaths. This chapter explores some of this literature and asks whether there are exceptions to this notion about the benefits of anticipating the death of a loved one.

The major causes of death in the developed world come from some form of chronic, lingering situation produced by a degenerative disease. Major examples include cancer, heart disease, cerebrovascular disease, and chronic lower respiratory disease. These chronic conditions produce either a slow, steady decline in health or a slow, ambiguous decline. On the whole, these chronic conditions allow all the persons involved to anticipate the death and, thus, to prepare. The deaths of older family members—typically from illnesses and "old age"—are ones that college students can anticipate.

The causes of friends' deaths are more than likely going to be sudden and unexpected. Mortality rates for adolescents and young adults are relatively low, but the major causes of death for this age group are all sudden and violent: vehicular accidents, homicides, and suicides are the three top causes of death in this age group. Bereavement literature and clinical lore attest to the problems grievers face when coping with a sudden, unanticipated death. The chapter looks at the impact on grieving when death was anticipated and when it was unexpected.

## CAUSES OF DEATH REPORTED BY BEREAVED COLLEGE STUDENTS

To preview material coming in the next chapter, the great majority of college students report that the family members who have died are grandparents and great grandparents. About one-fifth report multiple family deaths. Most family members' deaths were anticipated, illness or "old age" being the causes (83%). Other causes of death were sudden: accidents (8.6%), suicide (2%), and murder (1.2%). When I examine these data about causes of death, it seems plausible that the students had opportunity to prepare for the deaths of most family members who had died.

Over 60% of surveyed college students reported that a friend died. Most of the friends' deaths (62%) were due to injuries suffered in accidents (primarily vehicular accidents), 11.3% were suicides, and 6.2% were murders. Thus, nearly four-fifths of all friends' deaths were due to sudden, violent causes. Illness took 18% of the friends who had died; in most cases, the illness was a form of cancer.

## EVENT-RELATED FACTORS OF A DEATH IMPACTING GRIEF

Two overarching event-related factors that impact the intensity and duration of grief are whether the death was anticipated or happened unexpectedly. Much of this chapter looks at these two overarching factors. Other event-related factors of import include

1. whether the death was preventable,
2. the extent of intentionality,
3. how much suffering the person endured before dying,
4. how many persons the death affects,
5. whether the death occurred on-time or off-time, and
6. whether the death was due to natural causes or human involvement.

I have taken up each factor briefly.

### Preventability

This factor centers on grievers' assessments of whether something could have prevented the death. We see these assessments occurring primarily in deaths that are the result of negligence or malice. The issue of preventability clearly comes to the fore in deaths due to accident, homicide, and suicide. It also enters the picture with deaths due to some illnesses, such as heart disease or lung cancer: A person could have taken better care of himself or herself, could have lowered the cholesterol level, could have had regular physical checkups, or could have stopped smoking. My daughter, who deeply loved my father, still expresses consternation knowing he smoked cigarettes even though he was a physician and knew better.

Preventability raises issues of blame and guilt: "I should have taken Mom to the doctor when she said she didn't feel well," "I should not have let my daughter take the car when the weather was so bad," "I should have seen the warning signs that she was suicidal," and "Why did the judge let that drunk back out on the streets?" are four examples of assessing blame arising out of the realization that a death could have been prevented.

When a person understands a death was preventable, the prospects for posttraumatic stress disorder (PTSD) increase, as do the chances for major depression, intense anger, and guilt. These deleterious outcomes become even more likely when the death not only could have been prevented but occurred intentionally.

## Intentionality

Some deaths occur because of direct choice, as in the murder of a person during a robbery. Other deaths occur because of negligence, as in the case of a young woman who texts while driving a car and kills a pedestrian she would not have hit had she been paying attention to the road. She cannot be excused because she asserts it was an accident and she didn't mean to kill anyone. A more frequently occurring scenario of vehicular death involving intentionality comes from persons driving under the influence of alcohol. A person who gets in a car while under the influence has made a choice; although he (she) did not set out to kill someone, there is still a degree of intentionality. Mothers Against Drunk Driving (MADD; www.madd.org/) has waged a highly successful campaign to have vehicular deaths due to drunken driving considered homicides.

Deaths caused by murder are highly intentional, and deaths caused by human negligence are less marked by intentionality but still are marked by culpability. The more intent there was to take a life, the more focused the anger and hostility of the bereaved toward the perpetrator. And then, there are deaths due to suicide. It may be wrenching to accept that someone who took his or her own life did so intentionally; part of that completed suicide's intent involves the choice of abandoning the bereaved person.

## Extent of Suffering

Some anticipated deaths involve debilitating diseases that produce increasing amounts of suffering. Seeing a loved one in agony is dreadful, so that when death finally does come, a person may actually feel relieved. Accidents can lead to excruciating pain before the person dies, as in the horrendous deaths of persons burned alive. Deaths of the innocent caused by some human monsters—think of serial killers—nearly always involve terror and inflicted suffering. Knowing the person suffered before death can add to grief's intensity and duration.

## How Many Persons the Death Affects

This event-related factor is sometimes called "scope." The number of persons affected by a death may create natural social support systems. It may not be a specific death that leads to increased scope but the fact that so many persons grieve similar deaths and band together in support of one another. Examples are The Compassionate Friends, a support group formed by bereaved parents (www.compassionatefriends.org/home. aspx); the Tragedy Assistance Program for Survivors (TAPS), a resource for persons grieving the death of a person in the military (www.taps. org/); Parents of Murdered Children, a national organization providing support to survivors of homicide victims (www.pomc.com/); and the National Students of AMF Support Network, an organization whose mission is to assist bereaved college students (www.studentsofamf. org/). Scope links to the adaptive coping task of maintaining interpersonal relationships in the midst of a crisis and to the human sentiments of belonging to a moral order and of belonging to a distinct human group.

## On-Time Versus Off-Time Events

Life-span developmental psychologists have noted that one of the structural features of any life transition is whether the event occurs on-time or off-time. An infant learning to walk around the age of 12 months illustrates an on-time event. A child dying prior to her parents' dying, regardless the age of the child, illustrates an off-time event. The deaths of grandparents mark on-time events in the lives of many college students.

The deaths of a college student's peers or siblings—or even middle-aged parents—represent events occurring off-time. The deaths may be sudden or anticipated, but social expectations say the persons died before their time.

## Natural Causes Versus Human Action

Deaths due to tornadoes or floods are due to natural causes, whereas deaths caused by reckless driving, terrorist attacks, drive-by shootings, or road side bombs are due to human action. Deaths from natural causes may lead to anger, such as blame directed at public officials who respond poorly in the face of severe weather or resentment toward God for allowing a tsunami to destroy so many lives. When deaths are attributable to human action, then it is common to identify the persons at fault and hold them accountable. At times the person at fault and held accountable is the person left bereaved, as in the case of a college student who drove under the influence, had an accident, and killed friends riding in the car with him or her.

## ANTICIPATED DEATHS

Folk wisdom, perhaps simple common sense, asserts that anticipated deaths are easier to cope with than are unexpected deaths. My mother indicated knowing my father was going to die helped her to cope. Certainly being forewarned about my father's and my mother's deaths allowed me to prepare for the impending, irrevocable losses. I suspect the same is true of my sisters, though interestingly enough I have never asked them.

Being able to prepare for a coming death is not quite the same as grieving it ahead of time. Two theoretical constructs—"anticipatory grief" and its close cousin "anticipatory mourning"—assert that anticipating a death leads to grieving that death even before it occurs. First mentioned by Lindemann, anticipatory grief was seen as the process of grief work taking place in expectation of an irrevocable loss, specifically for one of Lindemann's patients, a woman whose husband was a soldier in World War II. For Lindemann, the ultimate outcome of anticipatory grief work would be emotional detachment from the person whose death was expected. Oddly, Lindemann cited only one case of anticipatory grief, the woman who said the extensive absence of her husband in a war zone led her to grieve his death and detach her emotional investment in him. Lindemann accepted the woman's comments at face value rather than consider alternative explanations, for instance, perhaps she wanted to be rid of her husband.

Do persons who anticipate a death begin grieving and mourning in expectation of the death? We may mentally and emotionally prepare ourselves for the loss, but do we take part in grieving the death before it happens? The implications of what we do in anticipatory grief are clear depending on which model of grief is in play. Do we begin confronting the distress of our impending loss, emotionally detach from the person who is dying, and form an emotionally neutral mental image of that person? I know I did not do any of those things prior to either of my parents' deaths. If anything, I felt closer to them in their final days. Do we oscillate between a loss orientation and a restoration orientation as we anticipate a death? I know I did not when my parents were dying. Maintaining a continuing bond as though the person is deceased seems too absurd to even grant credibility.

Crisis management theory teaches that being forewarned of an impending critical life event proves beneficial when the situation actually happens. It allows a person to get ready rather than be caught off guard. I believe there is benefit to having the opportunity to prepare for the death of someone loved. I am not convinced anticipating a death triggers grieving. I believe it can trigger anxiety, as well as care and compassion.

Empirical research is at best equivocal comparing bereavement following anticipated deaths and sudden deaths. Most research says sudden deaths have a much more negative impact on the griever than do anticipated deaths. Some research indicates the bereaved are worse following an anticipated death than are persons grieving a sudden death. Some research says that over time (2 years or more) there are no differences in the grief for sudden and anticipated deaths, whereas at the onset of grief the persons grieving a sudden death are worse off; in other studies, the persons worse off at the onset of grief are the ones grieving a death that was anticipated. Some research says it all hinges on the internal locus of control, with higher levels of control buffering the person and lower levels of control making one more vulnerable to the vicissitudes of bereavement, whether the death was sudden or anticipated.

I don't think anticipating a death triggers grief. I admit I may be wrong in this belief, and I recognize that many scholars take a different view, but too many factors militate against giving the construct of anticipatory grief credence. Operational definitions of the construct have been elusive, to put it generously, and thus gathering valid, reliable data on anticipatory grief has been obstructed. Methodological problems stemming from retrospective speculations on how people responded before the death are fraught with wishful thinking. Further, the notion of anticipatory grief assumes linearity to grieving that empirical data demonstrate is not the case. The notion of anticipatory grief assumes that once we begin to anticipate the loss, we thereby begin reducing the amount of grief associated with that loss. Much research demonstrates that anticipating a death does not lead to lessened grief when the death occurs.

There is a dark side to anticipated deaths. Lingering deaths in which the dying person wastes away place relentless emotional and physical pressures on caregivers, on finances, and on the psyches of loved ones. Witnessing the physical deterioration and the increasing pain of someone dying of cancer, or witnessing someone slip deeper and deeper into dementia or Alzheimer's can be devastating. In such cases, one wonders whether a sudden death would not have been a blessing to all concerned.

Other influences than whether the death was anticipated bear consideration. These influences include cultural values, the relationship to the person who died, ego strength of the person anticipating the death, the scope and meaning of the relationship in the life of the griever, the person's developmental maturity, social support, and the kind of attachment between the persons.

## UNEXPECTED DEATHS

Unexpected deaths occur in many guises, but have at least two properties in common. One, these deaths happen suddenly. Two, persons are unprepared. Thus, fatal accidents, completed suicides, and homicides come under the umbrella of unexpected deaths. Obviously, there are situations when persons can linger following a homicidal attack, a suicide attempt, or an accident and die several weeks later from their injuries; and in that sense there would be some prospect to prepare for the eventual death.

Cruel twists of fate can lead to the unexpected death of a person who has a terminal illness, a person whose death people were preparing for as something that would happen down the road once warning signs were emitted. As two examples, consider the case of Regina, whose older brother had osteosarcoma, was pronounced in remission following a check-up with his oncologist, but died less than 2 days later from the disease. Consider the case of Arthur, whose father had been diagnosed with colon cancer, had been in remission for several months, and one day while out walking his dogs was killed by a hit and run driver.

Catching people by surprise, unexpected deaths by definition give no chance to prepare. The preponderance of evidence indicates that sudden deaths are more likely than anticipated deaths to elicit bereavement of greater intensity and duration. The very shock of the death appears to extend the intensity and duration of grief. Colin Murray Parkes, a leading international figure in bereavement research, has identified an unexpected loss syndrome marked by continued perplexity, refusal to accept the death, and social isolation. The prospects of PTSD are more likely following sudden deaths.

Some sudden deaths (murder, suicide) are colored by stigma and lead to feelings of victimization as others place blame on the person who was murdered ("He must have done something to get killed" or "She ran with the wrong crowd") or on the family of a completed suicide ("It goes to show how messed up those parents are"). An elegant explanation is that stigmatizing murders and suicides is an effort to gain control over what otherwise remains random and chaotic and therefore scary.

Carefully designed longitudinal research with parents bereaved over the sudden deaths of children determined two factors were of great benefit to the survivors. Both factors assisted the parents in finding meaning, a very difficult task. One factor was the power of religion to help the person cope and the other factor was participating in support groups for bereaved parents. The astonishing fact was that bereaved parents who took part in support groups were four times more likely to give meaning to the death than parents who did not attend support groups. However, deaths due to murder or to suicide left parents less likely to find meaning than deaths due to unintended injuries. Major factors complicating the matter for grief over homicides and suicides were the perceptions of intentionality and preventability. And, when the bereaved considered the deaths preventable, the incidence of PTSD increased.

## Accidents

World Health Organization (WHO) data show the most prominent cause of death for children, adolescents, and young adults is accident, called in some quarters an unintended injury. The most common form of death due to unintended injury comes from vehicular accidents. This fact holds throughout the world and is not just a statistic peculiar to countries of the developed world.

Whereas research findings from the 1960s had indicated bereavement following the death of a spouse or child, regardless of the cause, ameliorated significantly within 4–6 months, careful analysis suggested that such optimism was unwarranted. A highly respected and often cited study of responses over time to the sudden death of a spouse or child in a vehicular crash clearly put to rest assertions about quick recovery.

The study used multiple measures that assessed depression, psychological distress, personal well-being, physical health, alcohol and drug use, finances, mortality, and acceptance of the loss, for example. Four to seven years following the accidental deaths, the persons in the study were still experiencing notable problems. As compared to carefully matched control group members, the bereaved study participants were more likely to be depressed, experience greater psychological distress (such as anxiety, psychosomatic difficulties, and hostility), have a decreased sense of well-being, increased mortality rates, lower finances, and difficulty accepting the death. Physical health did not differ for the persons in the control and bereaved groups, nor did alcohol and drug use. The bereaved individuals found themselves continually thinking about the death; in short, intrusive thoughts about the death preoccupied their conscious moments.

Longitudinal research since that groundbreaking study has confirmed the long-term difficulties that parents experience following a child's sudden, violent death. One year after the death, 88% could find no meaning in the death, and 5 years after the death, more than 40% still found meaning eluded them. As noted previously, parents who attended support groups were much more likely to find meaning than parents who did not attend.

## Homicides

Homicides in the United States occur at an alarming rate, attributed by most analyses I have read to the ready accessibility of firearms. Take these examples for comparison: In New Zealand in 1999–2000, the total number of homicides of 15–24 year olds was 6 for a prevalence rate of slightly less than 1 murder for every 100,000 New Zealand youths; in Norway it was 7 for a prevalence rate of slightly less than 1 murder for every 100,000 Norwegian youths; in Australia it was 44 for a prevalence rate of around 1½ murders for every 100,000 Australian youths; and in Canada 87 for a prevalence rate of slightly more than 2 murders for every 100,000 Canadian youths. In the United States, the total was 4,983 for a prevalence rate of nearly 13 murders for every 100,000 American youths. The rate was even higher for African American youths: around 18 murders for every 100,000 in the population of African American youth.

The murder of a family member or of a friend is not unknown to college students in the United States. This fact caught some European researchers with whom I was corresponding completely by surprise. They were interested in surveying bereavement among college students in Europe and had not listed murder as a type of death a college student would be grieving. Looking at mortality statistics for Western European countries, you can understand the reason for not listing homicide: Murders of youth are uncommon in these countries.

As in all other types of sudden death, males are more likely than females to be murdered, and males are much more likely than females to be perpetrators; this fact is found throughout the world. Seen in terms of youth homicides in the United States, around 83% of 15- to 24-year-old murder victims are male, and 93% of the murderers are male. The great majority of adolescents who murder are between 15 and 17 years old, and their victims are typically strangers or acquaintances, not family members. Adolescent girls who kill seldom murder strangers but, more typically, family members or acquaintances. There is a substantial correlation between child abuse and subsequent adolescent homicide. A legacy of the epidemic of child abuse in this country is a corresponding increase in the numbers of adolescent homicides.

A variety of very intense reactions characterizes grief over a murder. The reactions linger, as does their force, so that this adage proves true: Outsiders seldom appreciate the intensity and duration of bereavement over a murder. Among these very intense grief reactions are nearly total bewilderment, fear, anger, shame, and cognitive dissonance. There are powerful desires for revenge, even homicidal impulses, focused on the perpetrators of the homicide. The homicidal impulses, accompanied by intrusive and vivid images of what the griever wants to do to the murderer, can elicit shame and fear. The person was not aware of these capabilities lingering in his (or her) psyche. "I'm just as bad as these monsters who killed my sister" can become a concern. The hostility aroused in the bereaved summons one of the essential human sentiments that Leighton identified; fulfilling this sentiment, however, is problematic, particularly if it leads to committing a criminal assault rather than sublimating the expression of hostility through some indirect manner, such as constructing a memorial to the person who was murdered or starting an organization such as MADD or TAPS. Longitudinal research with parents of murdered children determined that psychological outcomes were worse for them than for parents of children who died in accidents or who took their own lives.

Murder makes the case a legal matter. It becomes a matter for public display in various media. The person who was murdered may be victimized by defense attorneys for the accused. The bereaved find their grief opened and re-opened as the case makes its way through the judicial system. There may be a stigma attached to the death, as the family is blamed for what happened.

In some cases, the perpetrator is never apprehended, or is found not guilty. Such realities scream at the grievers for the utter lack of fairness and justice, and compound the difficulties of coming to any sense of the meaning of this dreadful event. The murder itself assaulted the sentiment of belonging to a moral order, and when the murderer gets away with the act, the violation of belonging to a moral order is more pronounced. A death by murder clearly calls on bereaved persons to rethink what they believe about human values, about what is right, perhaps about whether there is ultimate meaning to existence. Finding meaning is a formidable challenge for persons grieving a death by murder.

## Suicides

Suicide has become a worldwide public health concern. The WHO (www.who.int; see also www.befrienders.org) argues that data collected since 1959 show an ever-increasing surge in attempted and completed suicides. For instance, rates of completed suicide around the world are up 60% since 1959; suicide ranks as one of the three leading causes of death for persons between the ages of 15–44; and suicide attempts are 20 times more common than completed suicides. Why this concern over the burgeoning number of suicide attempts? Data indicate a history of suicide attempts is a major risk factor in the lives of persons who do kill themselves.

The WHO considers adolescents and young adults as the age groups in many countries at greatest risk of committing suicide. Suicides Outstrip deaths due to traffic accidents in some countries, and in many other countries deaths due to suicides are second only to deaths due to accidents. Suicide has emerged as the second leading cause of death for youth and young adults in the United States, preceded by accidents and followed by murder. In addition, clinical and epidemiological data have shown that in 90% or more of all cases of attempted and completed suicides, severe emotional issues and substance abuse have been implicated. As a matter for concern, consider that on college campuses in the United States counseling centers report an overwhelming increase in the numbers of students who come seeking help for significant mental health problems; such severe psychological difficulties make college students vulnerable to stressors common to college life, and they place these late adolescents at risk for taking their own lives should distress overwhelm them. There is considerable evidence that substance abuse, particularly abuse of alcohol, including frenzies of binge drinking, are epidemic on college campuses in the United States and thus present an institutionalized set of dangerous behaviors that increase impulsivity and militate against the welfare of those youth distressed over life circumstances. Reconstructing what led a person to complete a suicide often reveals the final act occurred impulsively with impaired judgment due to heavy drinking or use of drugs and with access to the means to take one's life.

In the contemporary United States, the use of firearms has emerged as the leading method of suicide over the past 100 years. Prior to 1910 use of self-inflicted poison was the most recorded method of suicide in the United States. The primary methods of committing suicide in the United States are using firearms, poison, hanging, and strangulation. In all cases, men are more likely than women to use each method. Perhaps it is a myth that women are more likely than men to use poisons to kill themselves; United States census data gathered each decade since the 1930s indicate male-completed suicides by poison are more common than suicides by poison completed by females.

By far the greatest number of completed suicides in the United States is due to use of firearms, with men using firearms about seven times more often than women. Men use hanging and strangulation about three to four times more often than do women, and they use poison 1.5 times more often than do women. It is not much of an inference to conclude that males complete suicide more often than females because more males than females consistently use methods likely to prove lethal.

Grief following a suicide is more than likely going to be arduous. I garnered these ideas about coping with bereavement following a suicide from an excellent book produced by two clinical experts (Bob Baugher and Jack Jordan) who work with suicide survivors (the term used to denote people who are grieving the death of a loved one to suicide). They divide their very helpful comments into four time frames:

1. The first few days after the suicide.
2. The first few weeks after the suicide.
3. The first few months after the suicide.
4. The first year after the suicide and beyond.

### The First Few Days After the Suicide

People typically are in shock in the first few days following a suicide. Baugher and Jordan advise that it is important to accept that these reactions are normal, that the suicide survivor needs to take things one at a time and do what is needed to get through to the next day.

If the person witnessed the suicide or discovered the body, a sense of trauma is typical, with all the sequelae that accompany being traumatized: intrusive thoughts and images, reliving the experience, intense physical and emotional reactions, and emotional detachment from others. Reliving the experience may even take the form of flashbacks in which the person thinks he (or she) is back in the episode once again.

Suicide survivors face a crucial decision in the first few days following a suicide. They need to decide whether to view the body at the morgue or funeral home. Most suicide survivors who decided to view the body later said they had made the correct decision. However, rather than impulsively making this crucial decision, there are some important questions to ask. Asking these questions not only gains important information but also places a sense of self-efficacy back in the life of someone who may be afraid all control is lost. Here are the questions Baugher and Jordan recommend the suicide survivor ask about viewing the body:

1. What is the setting where I will view the body?
2. Will the body have visible wounds?
3. Will you describe for me the condition of the body?
4. Will I be able to touch the body?
5. Will I be able to take and keep personal effects?
6. What else should I know before I arrive for the viewing?

### The First Few Weeks After the Suicide

Here are three important maxims: There are many approaches to grieving, reactions to a death are individual, and there is no correct way to feel or to grieve. In addition to those maxims, Baugher and Jordan offer some ideas of what a suicide survivor may experience in the first few weeks after a suicide. One can see in this list links to Lindemann's idea of an acute grief syndrome. Here are common symptoms that suicide survivors experience in the first few weeks after a suicide:

1. Difficulties concentrating, remembering, and making decisions
2. Feeling helpless
3. Anger
4. Guilt
5. Feeling betrayed and abandoned
6. A variety of somatic reactions such as chills, fatigue, diarrhea, trouble sleeping, and trouble eating
7. Continuing psychological shock.

A crucial decision the person may face is whether to take prescribed medication to reduce feelings of anxiety and/or to reduce feelings of depression. Four reasons supporting taking such medications include (a) regaining a sense of self-control, (b) gaining focus on demands of daily living, (c) getting an extended sleep, and (d) coping with high levels of anxiety and depression. Three reasons against taking such medications include (a) some antianxiety medications can become habit forming when not used as prescribed, (b) some antidepressant medications can have distressing side effects (for instance, feeling out of touch with your own experiences), and (c) some suicide survivors report antianxiety and antidepressant medications suppressed grief reactions that the persons needed to address.

### The First Few Months After the Suicide

As time passes, suicide survivors become increasingly aware of what has happened. The shock and numbness dissipate. However, the pain of the grief remains intense. In particular, guilt is frequently prominent, and Baugher and Jordan emphasize there is no simple fix for the guilt a person feels. They point out some facts that may put the suicide into perspective.

1. Nearly all completed suicides are due to feelings of being trapped, extreme despondency, and a sense of being both helpless to bring about desired changes and a feeling of hopelessness toward the future. The person was under extreme duress and emotional pain. There were limits to what anyone could have done to fix the loved one's pain; this conclusion is particularly true if the person was convinced that suicide was the only source of relief available.

2. Once a person has decided suicide is the answer, there are limits to how much anyone can do to stop the act. A psychiatrist I knew once shared, "The only way to keep a person intent on killing himself from taking his life is to be with that person 24 hours a day." I can see how this second fact may be of no comfort and actually fan the flames of guilt. Baugher and Jordan address this matter by telling suicide survivors about the importance of getting a realistic perspective on how preventable was the suicide given the fact that the loved one had made a choice and figured out a way to carry out the choice.

3. It may be the case that you had some responsibility for the suicide. The person may have come to you and you were too busy to take time. The person may have given you a clue about her intentions, and you did not take her seriously. Even if suicide survivors hold some responsibility in the death, Baugher and Jordan encourage them to

work toward self-forgiveness. Such self-forgiveness involves accepting limitations and imperfections. Self-forgiveness involves as well intellectually and emotionally accepting that punishing oneself will neither bring back the person who died nor even erase mistakes that contributed to the death. A suicide survivor needing self-forgiveness faces a very formidable challenge.

### The First Year After the Suicide and Beyond

Anniversaries of deaths are important dates for the bereaved. The 1-year date of the completed suicide is a significant milestone. As in other bereaved persons' lives, the suicide survivor has made it through a whole year's calendar of important events (birthdays, holidays, ordinary days, and days that may have been special for the survivor and the person who completed a suicide).

Unrealistic expectations may be set around the 1-year date. The person may expect that the grief over the suicide will now be over; however, as in so many other cases of bereavement, ongoing grief is normal, particularly for persons in the recovery trajectory—and obviously for persons in the enduring grief trajectory.[2]

Persons dejected over the suicide may anticipate that the sadness will be gone. Some suicide survivors find that not only do they continue to feel dejected, but they have slipped into feeling chronically confused, angry, and fatigued. These developments may indicate the person is sliding into a major depressive episode.

Early on in the beginning of bereavement, the feelings of grief are difficult to distinguish from depression (except that bereaved individuals seldom think of themselves as utterly worthless and not deserving to live). The American Psychiatric Association for decades has identified bereavement as a clinical condition that is not a mental disorder and that depression should not be diagnosed in the first 2 months of a bereavement unless certain symptoms not characteristic of a normal grief reaction are present. These symptoms include

1. guilt related to matters other than actions taken/not taken by the survivor at the time of the death;
2. thoughts of death other than the survivor vs. belief that he (she) would be better dead or that he (she) should have died along with the deceased person;
3. morbid obsession with worthlessness;
4. pronounced psychomotor retardation;
5. protracted and pronounced functional impairment; and

6. hallucinations other than the belief that he (she) hears the voice of, or fleetingly sees the image of, the person who has died (adapted from American Psychiatric Association, 2000, p. 741).

Baugher and Jordan urge a suicide survivor to seek out a competent therapist if the intensity and quality of grief have not lessened or actually are getting worse over the year since the suicide.

A support group of suicide survivors will likely be helpful for persons struggling with grieving. Such groups offer a safe place in which the suicide survivors can openly share their stories and their feelings and be with persons who listen to and accept the persons telling the stories. Baugher and Jordan offer a caveat: If a person decides to attend a suicide survivor's support group, attend at least two if not three meetings before deciding whether to remain or leave. The first meeting in particular may be so intense and emotionally wrenching that the person may decide to flee. Veterans of these support groups for suicide survivors warn that persons experience an emotional hangover after the first meeting.

## CONCLUDING COMMENTS

This chapter has been about bereavement reactions tied to anticipated and sudden deaths. While experience and common sense say people are better off when able to prepare for someone's death, research data are at best equivocal on the short- and long-term bereavement effects of anticipated versus sudden deaths. Many persons accept the idea of anticipatory grief, but there are reasons for skepticism.

Various aspects of a death impact grief reactions. These aspects include (a) preventability, (b) intentionality, (c) the extent of suffering, (d) how many persons the death affects, (e) whether the death occurred on time, and (f) whether the death was due to natural causes or to human action. Deaths considered preventable and due to intentional actions particularly create distress for grievers.

Unexpected deaths fall into three categories: accidents, homicides, and suicides. The great majority of causes of death around the world for children, adolescents, and young adults are some form of unexpected violence. By definition, preparing for a sudden death is impossible. Intentionality and preventability come into play in deaths due to accidents, suicides, and homicides. Some wise, gentle suggestions were given for dealing over time with reactions to a completed suicide.

## NOTES

1. I have been asked by some persons who have read the manuscript to let them know what she told me, but I don't want to disclose any more than that we were "present" to one another and what she told me matters greatly to me.
2. See Chapter 3 for discussion of grief trajectories.

## FURTHER READING

American Psychiatric Association. (2000). *Diagnostic and statistical manual of mental disorders. DSM-IV-TR* (4th ed.; test revision). Washington, DC: Author.

Balk, D. E. (1997). Death, bereavement, and college students: A descriptive analysis. *Mortality, 2*, 207–220.

Baugher, B., & Jordan, J. (2002). *After suicide loss: Coping with your grief.* Available from b_baugher@yahoo.com

Berman, J. (2011). *Death education in the writing classroom.* Amityville, NY: Baywood.

Bernat, F. P. (2003). Negligent death and manslaughter. In C. D. Bryant (Ed.), *Handbook of death & dying. Vol. 2. The response to death* (pp. 968–973). Thousand Oaks, CA: Sage.

Cleiren, M. (1993). *Bereavement and adaptation: A comparative study of the aftermath of death.* Washington, DC: Hemisphere.

Curran, D. K. (1987). *Adolescent suicidal behavior.* Washington, DC: Hemisphere.

Doka, K. J. (Ed.). (1996). *Living with grief after sudden loss: Suicide, homicide, accident, heart attack, stroke.* Washington, DC: Hospice Foundation of America.

Fish, W. J. (1986). Differences of grief intensity in bereaved parents. In T. A. Randle (Ed.), *Parental loss of a child* (pp. 415–428). Champaign, IL: Research Press.

Fulton, R. (2003). Anticipatory mourning: A critique of the concept. *Mortality, 8*, 341–351.

Gilliland, G., & Fleming, S. J. (1998). A comparison of spousal anticipatory grief and conventional grief. *Death Studies, 22*, 541–569.

Haas, A. P., Hendin, H., & Mann, J. J. (2003). Suicide in college students. *American Behavioral Scientist, 46*(9), 1224–1240.

Jordan, J. R., & McIntosh, J. L. (Eds.). (2011). *Grief after suicide: Understanding the consequences and caring for the survivors.* New York: Routledge.

Lehman, D. R., Wortman, C. B., & Williams, A. F. (1987). Long-term effects of losing a spouse or child in a motor vehicle crash. *Journal of Personality and Social Psychology, 52*, 218–231.

Marcey, M. M. (1995). *A comparison of the long-term effects of bereavement after four types of death: Anticipated death, sudden death, drunk driver crash, and homicide.* Unpublished doctoral dissertation, George Mason University, Fairfax, VA.

McIntosh, J. L. (2001). *USA suicide: 1999 official final data.* Washington, DC: American Association of Suicidology.

McIntosh, J. L. (2003). Suicide survivors: The aftermath of suicide and suicidal behavior. In C. D. Bryant (Ed.), *Handbook of death & dying. Vol. 1. The presence of death* (pp. 339–350). Sage: Thousand Oaks, CA.

Murphy, S. A., Johnson, L. C., & Lohan, J. (2003). Finding meaning in a child's violent death: A five-year prospective analysis of parents' personal narratives and empirical data. *Death Studies, 27,* 381–404.

Parkes, C. M. (1975). Determinants of outcome following bereavement. *Omega, 6,* 302–323.

Peck, D. L. (2003). Suicide and suicide trends in the United States, 1900–1999. In C. D. Bryant (Editor), *Handbook of death & dying. Vol. 1. The presence of death* (pp. 319–338). Thousand Oaks, CA: Sage.

Rando, T. A. (2000). *Clinical dimensions of anticipatory mourning: Theory and practice in working with the dying, their loved ones, and their caregivers.* Champaign, IL: Research Press.

Redmond, L. M. (1996). Sudden violent death. In K. J. Doka (Ed.), *Living with grief after sudden loss: Suicide, homicide, accident, heart attack, stroke* (pp. 53–71). Washington, DC: Hospice Foundation of America.

Saldinger, A. L. (2001). *Anticipating parental death in families with school-aged children.* Unpublished doctoral dissertation, University of Michigan, Ann Arbor.

Saldinger, A. L., Cain, A., Katter, N., & Lohnes, K. (1999). Anticipating parental death in families with young children. *American Journal of Orthopsychiatry, 69,* 39–48.

Shackleton, C. H. (1984). The psychology of grief: A review. *Advances in Behavioral Research and Theory, 6,* 153–205.

Shneidman, E. S. (1980). *Voices of death.* New York: Harper & Row.

U.S. Public Health Service. (1999). The *Surgeon General's call to action to prevent suicide.* Washington, DC: Author.

Vera, M. I. (2003). Social dimensions of grief. In C. D. Bryant (Ed.), *Handbook of death & dying. Vol. 2. The response to death* (pp. 838–846). Thousand Oaks, CA: Sage.

# II

## Introducing the Bereaved College Student

Part II of the book presents what is known about college student bereavement. Prevalence data are the initial focus, with a review of what we know, how we learned this information, and why I consider the results persuasive. Then specific chapters look at topics central to what college students report about their experience of bereavement: how bereavement affects them and what they need. I use a holistic framework to organize these ideas, look at family dynamics and bereavement, and review what students report help them, what has proven difficult, what they wish were available, and what has surprised them. Once these chapters are completed, readers will have the basic information for describing reliably what is at stake for bereaved college students and the institutions they attend.

# 6

# *What Do We Know About Bereavement and College Students?*

Bereavement is a cross-section of the moment, a critical life experience, with which many college students are familiar. Bereavement is not an anticipated developmental transition considered normative for later adolescence and young adulthood. Yet bereavement happens to such a significant proportion of traditional-aged college students that it deserves attention. In this chapter, I have provided information on what we know about the incidence and prevalence of bereavement within the undergraduate population and how this information came to light.

College campuses annually witness numerous encounters with death. On average, for every campus at least four students die each year; in some cases, there have been annual incidence rates as high as 15 student deaths. Every year on many campuses there will be one or more suicides. The national suicidal rate for 17- to 19-year-old college students is 3.4 per 100,000 students. For students 20–24 years old, the suicidal rate is 7.1 per 100,000 students. And, of course, there are unusual outlier events such as deaths of a whole planeload or busload of students or a gunman's spree of killing, such as the one that occurred on April 16, 2007, at Virginia Tech.

Given the prevalence of student deaths and of student bereavement, one wonders why the existential reality of death and bereavement remains camouflaged and why the significant number of grieving college students remains a hidden population. In the next section, I provide an overview of what we know about the frequency of college student bereavement and how we learned about it.

## THE PREVALENCE OF COLLEGE STUDENT BEREAVEMENT: ANECDOTAL EVIDENCE

Before I began research on college student bereavement, conversations I had with college counselors and some faculty members indicated that bereavement over deaths to family members or friends could be a larger issue on campus than most persons realized. For several years, counselors and mental health professionals at college counseling centers had told me that loss often formed the presenting problem for many students who came for help; if loss was not the presenting problem, it frequently comprised a crucial part of the person's back story. When asked to estimate the presence of bereavement as an issue for college students, these professionals said it would not surprise them if 40% of the students were dealing with loss, grief, and mourning. They doubted that many of these students needed professional help with bereavement. Few of them said they had been educated on how to work with bereaved clients.

## THE PREVALENCE OF COLLEGE STUDENT BEREAVEMENT: THE FIRST ROUND OF EMPIRICAL STUDY

Review of this anecdotal information took me back to my first years as an assistant professor on the Kansas State University campus. Joan McNeil, one of my department colleagues, a woman who had been the President of the Association for Death Education and Counseling and who introduced me to that professional association, taught a popular survey course about human development over the life span; students from across the campus enrolled each semester, and on average the course never had less than 250 students. One semester Joan invited me to devise and administer a self-report instrument focused on the students' experiences with death and bereavement. Participation in the survey was voluntary and was one of several extra-credit options Joan offered her students.

The survey I developed asked students whether a family member had died and whether a friend had died. Details were then pursued about who had died, when the death happened, how old the person was at the time of death, the cause of the death, whether the student attended the funeral, the persons talked with about the death, and how helpful discussing the death had proven. Typical demographic data obtained included age, gender, ethnic/racial identity, and religious preference.

The survey was administered in five separate semesters. Thus, it was replicated four times. Here are some descriptions of the participants in the surveys.

- Out of a total of 1,442 students enrolled over those five semesters, 994 students completed the survey (68.9%).
- The mean age of respondents was 20.6, with a modal age of 19 and a median age of 20.
- Nearly 80% of the respondents were female.

As one would expect in a land-grant university drawing most of its enrollment from within the state of Kansas, nearly all the respondents to the survey were White (94%) and Christian (59.6% were Protestant and 31.7% Catholic). Other than the disproportionate number of females to males in the study, the sample was very much like the overall student body on the Kansas State campus.

## Deaths of Family Members

The great majority of the 994 respondents ($n = 813$, 81.8%) indicated that a family member had died, but only a few reported the death of an immediate member of the family: mother, father, sibling. Most of the family members who died were grandparents or great grandparents (67%). Nearly 20% reported multiple family deaths: 139 students reported two deaths, 30 reported three deaths, 8 reported four deaths, and 3 reported five deaths of family members. Here are three examples of students with multiple family deaths.

- A 22-year-old student reported her father, two brothers, and one grandparent had died. She also reported a close friend had died in a car accident.
- A 21-year-old student reported her father, brother, and grandparent had died.
- A 21-year-old student reported her father and her brother had died in separate years of the same form of cancer. Recently, her mother was showing the same symptoms.

The family deaths had occurred on average nearly 4½ years prior to the survey, and the median time since a family member's death was

3 years. Here are the prevalence data that grabbed my attention and Joan McNeil's.

> **294 respondents (29.6%) reported a family member had died within the past 12 months.**

Remember I said the survey was administered five times. It was after the first administration of the survey when 22% of the respondents reported a family death (or a friend's death) within the past 12 months that doing a panel study over more semesters was deemed crucial. The reactions to the first survey results were outright skepticism on the part of colleagues and administrators, except from Jon Wefald, at that time early in his lengthy term as president of Kansas State University.

The principal cause of family members' deaths was illness or "old age" (83%), not surprising as grandparents and great grandparents comprised most of the family members who had died. Other causes of death were accidents (8.6%), suicide (2%), and murder (1.2%). When I examine these data about causes of death, it seemed plausible that the students had opportunity to prepare for the deaths of most family members who had died.

Most students (82.2%) talked to their mothers about the death, a communication pattern also reported by high school students when I studied their reactions following the death of a sibling. Nearly 60% of the college students talked about their family member's death with their fathers. Practically the same percentage talked with a close friend about the death. Very few talked with a minister (7.7%) or with a counselor (5.7%).

Most students (87%) said they found talking about the death had helped: 44% said talking had been very helpful, and 43% somewhat helpful. A notable percentage (12.5%) said talking about the death had had no effect (that is, it had not proven helpful or unhelpful), and a very small percentage (1.2%) said talking had not been helpful.

### Deaths of Friends

Over 60% ($n = 594$) of the 994 respondents said a friend had died, and for many (47%) the person had been a close friend. It had been on average 2½ years since the friend's death. Once again we had prevalence data that surprised us.

A significant percentage of the 994 respondents (27%, $n = 268$) was in the first 12 months of bereavement over their friends' deaths.

Most of the friends' deaths (62%) were due to injuries suffered in accidents (primarily vehicular accidents), 11.3% were suicides, and 6.2% were murders. Thus, nearly four-fifths of all friends' deaths were due to sudden, violent causes. Illness took 18% of the friends who had died; in most cases, the illness was a form of cancer.

Comparing the causes of family members' and friends' deaths is instructive (see Table 6.1). Time to anticipate a death, and thus time to prepare for a death, is nearly in reverse for deaths to family members and deaths to friends: 83% of family members died from an illness, whereas 18% of friends died from an illness. About 80% of friends died because of sudden and violent causes, whereas 12% of family members' died because of sudden, violent means. Students were more likely to know the cause of friends' deaths, whereas in more than 5% of the family members' deaths, the students did not know what had happened in all cases of the deaths of distant relatives.

All but 25 of the 594 students bereaved over a friend's death talked to someone else about the death. Close friends were the persons most of the students talked to (87%). In descending order, the other persons the students talked to about the death were the students' mothers (62%), fathers (35.1%), sisters (23.6%), and brothers (20.8%). Some students talked to counselors (9.1%) and some to ministers (6.6%).

Students primarily talked about the deaths of family members and of friends with their mothers, close friends, and fathers. They were more likely to talk with siblings about family member deaths than deaths of friends. Counselors and ministers are not chosen by many

**TABLE 6.1** Causes of Death of Family Members and of Friends

|  | Family Members (%) | Friends (%) |
|---|---|---|
| Accidents | 8.6 | 62.4 |
| Illness | 83.0 | 18.0 |
| Murder | 1.2 | 6.2 |
| Suicide | 2.0 | 11.3 |
| Unknown | 5.2 | 2.1 |

**TABLE 6.2**   Persons Talked to About a Family Member's or Friend's Death

|  | Family Member's Death (%) | Friend's Death (%) |
|---|---|---|
| Mothers | 82.2 | 62.0 |
| Fathers | 58.9 | 35.1 |
| Sisters | 42.9 | 23.6 |
| Brothers | 39.2 | 20.8 |
| Close friends | 58.8 | 87.0 |
| Ministers | 7.7 | 6.6 |
| Counselors | 5.7 | 9.1 |
| Nobody | 7.2 | 4.2 |

students as someone to talk with about these matters. It is instructive to place side by side the information about who the students talked to (see Table 6.2).

Most students (83%) said they found talking about their friend's death had been helpful: 40.2% found it very helpful and 42.8% found it somewhat helpful. For 15.6% of the students, discussing the death had been neither helpful nor unhelpful, and, as in the case of discussing a family member's death, only a small percentage (1.4%) said these conversations were not helpful at all.

## THE PREVALENCE OF COLLEGE STUDENT BEREAVEMENT: THE SECOND ROUND OF EMPIRICAL STUDY

When I got to Brooklyn College in 2004, I had been doing more and more thinking about college student bereavement. I had directed a 2-year study into a social support intervention and had written numerous journal articles and book chapters. I had made presentations at annual conferences of the Association for Death Education and Counseling and found there a cohort of colleagues with similar interests. We were all convinced that college student bereavement remained under the radar as far as most colleges are concerned.

A task that appealed to me was to get beyond anecdotal evidence and convenience sampling to a prevalence study using a random selection of the students. It bothered me that findings based on convenience sampling were open to question about their representativeness. What

I wanted was to nail down once and for all prevalence data on college student bereavement. Random sampling opened such a possibility.

It is not often that one gets access to a sampling frame permitting use of random sampling procedures. But a college has at its electronic fingertips the list of all students enrolled at any one time. I wrote a small grant to carry out a stratified random sample to examine the prevalence of bereavement on my campus. The college's Institutional Review Board (IRB), which is tasked with appraising whether research participants are protected from harm, approved the study, and off I went to get data on the prevalence of bereavement among the Brooklyn College undergraduates.

Letters were sent to students selected at random from a full list of all undergraduates enrolled in the college, and in the letters students were informed of the study and offered US$22.50 for taking part. I had been warned by several persons to be prepared for a small turnout. They were so right. Of the many letters sent, less than 20 students contacted me to participate; Brooklyn College had approximately 10,000 undergraduates enrolled at the time. The explanation offered for such a small turnout was that Brooklyn College is not a residential campus, and most students come to the college to go to class and then they leave for their jobs or to go somewhere else. When I asked students, they said that explanation captured their attitude. Two more efforts to obtain a sufficient number of students using random sampling fell flat.

With permission from the funding source at the City University of New York (CUNY), I approached Andrea Walker, a colleague I met when I was a professor at Oklahoma State University. Andrea had already published some unique research on bereavement, grief, and mourning among Muscogee Creek Indians, so I knew she was familiar with issues in bereavement research. She was now teaching at a college in the Midwest. I asked her if she would like to collaborate on this effort to get prevalence data on college student bereavement. To my great pleasure, Andrea said yes to my offer.

Andrea approached the administration of a private university in her hometown about the proposed study and received their permission and the approval of that university's IRB committee. She drew a random sample based on the list provided by the registrar of all undergraduates at the school. She and her research team used email and phone to contact the students identified and obtained 118 participants (out of 433 contacted).

The sample consisted of 70 females and 48 males. Most of the participants (69%) were White, 12% were African Americans, 3% were American Indians, 4% were Hispanic, 3% were Asian Americans, and 9% from various combinations of other ethnic/racial groupings. An overwhelming majority (94%) of the students indicated they were Protestant. Andrea and I considered that the homogeneity of the respondents, while typical of the university they attended, did present limitations.

Our main hypothesis was that there would be a 22–30% prevalence rate for bereavement among the students. Despite the limitations mentioned above, it struck me that confirmation of the hypothesis would go a long way to establishing confidence that the earlier estimates were in fact correct.

Thirty-five of the 118 study participants (29.7%) indicated a family member or a friend had died within the past 12 months. These data clearly demonstrated that the 22–30% prevalence estimate was correct, and in fact the data said the rate is much closer to 30% than we had realized. An additional 46 (39%) noted that a family member or friend had died within the past 24 months.

One of the approaches Andrea used was to gather data on four separate occasions from different samples. These data nailed down for me that college student bereavement in the first year clearly is prevalent in nearly 30% of the undergraduate student body. Here is what Andrea uncovered:

- In the first round of data collection, 28% of the respondents reported they were in the first 12 months of a family member's or friend's death. The total number in this first round was 54.
- In the second round of data collection, 29% of a new set of respondents were in the first 12 months of bereavement. The total number in this second round was 27.
- In the third round of data collection, the percentage jumped to 39% of that group of respondents. The total number in this second round was 14.
- In the fourth round of data collection, 23% of this new sample reported a family member or friend had died within the past 12 months. The total number in this second round was 23.

The primary cause of death for family members was illness, though two persons were said to have died of "old age." More grandparents than any other family member had died. Two parents had died, but no other immediate family members had. Friends' deaths saw the same principal causes as seen in the research gathered at Kansas State: accidents, suicides, and murders.

## CONCLUDING COMMENTS

Anecdotal data, research findings from convenience sampling, and results from stratified random sampling have converged on this point: The prevalence among college students of first year bereavement over the death of a family member or a friend approaches 30%. Grandparents are the most common family member deaths, and the usual cause is an illness. Some sudden deaths occur to family members, but to a much smaller extent than anticipated deaths. Deaths of friends occur primarily from sudden, violent causes, and deaths of friends due to illness occur in slightly less than 20% of the cases.

Conversations about deaths of family members or of friends occur fairly commonly with mothers, fathers, and close friends. Ministers and counselors are not often selected. Between 4% and 7% of bereaved college students do not talk with anyone about the death they are grieving. On the whole, students say talking about the death helps.

## FURTHER READING

American College Health Association. (2002). *Safeguarding your students against suicide. Expanding the safety net: Proceedings from an expert panel on vulnerability, depressive symptoms, and suicidal behavior on college campuses.* Retrieved November 6, 2010, from www.acha.org/Topics/docs/Safeguarding_Against_Suicide_fullreport.pdf

Balk, D. E. (1997). Death, bereavement, and college students: A descriptive analysis. *Mortality, 2,* 207–220.

Balk, D. E. (2008). Grieving: 22–30% of all college students. In H. L. Servaty-Seib & D. J. Taub (Eds.), *Assisting bereaved college students. New Directions for Student Services.* No. 121 (pp. 5–14). San Francisco, CA: Jossey-Bass.

Balk, D. E., Walker, A. C., & Baker, A. (2010). Prevalence and severity of college student bereavement examined in a randomly selected sample. *Death Studies, 34,* 459–468.

Servaty-Seib, H. L., & Taub, D. J. (Eds.). (2008). *Assisting bereaved college students. New Directions for Student Services.* San Francisco, CA: Jossey-Bass.

Wrenn, R. L. (1989, November). *College student death: Postvention issues for educators and counselors.* Paper presented at the International Conference on Children and Death, Athens, Greece.

Wrenn, R. L. (1999). The grieving college student. In J. D. Davidson & K. J. Doka (Eds.), *Living with grief: At work, at school, at worship* (pp. 131–141). New York: Brunner-Routledge.

Zinner, E. S. (Ed.). (1985). *Coping with death on campus. New Directions for Student Services.* San Francisco: Jossey-Bass.

# 7

## Bereavement's Impact on
## a College Student

### BEREAVEMENT AFFECTS PEOPLE DIFFERENTLY

As a starting point, I think it prudent to accept that bereavement does not affect all students the same way. I can imagine readers saying that observation seems obvious to them; actually, my students would say "duh." You will find backing for this notion of diversity to grief responses from at least three sources: (a) the folk wisdom that each person grieves in her (or his) own way; (b) intuitive understanding built on interactions with a variety of individuals who have been hit with bereavement; and (c) empirical evidence from several research sources, both qualitative and quantitative, into bereavement. We now have persuasive data that adults' responses to bereavement, and children's responses as well, group into three distinct trajectories (resilience, recovery, enduring grief), and thus we should expect that bereavement's impact on college students will mirror those three patterns. There is no archetypal blueprint to the college bereavement experience, but I believe there are enough commonalities for us to recognize patterns and similarities in someone else's coping with the distress of bereavement. This recognition seems particularly to occur if we are or have been bereaved ourselves. An important aspect is to be sensitive to, and accept, experiences unlike our own.

In this section of the book I am going to look at what research tells us about the holistic impact of bereavement on college students. This framework has considerable scope and encompasses the vast variety of consequences following bereavement. As one examines a living case, it becomes apparent, however, that the holistic indicators, while offering distinct categories, typically overlap and interact.

## Two Students With Very Different Reactions to Sibling Death

I will provide two examples of distinctly different responses to the death of a sibling, and then compare them using the holistic framework as a guide. Take for instance this example of what happened to Doris at the beginning of her sophomore year, when her brother died in a boating accident.

> Doris was a 19-year-old sophomore majoring in mathematics at a large, private university, about 2000 miles from her home town. She was a very good student, and with a 4.0 GPA had made the Dean's list for both the fall and spring semesters of her freshman year. The new semester was going well, and then 2 weeks after the start of her sophomore year she learned that her brother had died when out with friends on the lake. He had been sitting on the front of the power boat, lost his balance and fell into the water, and was severely lacerated by the boat's propellers. He died within minutes of the accident.
>
> Doris found herself walking around in a daze. She stopped studying, and found it nearly impossible to concentrate on what was presented in her classes. Writing coherent papers became a chore, and one she only half-heartedly threw herself into. Her grades fell precipitously. She found herself thinking about her brother and how he died, even when she did not want to, and these thoughts distressed her. She cried when she did not want to, at times sobbing uncontrollably, wondering why she could not stop. She was not sure what she was feeling; she had never before had such a devastating thing happen to her, and it left her uncertain how to name her feelings. Besides feeling very sad; she felt confused. She lacked energy, and found climbing the stairs to her second floor apartment wore her out. She closed in on herself and isolated herself from her roommates. She had been raised a devout Catholic, and now found prayers and church services grated on her nerves. Whereas before she had trusted in God's benevolence, there seemed ample room to doubt now.

Here, however, is a different case of a student whose brother died. You met her earlier in Chapter 1. I am talking about Sarah, the young woman who took the job at the bar near her campus and learned her fellow employees could not talk with her about her dead brother.

> Sarah went to the land-grant university in her state. The school was about 3 hours from where she had grown up. She was a senior studying psychology, and she had plans to become either a counselor or a clinical psychologist and work with children and adolescents. She was a better-than-average student, with a 3.4 GPA.

Her brother Jimmy died toward the end of the first semester of her junior year. He was out riding with friends after a high school basketball game. His death occurred 2 weeks before Sarah's final exams. Sarah returned for Jimmy's funeral, and then came back to school and dug into her studies. She aced her finals. Her roommates were worried she would be so devastated by Jimmy's death that she would function poorly. She actually surprised them and perhaps herself. As she told me, "I love Jimmy and miss him. I wish he had not died. What a waste. He had so much promise. And we were close. But he would not want me to give up my life, and the only way I will be able to get my dream is to keep working hard here in school. Other people are counting on me, and I have obligations to myself... and obligations to Jimmy, actually."

It was not as though Sarah was untouched by Jimmy's death. For a couple of weeks she found it difficult to sleep, but those problems passed. Some persons thought she was suppressing her grief, but she did not believe them. She scoffed at the suggestion that she see a counselor. Rather than isolating herself from friends, she remained involved. She was a member of the student government, and carried out her responsibilities. She finished her class assignments on time, and continued to tutor middle school children in an outreach program between her university and a local public school. Her grades remained mostly As and Bs. She did not question how God could let her brother die; she did not think God controlled each and every event that occurs in this world. She did believe that when a car is going 85 miles an hour and hits a tree, people are more than likely going to be hurt, probably killed. She found it easy and comforting to think about and talk about her brother, to laugh when remembering some of the crazy things they had done together, but found few people felt comfortable talking about her brother when they learned he had died.

## Applying the Holistic Framework to the Two Cases

In these two stories, you can see the various indicators of the holistic template present in different ways for Doris and for Sarah. Consider, for instance, physical reactions: Doris became easily fatigued, a situation that continued for her; Sarah had some early problems sleeping, but those difficulties soon disappeared and her sleep returned to normal. Consider behavior: Doris stopped studying and cried at times uncontrollably, but Sarah not only continued to study for her courses but also remained active in student affairs on campus and seemed so calm that people mistakenly thought she was suppressing her grief.

Consider the emotional aspects of the holistic template: Doris felt both very sad and confused; Sarah missed her brother but did not find that her feelings overwhelmed her. Consider the interpersonal aspects: Doris cut herself off from her friends, whereas Sarah maintained her connections with other people. Consider the cognitive aspects: Doris's grades plummeted, whereas Sarah's stayed at a high level; further, when Doris thought of her brother she did so at times unwillingly and the thoughts distressed her; Sarah thought of her brother when she wanted to, and thinking about Jimmy was comforting, even producing laughter at times. Consider the spiritual aspects. Doris began to question her basic assumptions about God, whereas Sarah did not find what had happened altered in the least what she believed about God and how this world works.

## THE HOLISTIC IMPACT OF BEREAVEMENT IN THE WORDS OF COLLEGE STUDENTS

A principle guiding my thinking about bereavement is that it has a holistic impact. Evidence demonstrates that bereavement affects people in several dimensions fundamental to human existence. I introduced this framework in Chapter 3 and used it in this chapter to discuss the two cases of Doris and of Sarah. In short, the holistic framework allows us to look at the impact bereavement has on people physically, behaviorally, emotionally, cognitively, interpersonally, and spiritually. After presenting some overview comments on each of these aspects in the holistic framework, I will quote what some bereaved students said about each aspect in their lives.

### The Physical Impact of Bereavement on College Students

In what he labeled the acute grief syndrome, Lindemann noted that one of the typical responses to bereavement is physical. Loss of energy, problems with sleeping, chills, and diarrhea are some manifestations. When asked how bereavement affects them physically, what do college students say? Here are quotes from college students.

> Physically bereavement is feeling ill in my stomach, headaches and trouble eating. I can't eat because I feel sick to my stomach and when I don't eat I get headaches. I think about the death and go over and over

it in my mind and then I get bad headaches. I cry at times and it can be disturbing to others because I am usually a very happy person.

> Phyllis, 21 years old, Social Work major. Her best friend completed suicide nearly 8 years ago. In addition to her friend's suicide, a man who became like a second grandfather to her died of respiratory ailments shortly before Phyllis went to college.

Once I began to properly grieve,[1] I was often fatigued, but still had trouble sleeping at night. In college, it was much more work to keep up the facade I had maintained through high school. I was meeting new people and new challenges, and trying to disarm all of my emotions left me exhausted by the end of the day. But at night, my mind would reel. I'd try to process everything from the day at that time. And then, on top of that, I would try to process everything since my mother's death. This kept me up late at night, adding to my fatigue. Also, sometimes when I thought of my mom and felt particularly sad, my fingers would tingle. That was very odd.

> Rebecca, 22 years old, just graduated with her BA in English. Her mother died about 8 years ago due to a chronic, debilitating disease. Both of her grandfathers died about 3 years ago.

I really haven't had too many physical problems. At first I did have trouble eating when my mom was in the hospital and she was about to die. I couldn't swallow or keep anything down. There have been nights when I miss my mom so much that I can't sleep well. I remember one night I had a dream with my mom in it and I was crying in my sleep. That was the first time ever I had cried in my sleep, and never knew that was possible before.

> Susan, 19 years old, a Chemistry major. Her mother died 2 years ago after complications from a hiking accident. Her grandmother died 5 years ago from breast cancer.

Physically I have been fine. Just every once in a while I might have some problem sleeping due to memories coming back.

> Tara, 20 years old, a Physics major. Her father died of prostate cancer 1½ years ago.

## A Brief Synopsis

In the examples presented above, you can note that students mentioned reactions that correspond to what Lindemann reported as somatic responses to bereavement.

## The Behavioral Impact of Bereavement on College Students

Lindemann noted that bereaved persons he treated functioned poorly. They had difficulty keeping to regular patterns of conduct (for instance, going to class, making decisions, finishing assignments, and keeping appointments). Other behaviors noticed include restlessness, crying, and sighing. Here is what some students said about how bereavement affected their behavior.

> When I am feeling particularly bereaved I have to keep moving. I'm restless so I go out to do stuff with friends, but when I'm with those friends I want to be alone. I like to get my school work and other stuff done to pass my time and to get my mind off things.
>
> Phyllis

> Ever since my mom died, I have kept busy. I hate to sit still, and I often focus my efforts into my school and extracurricular activities. I often hope that what I do is something my mom would have encouraged or been proud of.
>
> Rebecca

> I have become more independent in my decision making. When my mom was alive I would go to her for advice, but since she is not physically in my life, most of the time I have to problem solve on my own.
>
> Susan

> As a result of my father's passing I have been trying really hard to succeed in life like he did. I have been more aggressive when it comes to gaining experiences and opportunities that will help to advance my career. I got into research because I wanted to try and make a difference when it comes to fighting the disease my father died from. I recently got a major science scholarship which I don't think I would have pursued if my father was still around.
>
> Tara

### A Brief Synopsis

Again, as in their description of physical reactions, students' reports of behavioral responses to bereavement coincide with some phenomena that Lindemann mentioned as part of an acute grief syndrome. However, the students are beyond feeling paralyzed when making decisions and they are taking initiative to achieve outcomes that matter to them. At times, their initiatives are directly related to the death that they grieved.

## The Emotional Impact of Bereavement on College Students

Emotional responses to bereavement are legion. For instance, bereaved persons mention such emotions as fear, sadness, confusion, guilt, anxiety, dread, anger, loneliness, and in some cases relief. In the midst of grief, a memory may provoke laughter so that some people find themselves actually feeling joy, not that the person died, but at some enjoyable, humorous episode or even at the delight the person evoked in others. Here is what some students said about how bereavement affected them emotionally.

> Bereavement has been confusion and loneliness for me. I felt guilty when my friend committed suicide because I did not see that he was depressed or unhappy with himself. I was also angry because he left me rather than fighting to live. The losses I have had have made me feel uncertain about the future. I don't know how to move on or I am having trouble keeping up with life because I am frazzled and forget things.
>
> Phyllis

> Bereavement has been a rocky experience. It took me about a year and a half to move forward and accept that the people I loved are no longer physically in my life. There were times when I felt guilty thinking, "Could I have been more helpful so that she could have recovered?" or "If I was just looking out for her she probably would be alive today." I have been afraid of not knowing what will happen to my family next week or a year from now, though there is this feeling of appreciation of how amazing the people I have lost are to my life. I gained so much knowledge of how the world is and how to be a good friend to others.
>
> Susan

> Bereavement has been very random. Sometimes I'll be fine and then other times something simple like a fire truck or a TV show will bring back memories and cause me to become very upset. Sometimes if I'm alone in the house I'll just start crying and/or screaming because my father isn't there.
>
> Tara

### A Brief Synopsis
The primary emotions mentioned are ones associated with distress. There are issues over uncertainty, but there are also aspects of benefit finding

such as appreciating what people loved mean to the students and how to be and remain a friend. Some persons' emotional experiences involve the regrief phenomenon when something unexpected or seemingly neutral elicits memories of the loss.

## The Cognitive Impact of Bereavement on College Students

Problems concentrating and remembering are common difficulties people have when challenged by distressing events. Bereavement commonly is a distressing event. There are also some reports that thoughts about the death can intrude on consciousness; it can be very scary to be unable to get rid of troubling, unwelcome thoughts. It is not difficult to understand how coping with the distress that bereavement causes would challenge a college student's studies and, ultimately, the student's overall academic performance, perhaps jeopardizing completing a semester and jeopardizing career options as low grades imperil one's potential.

> I have had many problems thinking and remembering school work because I keep going over and over the deaths in my life. I also worry about other people I love dying or me dying. I worry about forgetting the good times with my loved ones and how they smiled or laughed.
>
> Phyllis

> I was often distracted in college. On high stress weeks, I would feel like too much was happening. I could not process it all and I would be bombarded by feelings and emotions that I could not disarm or control. I would have nights when I would study and be so consumed by "real life" issues and by thinking about my mom, that I would have to quit studying completely and just take a walk. I felt unable to talk to people about what I was going through, perhaps because it was so long after my mom's death, and so it often took me a long time to process things on my own. I had, and continue to have, a large need to understand why I feel the way I do and to be completely self-aware of how people or situations affect me and why.
>
> Rebecca

> When I think about how my mother died, it does distract me school wise. I would continuously run all the events that happened within the 2 days that led to her passing away. It is lessened as time passes, but

if something triggers the fact that she is gone, many times I am unable to do school work and can't focus. Just recently was my mom's death anniversary and I was in summer school studying for a final a few days before. I got a call from my sister saying that they will be having a memorial service for her a day before she died and it was the same day as my exam and I broke down. They were able to change the day so I could make it, but I was not the same for the rest of the day. I couldn't focus and emotionally I was overwhelmed. In the end I didn't do as well on the exam as I could have.

Susan

As long as I'm focusing on a project then it is easy to keep the memories out of my head. The problem is though that when I'm not doing anything usually the memories come back. Unfortunately it's usually the memories of when he was sick, which makes me very upset. Not the memories from when he was healthier. I feel like I have to strain and try to remember what he was like before the illness.

Tara

*A Brief Synopsis*

Cognitions get linked to emotions for some of these students. Emotional responses would trigger difficulties concentrating on school work, and difficulties concentrating on school work would trigger emotions. Further, you can see the interconnection of other holistic aspects as well when the students talk about cognitive impacts. For instance, they will talk about interpersonal uncertainties or about restlessness. Keeping busy is used to keep undesired thoughts at bay.

## The Interpersonal Impact of Bereavement on College Students

A mainstay about successful coping with life crises is to maintain interpersonal relations. Contact with others provides escapes from getting hemmed in with narrow concerns and provides outlets for sharing. It is crucial to know one belongs and is accepted. It is crucial to be recognized, and to care about the welfare of someone else. Adolescents and young adults are expected to master the fundamental developmental task of developing and maintaining intimacy with others. Remaining connected to others keeps open the possibility of trying out ideas on others you trust, and it affords other people the chance to give you feedback and to answer your questions when you ask, for instance, "Jim, you dealt with your brother's death. What can I expect is going to happen to me now that my sister died?" Here are some quotes from students who discussed the interpersonal impact of bereavement.

Bereavement has been good in my life and has probably made others uncomfortable around me. I know that those who are my true friends will not leave me, and without actually knowing it I have surrounded myself with others who have lost loved ones. It has brought some of us together like my boyfriend and me, but it has also made others leave.

Phyllis

In high school, I kept mostly to myself, and I never talked about my mom. When I came to college, my first few years were spent enjoying the company of tons of new friends. I suddenly had an active social life. But internally, this meant I was living two lives. I had my self that was having an absolute blast learning and living in college. That part of me was outgoing, happy, and loving life. However, there was the other part of me that was freaking out because it was not used to this much emotional stimulation, even if it was positive stimulation. I could not keep up with my emotions, felt as if I was losing control, and I suddenly felt as if I was lying to my friends. Many of my new friends did not know about my mom. In fact, my roommate (who was one of my friends from high school) had to explain to all of my suite mates when I was not around why I never even mentioned my mother. This inability to talk about my mom kept me from getting really close to people. Sometimes, if I felt I was getting close enough to someone to talk about my mom, I would retract or pull away, spend time by myself again to try to figure out how I would take the next steps. But as the years passed, I slowly started to break down the wall that separated me emotionally from people. Therapy, good friends, and peer support groups helped me do this.

Rebecca

With my mother's death as I entered into college I would feel really lonely and depressed every time I saw parents. Inside I would be crying, missing my mom, and wishing she would be here to help me move in or see me on stage (at graduation). There is also a feeling of being uncomfortable around people I just met when they ask you about your family or if parents come up in conversation. It took me a long time to be comfortable to say my mom passed away in fear of creating an awkward situation. There also has been a feeling of disconnect with friends who have never lost someone so important in their life. They are unable to relate, and I sometimes get frustrated trying to make them understand.

Susan

When I am able to tell people what has happened in my life so far it has led to me being brought closer to them. Many have become like family and I am able to rely upon them. One of my friends I now consider a big brother. I feel that he took on this role to provide me with a male figure of support.

Tara

### A Brief Synopsis

New relationships that matter to the students are a common theme. They are attracted to persons who also have dealt with loss, and they have met persons they would likely not have met had it not been for their grief. For some students, coping with their loss led to secondary losses of their own making as when they would pull away from people rather than take the chance of getting close and then losing someone again. For all of them, there is the unease that is part of learning how, or whether, to tell people about the death when what in most cases is an innocent question is asked, such as happened to Sarah in Chapter 1 when asked if she had any brothers or sisters.

## The Spiritual Impact of Bereavement on College Students

Meaning making has become one of the principal activities proposed for recovery from bereavement. Within the literature on crisis coping, establishing the meaning and personal significance of an event is considered of fundamental importance. It is fairly common for spirituality to be seen as an aspect of meaning making, although when it comes to human decisions about the ultimate meaning of existence, there are emotional and cognitive aspects involved as well. For instance, a worldview that makes sense gives a person emotional coherence and cognitive harmony, whereas a loss of one's assumptive worldview creates emotional distress and cognitive dissonance. For those who have been there, you know the terrible situation of a person whose faith has shattered and there is nothing plausible to take its place. Within the practice of spirituality, there can be specific aspects of religion, such as the belief that nothing happens that is outside of God's plan. However, many persons now accept as a truism that a person can be spiritual without being religious. From the other point of view, do you think it is possible to be religious without being spiritual?

Here are comments some college students made when asked how bereavement affected them spiritually.

> Since I have never been religious I have kept mainly indifferent to going to churches for funerals and such. Other than that, I have not really thought about it.
>
> Phyllis

> I found a good church community in high school, but it was not at the church I grew up in. That church was often gossiping about my dad being an eligible bachelor, and I did not enjoy going and hearing about that. I felt like an outsider. My new church was small and inclusive, and I felt closer to God in that community. However, since college, spirituality has become less a part of my weekly routine, and more a source of greater questioning. I am still searching for answers.
>
> Rebecca

> It has actually strengthened my faith more than before. Having faith in God gives me a reason to believe that she is watching over me still affecting my life. I get out of losing my mom and grandmother a greater unknown understanding of why they died. I constantly think their life on this earth is over and God felt it was their time.
>
> Susan

> Mainly I wonder how God could have let this happen. I wonder why it had to be my father. I wonder if it would have been different if my father had a stronger relationship with God. I wonder if it was meant to happen so that I would accomplish certain things in college. Sometimes I even wonder if God really exists.
>
> Tara

### A Brief Synopsis

For these students, spirituality is linked to God and to religion. This perspective on spirituality is fairly common, but it is not the dominant point of view driving efforts to promote spirituality among college men and women today. The dominant point of view encompasses such topics as connectedness and meaning making. The chapter on spirituality and college student bereavement takes up this matter in detail.

## FAMILY DYNAMICS AND COLLEGE STUDENT BEREAVEMENT

It would seem obvious that bereavement affects a family. In this section of the chapter I look at what scholars have thought about bereavement's impact on a family. Extrapolating from these ideas to college student bereavement will occur with an exercise at the end of the chapter. Let's start with the story of Sherry and the impact that her mother's death had on her and her family.

---

Sherry was a 17-year-old high school senior when her mother died after a 6-month illness. This loss happened 2 years ago. Sherry was the youngest child in her family; her older sister, age 26, lived 200 miles away with her husband and one child; her brother, age 22, was finishing his last year in college, about 300 miles away. Following her mother's death, Sherry assumed all the major roles of caring for the household and of caring for her father.

Sherry's father became remote, and at times tearful and irritable, in his grief. A factory supervisor, he expected Sherry to care for the house and continue to do well at school. He did not want Sherry to talk about her mother, and he got angry if she cried, telling her that it made him more upset.

Sherry turned to her friends, three classmates who lived in the neighborhood and with whom she had been close since elementary school. Two of her friends stopped coming to Sherry's house after her mother's death. The third friend, Barbara, was still available and even spent more time than before with Sherry. They did things together, and Barbara listened to Sherry and often helped her with the additional responsibilities she had at home. Barbara's family continued to welcome Sherry to their home, where she could be an adolescent. She was often included in the family's activities and became their "adopted" member.

Sherry's relationship with her father was quiet but consistent. Her siblings were distant and often tried to tell her what to do. Sherry continued to do well at school, earning a scholarship to the state university, and was able to meet the responsibilities of her expanded roles at home. Although there was little overt support at home, she did know that her father cared about her.

Sherry often felt alone, both at home and because of the friends who had abandoned her. She was able to feel support from the friendship with Barbara and Barbara's family. She has remained close to them now that she has graduated from high school. She is living away from home in a dorm at the state university and likes what she is studying as well as the freedom she feels. She writes her father about once a month and calls him more often. He seems to her to be doing better than he was following the death. Her siblings are less understanding; they put pressure on her to stay at home with her father and not go to college.

The death of a family member—as well as its anticipation in cases of diagnosed terminal illnesses—is a family crisis that places excessive demands on a family's resources and capabilities to adapt. Many variables influence a family's ability to recover from a crisis, whether it be a death or some other challenging life event. The capability of a family to recover from a crisis is often referred to as the *regenerative power* of the family.

It is something of a paradox to talk of family grief because the traditional indicators of grief are manifest by individuals. Earlier in this book in the discussion of the multidimensionality of grief, I presented some traditional indicators of grief: difficulty sleeping, intrusive thoughts and images, restlessness, difficulty concentrating, a sense of hopelessness, sorrow, loneliness, anger, confusion, fear, startle reactions, and pining for the person who died. You might want to reflect on how it is possible to talk accurately—if at all—about family grief. We know what would indicate individual persons in a family are grieving; what would indicate *family grief*? Is there such a thing as family grief or is the term *family grief* just very loose and misleading use of language? The same question can be applied to bereavement. We know that a person who is bereaved has been thrust into a state of irreparable loss. Is it anything more than a metaphor to speak of family bereavement?

Among the variables which influence the family's ability to recover from a crisis are (a) concurrent life stressors, (b) family resources, and (c) the family's perception of the event. We will look at each in turn.

## CONCURRENT LIFE STRESSORS

The ability of the family to cope may be complicated by other events occurring at approximately the same time as an illness and death. Concurrent stressors of bereavement are typically grouped into two broad categories: (a) stressors directly related to an illness and a death and (b) other stressors that are not directly related to an illness and a death

## Stressors Directly Related to an Illness and a Death

Families experience a variety of these kinds of stressors when a family member is dying from a terminal illness. Examples include the physical and emotional demands of caring for someone who is dying, financial strains in terms of medical bills and decreased income if the "breadwinner" is the person who is dying, and the anxiety associated with anticipating the coming death. Overt and covert rules within a family for dealing with an impending death can create stress—for instance, the rule that everyone pretends nothing is the matter.

There are obviously other examples of concurrent stressors related to an illness or death, and the spotting of them may prove invaluable in the contributions of professionals and volunteers who are working with the family.

## Other Stressors Not Directly Related to an Illness and a Death

The possibilities of these other kinds of stressors seem limitless: the birth of a child, moving to a new town, change in jobs, the death of someone else, terrible news about a close friend, the marriage of one of the children. There are obviously other examples of concurrent stressors that impinge on a family and are not directly related to a family member's illness and death.

The notion of concurrent stressors has embedded in it the concept of "pile up." Pile up (sometimes called the "multiplier effect") refers to the accumulation of concurrent stressors in a crisis. As the pile up of stressors continues, a family's resources increasingly become strained—and the risk is that the family's resources will become bankrupt and the family's coping will become detrimental to recovery from the crisis.

## FAMILY RESOURCES

Resources effectively used to mediate a crisis can include both (a) support and strengths within the family and (b) support and services from individuals and organizations outside the family system. Studies of families have led to the conclusion that the families that respond most adaptively to life crises such as illness and death seek practical help and emotional support from persons inside the family and from individuals and organizations outside the family. Getting a family unused to turning beyond itself or unused to turning within itself is a very difficult challenge.

## THE FAMILY'S PERCEPTION OF THE EVENT

Two tasks considered fundamental to coping well with a life crisis are to establish the meaning of the event and to respond to the demands of the situation. These tasks involve how a family sizes up or perceives a life stressor. In fact, these two tasks may be the mechanisms whereby a family acknowledges its perception of the event.

There is evidence from some families that perception of the crisis even alters the feeling of being in a family. For instance, there are family members who perceive that a death is destroying their family or is taking from them the person who gave life to the family and kept it together. Bereaved mothers not uncommonly talk about "not seeming to be a family any more" after a child's death. Other families find the death leads to a rallying around each other and a greater commitment to the persons still living. They see that they are getting through this tragedy together.

For some families religious beliefs play a major part in how they understand and explain a crisis. They understand, for instance, the crisis as a test of their faith or a challenge whereby their faith will become stronger. They see their faith as a bulwark against concluding that a difficult death—for instance, the death of a young child from a painful illness—is proof that human existence is fundamentally absurd. Of course, some families explain crises as punishment for sins and a sign of their unworthiness and guilt.

### Adaptation by the Family

Life crises are sometimes called dangerous opportunities. There is the notion that within this life event that threatens well-being are the possibilities not only of dissolution but also of growth and positive change. Thus, to speak of the positive outcomes of death in the family is to speak of the side of a crisis that is *opportunity fulfilled*.

What are some examples of positive outcomes in a family dealing with the death of one of its members? Researchers have reported the following observations of positive outcomes following a death in the family:

- Closer bonds between the persons still alive;
- Better understanding for each other's strengths and needs;
- Enhancement of problem-solving skills;
- Greater empathy toward other persons' suffering;
- Increased willingness to help others in need;
- Greater grit in the face of trouble.

It has been my personal experience that adolescents who have coped with the death of a sibling and college students who have coped with the death of a family member or friend are more mature than their same-aged peers—and are not frightened by the pain and sorrow others manifest. They do not flee a room when someone in pain enters or feel a need to change the topic or feel compelled to fix the person's problem. Longitudinal research with adolescent boys has shown that the boys who had to cope with a family tragedy were propelled into young adulthood ahead of their same-aged, unaffected peers.

There is no guarantee that a family or each family member will respond positively to a death. This possibility accents the menace within a crisis—an opportunity fraught with danger. A family may not possess the coping strategies to deal with the stress and conflict that arise after a death or during an illness. One way to think of these negative outcomes is to place them in a special category called *incremental grief*. Incremental grief refers to the addition of new losses as a family is unable to cope effectively with the death of a family member. The crisis of this one person's death does not draw family members closer together but rather causes significant discord in the family. The discord leads to further losses and a sense of grief mounted upon grief.

One source of incremental grief is the refusal of family members to accept that some persons are grieving in different ways than they are. This issue arises from the mistaken notion that there is one acceptable way to grieve, and the refusal therefore to accept what are called *discrepant coping styles*. In the broadest sense, difficulties over discrepant coping styles arise from intuitive and instrumental approaches to grieving; some persons openly express their feelings while others turn inward and don't let others know how they are feeling. It is not an exaggeration that many persons understand intuitive approaches to grieving are the norm;

their conclusion when other persons don't openly express their feelings is that they are not grieving properly. You can see this problem playing out in the quote from Rebecca, a young woman whose mother died when Rebecca was in early adolescence. She told me this story when she was a 22-year-old college student.

> Bereavement has been confusing for me. My father was very upset after my mother's death, and showed his emotions vividly by crying often. I did not cry and did not fully understand the permanence of her death and how it would impact my life continually down the road. My mother had always told me everything was right, as it should be, and everything would always be alright. She and I were adapters. When my father confronted me just after the loss by pulling over our car, turning off the music, and asking why I was not grieving, I felt attacked and began to close up. I did not understand why I did not feel as everyone else was, and began to feel guilty. And so, when things started to change, I became an empty shell. Through my high school years, my exterior reflected the person I thought others expected to see at this time—happy, adjusted, and moving on. But inside, I was still a scared 13-year-old who did not know how to grieve and did not have a comfortable outlet to do so. This followed me all the way into college.

Discrepant coping styles may lead to what has been termed *dyssynchrony of grief*. This phrase means that individuals in a family can experience bereavement differently than do other family members and may need different amounts of time than others to cope with their sense of loss. Difficulties can emerge when some family members feel quite differently than others about a death—and when some have come to terms with the loss whereas others have not. Consider the case of a family in which the mother is wracked by sorrow and anger over the death of her son 18 months ago. The father has gained acceptance of the death, though he at one time felt considerable pain and confusion. His wife's anger pours over onto him because she does not understand why he feels differently than she about the death. He feels he has to walk on egg shells when around his wife because he cannot predict what will set her off. She wants to talk about the death, whereas he prefers to put this episode behind. He will talk about the happy memories of his son, but does not want to dwell on his son's death.

I have no formula or magic words whereby you can solve or fix problems arising when people reject each other's discrepant coping styles and their dyssynchrony of grief. I don't think of grief as a problem to be solved, but rather as a complicated process of attempting to recover from the irreplaceable loss of an important relationship in your life. Actually, I think attentive listening is often all you can do. When applied to discrepant coping and dyssynchronous grief, attentive listening can allow you to help family members angry at each other for not grieving in the same way to understand what their expectations and expressions of grief are doing to their understanding of each other. In their inflexibility they may be losing each other (what is sometimes called *secondary losses* following bereavement).

## FAMILY COPING TASKS

The single most important task is for the family members to talk openly about the death, its impact on them, and their emotional reactions to the death. A tension emerges when some persons are more comfortable than others talking about the death and their reactions to it. As a corollary, it is critical that family members be sensitive to the uniqueness of each individual's reactions. I will mention four family-oriented tasks: (a) maintain open communication, (b) reassign family roles, (c) provide support to each other, and (d) modify relationships with external networks.

### Maintain Open Communication

As you may have been able to surmise without conducting any expensive research, families are at risk for experiencing negative outcomes if the family members do not share their thoughts and feelings. There is a clear correlation between lack of open communication and increased guilt, blame, and conflict following a death.

### Reassign Family Roles

Two general types of tasks cover the kinds of roles people fill in families. There are *expressive tasks* and *instrumental tasks*. Expressive tasks are activities that have emotional and social functions and facilitate interactions between family members. Examples would be talking to others, encouraging others, listening to others, and giving hugs and other forms of affection. Instrumental tasks are activities that contribute to the effective day-to-day functioning of the family. Examples would be preparing meals, buying groceries, earning money, paying bills, doing the dishes, fixing stopped-up plumbing.

A death in a family may require that a family reassign the tasks that had been performed by the person who died. This reassignment of tasks means reassigning some roles. A rule of thumb: The number of roles to be reassigned and the centrality of these roles to overall family functioning affect the intensity of the family crisis. The person who died may have filled so many roles that the family is at risk of role strain as others attempt to assume these new roles. Consider the case of a family in which the father has died. The father fulfilled several instrumental tasks (income, basic maintenance of the car, handiwork around the house). The wife may begin to experience role strain by trying to assume too many additional roles. Or the 15-year-old daughter or the 16-year-old son may begin to assume roles for which they are inadequately prepared. The 20-year-old daughter in college may think she has to drop out of school and return to her family in order to take up several roles.

What is needed is assignment of roles based on open communication among the family members and by achievement rather than ascription of roles. Open communication enables family members to negotiate what roles need to be reassigned and identify who can fulfill them most effectively and thereby prevent roles from being assigned by default. Poor communication leads to roles being reallocated simply by default (or some roles simply go unfulfilled).

What is the difference between *ascribed roles* and *achieved roles*? An ascribed role is one assigned to someone by virtue of some characteristic over which the person has no control—for instance, a person's gender. An example would be ascribing to the 16-year-old son automobile maintenance because he is male, not because he shows interest in such tasks. An achieved role is acquired by the efforts and skills of the individual. In this family, the 15-year-old daughter tinkered with the cars all the time while her dad was alive, and learned auto mechanics from her father. Thus, she could be ready to assume the instrumental task of doing basic maintenance on the car.

## Provide Support to Each Other

One of the coping tasks identified by scholars for dealing with a life crisis is to maintain interpersonal relationships. One study examined how "strong" families dealt with crises. The investigators concluded that the family members most commonly saw the family as a major resource for each other during the crisis. Families in which an adolescent was grieving the death of a sibling did much better over the long haul when they were marked by strong emotional attachments to each other and by conversations about things that mattered; families marked by distant emotional relationships and lack of personal conversations fared much less well over time with the death of a child and with their own family relationships.

## Modify Relationships With External Networks

Surviving family members need to establish or modify relationships with social networks. Families often do not possess all the resources to deal with severe crises. The role of formal and informal social support systems becomes prominent as a means of coping. Formal support includes organizations and professionals that provide needed services to people. Examples would be services provided by the legal profession, hospitals and medical organizations, lobbying organizations such as Mothers Against Drunk Driving, counseling centers, and banks and other financial institutions. Informal support includes support networks comprising extended family members, friends, and neighbors. For many persons, involvement with their church, synagogue, or mosque provides an extensive informal support network. Groups such as Compassionate Friends provide support to bereaved parents.

## USING A GENOGRAM

Family therapists have produced an intriguing tool called a genogram. This tool is used to increase understanding about the history of a family's dynamics. The genogram particularly casts light on emotional relationships across generations. Using the genogram depends upon understanding each generation in a family as a system that influences later generations and has been influenced by earlier generations. Another way of looking at genograms is to liken them to a family tree of relationships.

Genograms can disclose how certain patterns of conduct emerge in successive generations. For instance, some families teach their children to negotiate interpersonal difficulties and to develop close attachment bonds. A genogram may reveal that this style of interaction was present in earlier generations as well. There can as well be a history of denying conflict if present or pretending distressing events have not happened. A rule of conduct passed on from one generation to the next can be that discussions of distress do not take place in the family.

Genograms use symbols to identify individuals and to indicate relationships. These symbols are presented in the key to Figure 7.1. The figure

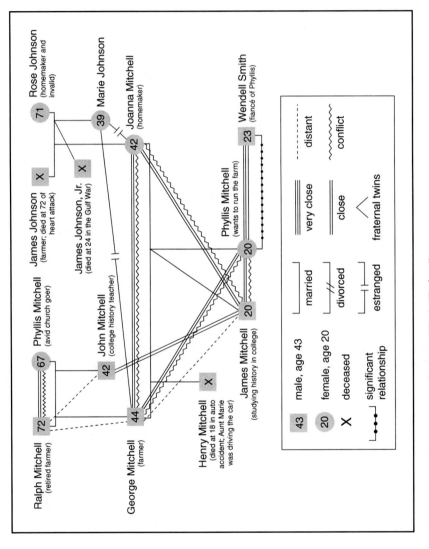

**FIGURE 7.1** A genogram of James Mitchell's family.

presents a hypothetical family, George and Joanna Mitchell and their two living children, the fraternal twins Phyllis and James. The Mitchells live on a farm. Our interpretation of the Mitchell family genogram focuses on James, the 20-year-old son; however, there is plenty of data in the genogram to examine the other persons identified in the figure.

The first lesson we learn concerns intimacy. Males in the Mitchell family for the most recent three generations have close but conflictual relationships with females. Through years of interacting within his family and observing others interact, James has learned that relationships with females are risky. He has learned males and females protect themselves by mixing intimacy with conflict. Like many sons, James perceives his father as distant; James also sees that his father and paternal grandfather are emotionally distant with each other.

The Mitchell farm has been in the family for five generations. Each oldest son has inherited the farm and improved it. James is expected to take over the farm from his father. The mantle of inheritance was passed to him when his older brother, Henry, died in an automobile accident 1½ years ago.

There is conflict for James and his family over this family tradition. James, first of all, entered the state university 2 years ago with the intention to become a college history professor like his Uncle John (Figure 7.1). James has no desire to study agriculture, and he does not want to return home to run the farm. Communication between James and his uncle is open, and the two feel close to one another. They email one another regularly.

Second, the family farm is in serious economic crisis, and James's father might lose it before the end of the year unless arrangements can be made with creditors. The level of distress in the family over the potential loss of the farm has three generations of Mitchells deeply upset. James feels guilty about his desire for an education in history at a time when his family is in such need. He feels pulled to change majors and accede to his parents' wishes about inheriting the farm. There is actually more pressure on James than wishes from his parents: The night after Henry's funeral, George became very autocratic and gave his younger son a lecture on family responsibility and on the need to sacrifice for what was in the best interests of the whole family. So far James is holding out against these pressures. If the farm is to remain in the family, George can see no alternative to James's managing the farm.

A third dynamic has entered the picture and might provide James and his family an outlet if they can get beyond gender stereotypes. Phyllis Mitchell, the 20-year-old twin of James, has expressed her desire to take over the farm and keep it in the family. She began to express her interests about a year after Henry's death. James and Phyllis are close, but argue a lot, particularly now over the future of the farm.

James's father is also close with Phyllis but, like other males in the Mitchell family, tempers this closeness with conflict. He is, however, beginning to say to others in the family that perhaps his daughter can help to save the family's inheritance. He respects Phyllis's fiancé, a young man who knows a great deal about farming and who last year earned a college degree in agricultural economics.

James is feeling confused about what is appropriate for men and women to do now that he knows his father's opinions about his sister's interest in taking over the farm. James is suspicious of Phyllis's fiancé, whom he thinks is an outsider more interested in getting the farm than in marrying his sister. Although he wants to follow in the footsteps of his uncle, he is confused about what his duty is to his family. Were it not for Henry's death, he would not have had the role of inheritor placed on him and could, without any distress, have been given the family's blessing to become a college history teacher.

John feels very torn about what advice to give his nephew. While he thinks James will make a very good college teacher, he feels hesitant to interfere in an issue that is so emotionally charged for his brother's family. He is also sure that many unresolved bereavement issues linger regarding Henry's death for George, Joanna, and their surviving children.

James would like to talk to his Aunt Marie about the confusion he feels. For some reason James cannot understand, he is relaxed around his aunt. However, the Mitchells have a family rule not to share family secrets with anyone the parents do not approve of. Relations between James's parents have cut off communication with Aunt Marie, and they expect their children to follow suit. They blame Marie for Henry's death. She was driving the car when Henry died. The car was hit by a sudden gust of wind, went out of control, turned over, and caused Henry to die of massive internal injuries. Marie suffered a broken arm and some cuts and bruises, but for the most part was unscathed.

James believes his parents are blaming Marie for something that was not her fault. James knows that Marie and her brother, who was killed in the Gulf War and after whom James was named, were very close. If you look at the genogram, you will see that Marie and her brother were twins, just as Phyllis and James are. In his physical appearance, James reminds everyone of his Uncle James.

Unresolved grief seems to haunt the Mitchells, preventing any closure to the death of their older son Henry. An unspoken but well understood rule in this family was that there would be no discussion of Henry's death after the funeral. The estrangement with Marie over Henry's death has made unwelcome one relative James feels at ease with. One wonders how Marie and her sister Joanna dealt with the death of James Johnson, Jr. when he was killed in the Gulf War.

The genogram in Figure 7.1 helps concisely to portray these family dynamics. A key example is the presence of so many close but conflictual relationships between males and females. It is little wonder that separation from his parents is a matter of difficulty for James given the family dynamics illustrated in the genogram.

Opening up to his family now about what he wants leaves James vulnerable to conflict and being pressured by his parents at a time when he wants to be his own person. He is beginning to become emotionally isolated from his parents.

---

### An Exercise to Use a Genogram

Take the genogram structure and depict your family back to your grandparents. Use the symbols in the key to the genogram to identify the various persons and their relationships with one another. Examine the dynamics that occurred around deaths in the family. Write out a brief narrative that explains what you have depicted in your genogram.

---

## CONCLUDING COMMENTS

This chapter began with the observation that bereavement affects persons differently. In other words, I accepted as a starting point that we all grieve in our own way. However, I don't completely believe that statement. If there were no commonalities to the human responses to loss, no patterns to discern despite the utter individuality of each person's grief, then we would be at a loss to talk about bereavement, grief, and mourning. I have posited that the holistic framework gives us one way of deciphering the mystery of how bereavement affects college students. Further, earlier chapters presented such research findings as the acute grief syndrome, the dual process model, three bereavement trajectories, and ideas for coping with stress. How grief will manifest itself for you and for me will be a matter of complexities that go to make up our own individual personalities. But we do have some guidelines for examining how bereavement impacts someone, and thus I applied the holistic framework as a means to organize thinking on bereavement's impact in the lives of four college students. You could take Leighton's sociocultural model as a template to examine how bereavement impacts college students. Look at the proposed exercise in Chapter 4 to get the basics for such an examination.

I ended the chapter with a look at the topic of families and bereavement. The family milieu changes when someone in the family dies, and there are various interactions that have been identified that mark what bereavement requires in order for a family to achieve a new equilibrium following a death. Using a genogram helps show persons visually the impact of a death on the family system.

## NOTE

1. It is not clear what this student meant about grieving properly. Perhaps she was an instrumental griever and had been concerned she was not showing affect or sharing her grief with other persons. Maybe she was an intuitive griever and she finally found persons who would allow her to share her grief with them. She suggests that properly grieving involved letting herself experience the distress that bereavement stirs up.

## FURTHER READING

Attig, T. (1995). *How we grieve: Relearning the world.* New York: Oxford University Press.

Balk, D. E. (1999). Bereavement and spiritual change. *Death Studies, 23*(6), 485–493.

Balk, D. E. (2008). A modest proposal about bereavement and recovery. *Death Studies, 32*(1), 84–93.

Bonanno, G. A. (2009). *The other side of sadness: What the new science of bereavement tells us about life after loss.* New York: Basic Books.

Bonanno, G. A., Boerner, K., & Wortman, C. B. (2008). Trajectories of grieving. In M. S. Stroebe, R. O. Hansson, H. Schut, & W. Stroebe (Eds.), *Handbook of bereavement research and practice: Advances in theory and intervention* (pp. 287–307). Washington, DC: American Psychological Association.

Cook, A. S., & Oltjenbruns, K. A. (1999). *Dying and grieving: Lifespan and family perspectives.* Fort Worth, TX: Harcourt & Brace.

Cook, J. (1988). Dad's double binds: Rethinking fathers' bereavement from a men's studies perspective. *Journal of Contemporary Ethnography, 17*(3), 285–308.

Lindemann, E. (1944). The symptomatology and management of acute grief. *American Journal of Psychiatry, 101,* 141–148.

McGoldrick, M., & Gerson, R. (1985). *Genograms: Assessment and Intervention* (2nd ed). New York: W. W. Norton.

Moos, N. (1995). An integrative model of grief. *Death Studies, 19*(4), 337–364.

Moos, R. H., & Schaefer, J. A. (1986). Life transitions and crises: A conceptual overview. *Coping with life crises: An integrated approach* (pp. 3–28). New York: Plenum.

Nadeau, J. (2001). Meaning making in family bereavement: A family systems approach. In M. S. Stroebe, W. Stroebe, R. O. Hansson, & H. Schut (Eds.), *Handbook of bereavement research: Consequences, coping, and care* (pp. 329–347). Washington, DC: American Psychological Association.

Neimeyer, R. A. (Ed.). (2001). *Meaning reconstruction and the experience of loss.* Washington, DC: American Psychological Association.

Oltjenbruns, K. A. (1991). Positive outcomes of adolescents' experience with grief. *Journal of Adolescent Research, 6*(1), 43–53.

Shapiro, E. R. (1994). *Grief as a family process: A developmental approach to clinical practice.* New York: Guilford.

Silver R. L., & Wortman, C. B. (1980). Coping with undesirable life events. In J. Garber & M. E. P. Seligman (Eds.), *Human helplessness: Theory and applications* (pp. 279–304). New York: Academic Press.

# 8

# *What Bereaved College Students Need*

What does a bereaved college student grieving the death of a family member or friend need in order to cope well? Great bereavement scholars such as Freud, Bowlby, and Bonanno have given their conclusions. Other impressive scholars such as Leighton have offered their notions about the holistic impact that recovery from a major life crisis demands. Bereaved students have offered their views. In this chapter, I examine these various strands of thought as directed toward the practical issue of what bereaved college students need.

## IDEAS FROM THE GREAT BEREAVEMENT SCHOLARS

The great bereavement scholars offer competing views in some regard, although there is more similarity than difference in the views of Freud and of Bowlby about coping with bereavement. For instance, it is not impossible or even implausible to consider that Freud's grief work can emerge in the phases Bowlby described. Confronting the distress that bereavement causes could occur in a process moving from shock to yearning to despair and disorganization before reaching resolution in a newly organized life.

An issue at stake for the bereaved college student is whether recovery from bereavement unfolds as a matter of natural development requiring confronting the distress of one's loss. If you accept what Freud and Bowlby (and Lindemann and Worden) claimed occurs as a natural response to bereavement, much of practical significance about what bereaved college students need takes a definite tack toward experiencing the distressing aspects of irreparable loss. If they are correct, then bereaved college students need time in which to reduce the distress caused by reminders of their loss and would profit from designed approaches permitting such confrontation. Confronting such reminders need not require professional intervention because grief work can be supported by strategies such as journal writing about one's loss and talking with friends and with bereaved peers about the loss.

Bonanno, of course, concluded that the theory of grief work has not been substantiated, that engaging in grief work is counterproductive, and that recovery from bereavement occurs when positive, happy experiences and thoughts naturally occur. Bonanno's research data indicate ruminating on what is distressing actually works against the griever.

Bonanno's three trajectories of bereavement point to three overall patterns whereby persons engage their bereavement: The resilient group apparently spends little if any time confronting the distress caused by irreparable loss, but the other two groups (the recovery group and the enduring grief group) seem incapable of ignoring their distress. Perhaps bereaved college students in the resilient trajectory do naturally what they need; however, the students who comprise the other two trajectories will profit from structures enabling them to engage in grief work—and, drawing on the wisdom of the dual-process model, of also engaging in living.

One structure to help bereaved students engage in grief work is offering workshops for residence hall assistants (RAs) and other interested parties on campus. Workshop topics can include training in facilitating groups, the basic facts known about bereavement, and the components of the dual-process model of coping with loss. There are persons on college campuses who understand very well how to design and present workshops, but they may not know very much about bereavement, grief, and mourning. Pairing these workshop experts with persons who understand the issues of bereavement strikes me as a union with considerable benefit to the college, the student body, and to the persons trained. It may be possible to link the workshops to education that will interest graduate students in particular majors, for instance, counseling psychology, school psychology, or social work. Completing a coordinated series of workshops would lead to campus certification of mastery of that knowledge; the person would understand an expectation of such certification to use the information—for instance, to facilitate groups on campus. The role of supervision would no doubt be discussed.

## THE VALUE OF THE HOLISTIC FRAMEWORK

Bereaved college students need the holistic impact of bereavement to be a focus of actions taken to assist them cope with grief. Alexander Leighton persuasively argued that individuals suffer when community influences obstruct reaching sentiments essential to being human (such as belonging to a definite group, receiving love, expressing love, and expressing hostility). Holistic interventions will address the comprehensive influence that bereavement exerts against achieving the essential human sentiments. College students grieving a death need opportunities that address their physical, emotional, cognitive, interpersonal, behavioral, and spiritual makeup. We need to listen to what bereaved college students say has helped them to overcome impediments to living as holistic beings and what they wish were in place to help them. The rest of this chapter looks at just such information.

## SOME WAYS OF HELPING THE BEREAVED

Here are six broad principles for helping the bereaved.

### Give Permission to Grieve

Rather than insisting that people hide their grief and pretend everything is all right, it can be both helpful to the bereaved and freeing for all parties concerned to share that grieving is normal and healthy, an adaptive response to circumstances. If you knew the person who died, giving permission to grieve can occur with such comments as "Tell me about your brother." I heard another person say to a grieving person, "I miss him too. I can imagine how hard it has to be for you." When you didn't know the person who died, you can still comment on the situation. I once heard a woman I have utmost respect for say to a college student whose father had just died, "Oh, Judy, this is just rotten."

### Encourage Expression of Grief

There is a widely held view that giving expression to one's grief not only helps people to identify what they are experiencing but also helps them to become reconciled to their loss. This view is found clearly expressed in Erich Lindemann's notion of the imperative importance to voice the distress one's bereavement causes. Shakespeare wrote about the value of giving expression to one's grief. Recall the line from *Macbeth*: "Give sorrow words, The grief that does not speak Whispers the o'erfraught heart and bids it break" (*Macbeth*, Act 4, Scene 3, line 209). Yet many persons are careful to share their grief only with persons they trust and insisting that the person express her (or his) grief with us can be intrusive and arrogant. Further, it is imperative to accept that some bereaved persons do not mourn through verbal expression. Nevertheless, it is very unlikely there won't be some manner in which they give expression to their grief, even if indirectly such as engaging in volunteer work or pouring themselves with more intent into their studies.

## Support Acceptance of All Aspects of the Loss

This strategy is a way to help the bereaved student accomplish Worden's tasks of accepting the reality of the loss as well as of adjusting to an environment in which the deceased is missing. It is helpful to get the person to talk about the person who died and all the multiple roles the person filled that now represent losses in the bereaved's life. Note that **it is the bereaved person who recognizes each loss**; this strategy does not say we need to hammer home to the person the losses he/she has yet to recognize. We don't need someone wanting to be the bereaved's friend in the worst way: "Well, Ethel, I have been hoping you'd recognize this loss, but since you haven't brought it up, I guess I'll have to make sure you don't miss the point." The strategy opts for a natural conversation in which, over time, the bereaved person will come to the recognition of losses that we may already see.

The bereaved do not find helpful responses that minimize the loss (for instance, saying to a woman after a miscarriage, "Just be grateful you can have other children"). And, the bereaved do not like "forced cheerfulness" from other people or inept, clueless statements such as, "I know how you feel."

## Listen to the Bereaved

There is little doubt that most persons feel at a loss for words or what to do when with a bereaved person. You remember the story of Sarah on her first day working at a bar near her campus. When two young men learned her brother had died, they abruptly left her standing alone. Her story captures the difficulties that some people experience when in the same room with a person who is bereaved.

While most persons would not literally flee the presence of someone who is bereaved, it is not uncommon for persons to change the subject abruptly when death is mentioned or to become visibly uncomfortable. At the same time, many persons would like to know what to say or do, as though there may be some magic words that fit such an occasion. There may as well be a desire to fix everything, to stop the person from hurting, and yet most of us know there is nothing we can say that will make the person's grief go away. Perhaps that realization is what leads some persons to literally or figuratively leave the room when a bereaved person enters. So, at least we can start from the perspective that the distress of bereavement cannot be made to disappear with some sort of magic spell.

## Share Information About the Grief Process

One thing many people don't know is what to expect from grief. Outsiders to bereavement typically underestimate the intensity and duration of grief feelings. "It's been six weeks. Aren't you over his death yet?" The intensity of the feelings leaves some people fearful they are going crazy, and the duration surprises them, especially if they have had a few good days and think the worst is past and then the grief returns seemingly in a fury. While there is no agreed upon time for grief to last, it is clearly unlikely to disappear in the first several months after the death. What is also helpful is for persons to know their grief does not have to fit some sort of prescribed method. Not grieving in the same way as others is common, but can be disturbing if a person thinks "There must be something wrong with me." Help people know that there are some commonalities to grief, but how each person experiences grief is unique to that person. If necessary, let them know that there are no prescribed stages to the grief process. People don't even grieve the same death in the same way, and persons recover at different rates than other persons.

## Assist in Practical and Concrete Ways

The needs of bereaved persons involve more than social interaction. In addition to keeping open interpersonal relationships, bereaved individuals have such practical needs as exercise, nutrition, sleep, and hydration. Some practical ways you can help is by taking the bereaved a meal, babysitting a young widow's children so that she can get some time to herself (or at least get a respite from parenting), and getting the person to take long walks with you as early morning exercise. Helping in practical, concrete ways means you need to make a practical, concrete offer. There is a huge difference between saying, "Call me if there is anything you need" and "I'll be coming over this afternoon and we'll go out to eat." You can call your friend and say, "I'm ordering pizza to be delivered. What do you want on yours?"

## WHAT BEREAVED PERSONS SAY THEY FIND HELPFUL

There must be some things that outsiders to bereavement can say or do that bereaved persons find helpful. What have researchers (as well as the bereaved themselves) reported?

Diaries of bereaved individuals and personal statements make it clear that one of the most helpful things others can do is simply being present. C. S. Lewis commented on that very fact in his moving diary *A Grief Observed* written in the days following his wife's death from cancer. Charles Corr and his colleagues (2001, p. 245) write, "It is not as important what such a person says or does—although there are better and worse things that one might do or say—as that the person does care and is available." Being an attentive listener is not only valued but becomes a way of being present to the bereaved. "Don't just do something, stand there" is at times the best action to take.

Research done on helping mourners and getting in their way has turned up some clear findings. The overall finding is that grievers are helped by behaviors that promote security and offer a sense of safety; however, those things that suggest uncertainties or danger make grieving more difficult. While outsiders to a loss may intend to be caring and compassionate, an amazing statistic is that 80% of all well-intended comments were in reality considered unhelpful by the bereaved individuals.

Three categories have been found beneficial. These categories are

- Safe places;
- Helpful or close persons;
- Comfortable situations.

We will take up each category in turn.

## Safe Places

One student wrote me that bereaved students need "a place to talk, time to process, and a safe place to connect with others in the midst of the fast-paced college life." The category *safe places* refers to where conversations take place rather than to conversations about places considered safe. A paradoxical place for many recently bereaved persons is their home. Home is a painful sanctuary. It provides a place of retreat and comfort as well as continual reminders of the person who used to live there.

An aspect of home as a painful sanctuary is that the reminders of the person who died provide an environmental means to come to terms with the person's absence. As an example, I will offer the following story told me by my mother who stayed in the home in which she and my father had lived for nearly 20 years prior to his death and in which she stayed for nearly 30 years after his death.

My parents had been married for nearly 25 years when they moved to Phoenix, Arizona, where my Dad became the head of the physical medicine department at the Veterans Administration Hospital. After my Dad retired in the 1970s from his position at the VA, he liked to sit in the kitchen in an old chair positioned in such a way that he had a view of other rooms in the house. Upon his death, this chair became a source of trouble for my mother. She would look at it and wonder what to do about it. She said she was almost afraid to be in the kitchen because the sight of the vacant chair brought pangs of grief that were wrenching; however, removing the chair seemed an act of betrayal to her husband's memory. What she did amazes me to this day. Instead of removing the chair from the room, she one day went over to it and sat in it. She stayed in it for quite a while. And the chair lost whatever power it had to make her panic. It is now over 30 years since that episode, and I inherited the chair upon my mother's death in April 2010. Anyone who wants can sit in the chair.

### The Internet as a Safe Place
It is likely the Internet affords a safe place for grieving students. There are some exceptions to consider that I will address in a page or two. Clearly, a major social transformation has occurred in the past 20 years. We now have cohorts of youth who live much of their waking moments hooked up to electronic media. A definite gap separates the younger generations from the persons of my generation. The younger people are digital natives, whereas my cohort's members are at best digital immigrants. Seeing youth furiously pounding away with their thumbs to text their friends is almost an all-pervasive social phenomenon. What

college and high school students have is access to friends and acquaintances via such Internet features as Facebook. To remain socially connected, they must use instant messaging and other electronic forms of contact. To drop out of this electronic grid leaves them clueless about what is going on socially and, if they do not reconnect electronically, socially isolated.

I am a digital immigrant. I don't do Facebook, nor do I send instant messages. I also don't use Twitter or use MySpace. Some years ago I mastered the rotary dial telephone and due to the care and nurturing of my wife I understand how to use my cell phone. My job requires I use a computer, but I mostly use it for word processing and email and designing and teaching online courses using Blackboard. I am clearly on the margins of the Internet revolution, not wrapped up in it full time. College students, however, spend a lot of time using the Internet, and the Internet affords an opportunity for assisting those students who are grieving.

There are numerous links on the Internet to the topic of grief, and it is unclear to me that users of these sites are aware of the dangers of linking to sources whose reliability is untested. It is imprudent to think the Internet presents no risks to persons who open up online about their grief. We have seen dreadful cases of cyber bullying that led to deaths of young people. While there are persons empathetic to other persons' suffering, the Internet provides camouflage for individuals who enjoy hurting people who are already vulnerable. Other persons may have incorrect information about bereavement on the Internet and mislead a grieving student.

Adolescents use the Internet as a main way to get information about death and bereavement, and at the risk of being out of date as soon as I post this information, here are some reliable Web sites that were established with a focus on bereavement:

- www.teenhealthandwellness.com
- www.beliefnet.com
- www.griefworksbc.com/Teens
- www.dougy.org/default.asp?pid=1276972

### Safe Places on Campus

Where are the safe places on campus for students in distress? You may recall that one of the functions of a university is to provide a sense of security for people on campus. An important aspect of gaining this sense of security comes from the campus police who remove worries about physical safety. A college's counseling center is built with the assumption that it offers safe places to talk; most students from what I can tell do not automatically think of finding a college counselor in order to talk about matters of import.

Student unions and college libraries and residence halls are built with the intent of providing quiet, safe places for conversation. For instance, college libraries and student unions have rooms students may reserve for small group study sessions. It is not much of a stretch of the imagination to see getting one of these rooms for a private talk. Meeting in one's dorm room offers a safe place. A meeting with a trusted faculty member in her (or his) office occurs in a safe place.

## Helpful or Close People

Persons who are known to be supportive are important topics for discussion. So are significant relationships. Thus, a topic for conversation can be persons the bereaved individual enjoys talking about. The deceased can be one of these safe people, and the bereaved commonly respond favorably to such requests in conversations as "Tell me about your brother" "What are some things you remember about your life with your husband?" "What do you most remember about your father?" and similar comments. It clearly opens up possibilities for an otherwise tongue-tied outsider to the grief to know that whereas most people are afraid to mention the dead person's name even though the bereaved do not want the name forgotten, most bereaved individuals are quite appreciative of the chance to talk about the person who died.

## Comfortable Situations

A widely held hypothesis proposes that social relationships are important in regulating many human responses, and are very influential helping people cope with life crises. Remember the discussion about coping with stress in Chapter 5. Obviously, comfortable situations provide a desirable milieu in which to interact. For several years, the National Institute of Mental Health had a standing call for research studies that would look into social support as an intervention with bereaved individuals.

Some of the most successful community responses to various sources of distress have been the social support groups that have emerged in the past several decades. Probably, the most famous such group is Alcoholics Anonymous. Other social support groups that have endured because they are clearly meeting a need include

- Society of Compassionate Friends, a support group for bereaved parents commonly just called Compassionate Friends (see the Web site http://www.compassionatefriends.org/);
- Mothers Against Drunk Driving (MADD), a support group with strong policy advocacy activities aimed at legislation concerning driving while under the influence of drugs or alcohol (see http://www.madd.org);
- Survivors of Suicide, a support group for persons bereaved by a completed suicide (see http://www.survivorsofsuicide.com/);
- Parents Without Partners, a support group for single parents (see http://family.surfwax.com/files/Parents_Without_Partners.html);
- Survivors Network of Those Abused by Priests (SNAP), a support group for persons wounded by religious authority figures, not only by abusive priests (see http://www.snapnetwork.org/).

Recently, a group developed by students for students has come to life. It is called the National Students of AMF Support Network. It is present on over 40 campuses in the United States. Its mission is to support college students grieving the illness or death of a loved one. Here is the Web address: www.studentsofamf.org

In terms of bereavement, emotional support comes from persons willing to be involved with the grieving individual, NOT from persons whose concerns are expressed as pity. Expressions of pity may leave bereaved individuals feeling weaker and more insecure than they already were feeling. Support groups have proven so successful because the participants find other persons who understand what they are experiencing, are not afraid of their pain, and can even provide mentoring for newcomers. These support groups also provide a safe place (because the people are safe) to experience and express the distress of one's bereavement. These groups allow the person to engage in the "loss orientation" of coping that is part of the dual-process model, and to engage in the "restoration orientation" by connecting with persons in ways beyond the issues of loss.

A phenomenon fundamental to social support's effectiveness is the willingness of participants to talk about themselves. A corollary requirement is for persons to be attentive listeners to what someone else discloses. A campus program to train peers in attentive listening will be presented in Chapter 9. I decided to spend some time examining the topic of self-disclosure and bereavement in Chapter 10.

## BEREAVED COLLEGE STUDENTS: WHAT HELPED THEM AND WHAT THEY WISH WERE AVAILABLE

When in the midst of a life crisis, it is surprising at times to discover what helps. Bereavement surely presents one of those times. We know what scholars say is needed. There are the adaptive tasks identified, and the dual-process model that talks about moving back and forth between confronting one's distress to going on with being alive. Two groups of activities seem to dominate: (a) being connected to others who understand and who care, and (b) being engaged in doing things for others, activities that involve people in concerns beyond their own individual interests.

The National Students of AMF, the support network for bereaved college students, has a multifaceted approach that involves getting persons to disclose about themselves and their grief in support group meetings and to become active in some form of community service. The community service is geared to engage bereaved students to continue living by doing something for someone else. Some of the activities in which AMF chapters have been involved include 10K walks for cancer prevention. At one campus, the University of Wisconsin at Green Bay, the Students of AMF chapter has developed Camp Lloyd, a camp for grieving children.

Here is what some bereaved students said helped them.

At my college a camp for grieving children has helped me deal with my bereavement by connecting me with others who have gone through similar situations. Helping children who are bereaved has helped me make peace with my own experiences and has taught me that by helping others you can help yourself.

Phyllis

Students of AMF helped me to find other people who were dealing with similar issues. When little or big things came up while I was at school, I had an outlet of attentive listeners who were there just to listen, with no other agenda. It was nice to have a community that always remembered the things you have experienced. It was also therapeutic to have your feelings validated by others who feel the same way. It was also nice to have 8 free therapy sessions at our Counseling and Wellness center and a service to refer me to a specialist in the local community when I asked for further sessions.

*Rebecca*

Meeting another person who has lost someone. They have helped fill a void that I had my first year of college. I felt that I really had no person my age to talk about the people I had lost in my life.

*Susan*

Talking to others my age about my grief has helped me cope. I don't feel so alone and the feelings I have are released because I don't have to bottle them up.

*Tara*

Writing has been a huge help for me. I like to write about what I feel and about my relationships affected by the loss. It helps me to process things and come up with solutions to problems or decisions I face.

*Phyllis*

Talking with my friends has helped. Traveling to new places and pursuing new interests has also been great for building self confidence. Having good friends to talk to and spend time with. Knowing that they will be there for me when times get extremely tough has been the best help.

*Rebecca*

School has helped me cope because that has not changed. The people at my school have not changed. And thus I can go about my day as if when I get home he'll still be there. It helps give me a sense of normalcy.

*Susan*

It is my assumption, based on reflections about the different bereavement trajectories, that students within a resilient trajectory will carry on and function well, probably not seeking or needing any special help. However, the students in the recovery trajectory will profit from programs that recognize the distress with which they are coping and offer outlets, starting with sensitively-run support groups; there is a growing push for leave time to be granted to students whose bereavement is marring their work in school. Then there is the group of students whose acute grief has not lessened. These students clearly need and will profit from expert clinical help; they also will appreciate the prospect of being able, if they wish, to have an official leave of absence that does not penalize them in any way once they return to their studies.

Here is what some bereaved students said they wish were available.

I think colleges should all have some universal rules on letting college students be absent due to bereavement and funerals. I know at the college I am at it is sometimes difficult to get excused absences or moved back tests or papers. I think most colleges focus on depression when they should also focus on grief.

Phyllis

I would like colleges to offer some free sessions, with immediate support for students in crisis. A peer support group such as Students of AMF has also been a huge help, and an important part of my grieving process. My loss was not during college, and so I do not think it would be recognized by the university for academic leniency, and luckily, I did not need such support. However, it may be nice if the counseling center had some kind of relationship with the student's professors to work with the student during the toughest times.

Rebecca

[I wish there was] a way to pair up students with other students who have lost someone. I go to a big school and there are so many people, but you don't really know of others who have lost someone. A way to connect with other bereaved students has helped me cope the most. Also, to be more open to students who are grieving and give them time to grieve.

Susan

Colleges should provide counselors who are experienced in dealing with grief for students to talk to.

Tara

## BEREAVED COLLEGE STUDENTS: WHAT HAS PROVEN DIFFICULT FOR THEM

Bereavement has its distinctive features. We pretty much expect bereavement will present difficulties in coping, although a surprisingly high percentage of persons apparently return to normal functioning despite the sorrow their loss evokes. We can trace the influence of bereavement by seeing how fundamental human sentiments are obstructed and by seeing the pervasive reach bereavement has in the holistic dimension of people's lives. Exactly how bereavement will affect an individual can be estimated, but what issues will prove difficult cannot be reliably forecast. Here is what some college students said had proven difficult for them in their bereavement.

> The most difficult thing for me has been watching those I love die slowly and painfully. And then afterward a lot of people in my life have moved on when I have not. We don't really talk about it because I feel if I talk to them I will make them uncomfortable since they never bring our loved ones up. Another difficult part was going to work when I could not get off to go to the funerals or to grieve.
>
> Phyllis

> The most difficult thing for me has been the loneliness I have felt in my grief. I do not have any siblings and for a long time was not comfortable discussing my mom with my dad. The year my mother died was also only a year after I had switched schools to another middle school, and I did not have many close friends. We moved to a new home, which wasn't far from my old home, but it was still 45 minutes from my school. I kept to myself most of the time, which I thought I enjoyed. But, in the end, I know it was very hard for me. It was also difficult for me to accept that my father was dating my godmother after my mother died. My godmother was one of my mom's best friends. I did not understand how she fit in my life after Mom died. My relationship with my father was also hard. I felt that he had trouble relating to me as an adult rather than as a parent and child. He also gave me very little guidance as to what I should strive for in my future. Also, because it took so long for me to open up to people, I was never in any romantic relationships in high school nor most of college. This was further isolating.
>
> Rebecca

> (The most difficult thing has been) keeping focused. Sometimes I miss my loved one so much that I become discouraged with my life and wished they were here to keep me going.
>
> Susan

> The most difficult thing for me has been acknowledging that my father is not coming back, ever.
>
> Tara

## BEREAVED COLLEGE STUDENTS:
## WHAT HAS SURPRISED STUDENTS
## ABOUT BEREAVEMENT

Despite the universality of death and bereavement, there are few if any mentoring activities to prepare one for grief and mourning. Perhaps there were such learning opportunities back in the early 20th century in the United States when most people died before they were 14, when persons typically died at home, and when youngsters could see how their adult role models dealt with bereavement.

We don't expect bereavement to be as intense or last as long as it typically does. You have read that statement before in this book. More than one college student has told me that prior to being bereaved, it would never have occurred to them what bereavement is like. "I'd have been one of those persons expressing surprise that it is taking so long" is what a student at Kansas State University told me. "But now I know different."

What has surprised scholars is that in the midst of bereavement, people can also express happiness and can laugh. Not all the time is filled with being somber and sorrowful, except for the persons whose acute grief just never lessens. Increased empathy and desire to give oneself for the benefit of others are sometimes unexpected results.

Here is what some college students said surprised them about their bereavement.

The fact that helping others has become so important to me and my grief has surprised me. I used to think I did not want to do anything because of my grief but now getting out there and doing stuff for my community and campus has really affected me.

Phyllis

Bereavement is one giant roller coaster of surprises. You are up, and then suddenly you are down. You are right, and then you are left. You feel like everything is right, and then just a phrase, a look, a sinking feeling, and suddenly everything is very, very wrong. I never knew that bereavement could and would occur 5 or 6 years after my mom's death. I was also surprised how much my friends wanted to listen once I began to open up.

Rebecca

The great emotional and psychological burden it puts on you. I pretty much knew I would be thinking about the person I had lost everyday, but I never imagined how overwhelming it can be at times.

Susan

How long it can hold a person.

Tara

## CONCLUDING COMMENTS

The pragmatic side of this chapter is crystal clear, just from looking at the title: "What Bereaved College Students Need." There is an unspoken assumption that by seeking answers to the question "What do bereaved college students need?" we will identify the steps, the resources, the activities to meet those needs. In the main—in fact, greatly in the main— I agree that we have the capabilities of addressing effectively these students' needs that we identify.

The great bereavement scholars are divided on what will be effective ways to respond to needs of grievers. I decided to take as my cue that bereavement trajectories found in adults and in children will be what is true for college students. I assume that students in the resilience trajectory are dealing well with their bereavement. We could still ask them what they need, but overall I suspect the real focus needs to be on the students in the recovery trajectory and the students in the enduring grief trajectory.

The ideas proposed in this chapter on meeting the needs of the bereaved make sense when the students are in the resilience trajectory and in the recovery trajectory. I doubt that the supportive methods mentioned will be of any help to a person bogged down for months in the intensity of acute grief. There could even be justifiable skepticism that students in the enduring grief trajectory are still in school if they did not obtain effective therapy. What these students need is a college environment aware of the presence of students with enduring grief, staff members who can refer the students for the professional help they need, and policies allowing students with such enduring distress a leave program from school. Policies should allow students in whatever bereavement trajectory the choice of an excused leave; I doubt college administrators or faculty want to start discriminating need on the basis of bereavement trajectory.

This chapter is rife with explicit and implicit ways to assist bereaved individuals. The greatest help will come from creating a culture in which steps are taken to develop programs that educate persons to be attentive in the application of the six broad principles for helping the bereaved. Some efforts are already at the touch of an electronic fingerprint, so about all we need to do there is provide WiFi spaces and advertise in prominent places addresses of reliable resources on the Internet for the student to explore.

Developing and offering formal training in facilitating support groups strikes me as such a logical and practical step. We have the persons who know about group dynamics. We have access to persons who know about bereavement. We have persons (both students and college personnel) willing to learn these group skills and to use them.

It seems clear that asking bereaved students what they need leads us to use skills and resources at our beck and call. Why would we wait, especially since it is in the interest of everyone concerned?

## FURTHER READING

Bonanno, G. A. (2009). *The other side of sadness: What the new science of bereavement tells us about life after loss.* New York, NY: Basic Books.

Bonanno, G. A., Boerner, K., & Wortman, C. B. (2008). Trajectories of grieving. In M. S. Stroebe, R. O. Hansson, H. Schut, & W. Stroebe (Eds.), *Handbook of bereavement research and practice: Advances in theory and intervention* (pp. 287–307). Washington, DC: American Psychological Association.

Bowlby, J. (1969–1980). *Attachment and loss.* New York: Basic Books. [Vol. 1, *Attachment*; Vol. 2, *Separation: Anxiety and anger*; Vol. 3, *Loss: Sadness and depression.*]

Cook, A. S., & Oltjenbruns, K. A. (1989). *Dying & grieving: Lifespan and family perspectives.* New York: Holt, Rinehart and Winston.

Corr, C. A., Nabe, C. M., & Corr, D. M. (2003). *Death and dying, life and living* (4th ed.). Belmont, CA: Wadsworth.

Davidowitz, M., & Myrick, R. D. (1984). Responding to the bereaved: An analysis of "helping" statements. *Death Studies, 8*(1), 1–10.

Freud, S. (1957). Mourning and melancholia. In J. Strachey (Ed. & Trans.), *The standard edition of the complete psychological works of Sigmund Freud* (Vol. 14, pp. 243–258). London: Hogarth Press. (Original work published 1917)

Lehman, D. R., Ellard, J. H., & Wortman, C. B. (1986). Social support for the bereaved: Recipients' and providers' perspectives on what is helpful. *Journal of Consulting & Clinical Psychology, 54*(4), 438–446.

Leighton, A. H. (1959). *My name is Legion: Foundations for a theory of man in relation to culture.* New York: Basic Books.

Lewis, C. S. (1961). *A grief observed.* New York: Seabury.

Lindemann, E. (1944). The symptomatology and management of acute grief. *American Journal of Psychiatry, 101,* 141–148.

Lynn, J., Schuster, J. L., & Kabcenell, A. (2000). *Improving care for the end of life: A sourcebook for health care managers and clinicians.* New York: Oxford University Press.

Moos, R. H. (Ed.). (1986). *Coping with life crises: An integrative approach.* New York: Plenum.

Moos, R. H., & Schaefer, J. A. (1986). Life transitions and crises: A conceptual overview. In R. H. Moos (Ed.), *Coping with life crises: An integrated approach* (pp. 3–28). New York: Plenum.

Richtel, M. (November 21, 2010). Growing up digital, wired for distraction. *The New York Times,* CLX (55,231), pp. 1, 26–27.

Silver, R. L., & Wortman, C. B. (1980). Coping with undesirable life events. In J. Garber & M. E. P. Seligman (Eds.), *Human helplessness: Theory and applications* (pp. 279–304). New York: Academic Press.

Sofka, C. J. (2009). Adolescents, technology, and the Internet: Coping with loss in the digital world. In D. E. Balk & C. A. Corr (Eds.), *Adolescent encounters with death, bereavement, and coping* (pp. 155–173). New York: Springer Publishing.

Stroebe, M., & Schut, H. (1999). The dual process model of coping with bereavement: Rationale and description. *Death Studies, 23,* 197–224.

Worden, J. W. (2009). *Grief counseling and grief therapy: A handbook for the mental health practitioner* (4th ed.). New York: Springer Publishing.

# Doing Something Constructive

This part of the book builds on materials from Parts I and II. Readers are now ready to review specific topics having to do with a diversity of proactive responses that can be implemented on college campuses and to examine three topics of paramount importance to college students' experiences of bereavement, grief, and mourning. The three topics are self-disclosure, recovery following bereavement, and spirituality. Once these chapters are completed, readers will have the basics needed for planning that is responsive to college student bereavement in their particular campus milieu.

# 9

## *What Can Happen on Campus*[1]

What is the campus like for a college student bereaved over the death of a friend or family member? For all students, bereaved or not, the college campus places expectations on them to stay on task, to meet multiple obligations from courses, friends, and jobs and to play. On the campus, there is little, if any, realization at all about the fact of someone's bereavement and little patience from the unaffected about the duration and intensity of grief. Life goes on, and the campus seems unfazed by the death the student is grieving. And yet, this lack of awareness flies in the face of the significant prevalence of bereavement in the student body.

College student bereavement is a secret, despite its significant rate of incidence and prevalence: Between 22% and 30% of undergraduates are in the first 12 months of bereavement. Consider that if the prevalence rate is 22% and the campus has an enrollment of 18,000 undergraduates, then nearly 4,000 students are in their first year of bereavement. You can do the math for campuses with other enrollments. Consider the implications should the prevalence rate be closer to 30%.

College students who are grieving may begin to question their own competence and self-worth. They may doubt that outcomes they desire are within their personal control. The intensity and duration of grief can lead to doubts that a sense of balance will return. College students who are grieving may lose ground in their studies, perhaps incurring academic probation, suspension from school, or even expulsion. Difficulties with bereavement produce severe problems in concentrating, studying, completing assignments, passing courses, staying engaged with school, and taking advantage of the multiple opportunities offered in a college's diverse social milieu.

Discussions with bereaved college students have disclosed what they need and want in order for the campus to become a place helping students in distress. Here in summary are some of what I have learned from students:

- They need a place on campus readily recognized as safe and providing support and information.
- They need to adjust to a college milieu that is unchanged by the death they are grieving.
- They need to know how to respond to people who ignore their grief, or who tell them that they need to get on with life and that it's not good for them to continue to grieve.
- They need to know what normal grieving entails and not become worried that the intensity and duration of their reactions mean they are going crazy.
- They need teachers to allow late work, make-up exams, or an incomplete for a class.
- They need to know they are not alone.

## CHANGING THE CAMPUS

The question arises, "How can we make college a place for helping bereaved students?" What is needed in a campus environment to foster acceptance of persons in distress? Here are goals that I consider both reasonable and appropriate to address the two questions just posed:

- Reach out to all students in distress, regardless of level of risk the student is facing.
- Change the climate on the campus toward assisting students in distress.
- Design a campus environment to foster acceptance of persons in distress.

## THE MISSION OF THE COLLEGE

Implementing strategies to meet these goals is in the best interests of a campus and goes to the very core of the mission of a college and a university. Let's discuss the mission of a higher education institution. Universities and colleges are devoted to scholarship. The mission is to discover new knowledge, to integrate disparate forms of knowledge, to extend knowledge through teaching, and to apply knowledge to help persons and communities and organizations in need.

But universities and colleges are more than institutions devoted to scholarship alone. Universities and colleges are communities that are obligated to offer care and compassion. In his reflections on the idea of the university, Jaroslav Pelikan, Dean of the Graduate School at Yale University, wrote:

> Any definition of the university that does not explicitly incorporate this dimension of personal caring betrays the deepest traditions and highest ideals of the university and is woefully inadequate, and any citizen of the university who feels squeamish about a definition of the university that includes this dimension should reexamine both the intellectual and moral imperatives that underlie the university in a community.
>
> (Pelikan, 1992, p. 54)

Building on these core beliefs about the dimension of personal caring within the very idea of a university, universities can make the campus a place for helping bereaved students. What are some possibilities? In this chapter, I offer several suggestions.

Students, faculty, and administrators can take an active role in addressing the needs of the significant proportion of college students who are grieving the death of a family member or friend. These actions can also work to the benefit of the college, and thus address the needs of the school. The actions I am considering cover grassroots initiatives by students to offer support groups, faculty actions, planned interventions grounded in theory, education programs to inform the student body, continuing education to augment counseling staff members' understanding of bereavement and college student needs, and policy decisions establishing protocols addressing student bereavement.

## STUDENT GRASSROOTS INITIATIVES

With a bit of enterprise and persistence, motivated students can set in motion initiatives to address the fact that many of their peers are bereaved. Articles can be written in the student newspaper about the prevalence rate of college student bereavement. Interviews can be conducted and posted online with bereaved students; care needs to be taken to determine whether the student wishes to remain anonymous.

## Support Groups

A support group is the intervention that most comes to mind as an initiative within the power of students to accomplish. Support groups get widespread endorsement from bereaved students. One student wrote to me that bereaved students "need people that they can talk to about their feelings and who understand what they are going through. They need someone they can rely on when the emotions become hard to handle by oneself." Support groups provide an answer to this need.

Models are available for running groups. It would be prudent to do homework on the structure and rules for the group before it begins. Here are some ideas to think about:

- Who will facilitate the group, and what are the person's credentials and skills with group discussion?
- How often will the group meet?
- Where will the meetings be held? A neutral place, even a classroom, is a good choice for meetings; support group meetings held at the counseling center seem not to attract students.
- How long will meetings last?
- How will the group meeting be advertised?
- Will the meeting have an open door policy?
- Will there be an experienced faculty member to serve as a sponsor and advisor for the group?
- What sorts of interpersonal dynamics may create problems, and what will be effective ways to deal with such problems?
- How will the group refer persons whose complicated grief is beyond the capabilities of a support group?

Support groups provide a means to address needs identified by bereaved students. One student wrote to me, "Bereaved students need to know they are not alone. Many times a bereaved student will not want to talk about their grief but they like to listen to others' stories and problems. This simple thing helps them to heal. They also need time to let their grief dissipate to get their work done and to do what they need to heal. They also need some way to begin to heal and to help others to get their mind off things and their hearts in the right place."

Support groups can run into problems. Five problems that need to be thought about ahead of time are (a) nonproductive silences or superficial discussions, (b) attendance problems, (c) domination or criticism by a group member or giving bad advice, (d) psychological disorder in a group member, and (e) running overtime. We'll take up each in turn.

### Nonproductive Silences or Superficial Discussions

Some silences are productive, and the worst thing that can happen is for someone to break in with chatter as persons are reflecting on what has transpired in a group. Some persons have difficulty tolerating silences, and they need to overcome the anxiety that leads them to impulsively talk when the group is silent. One guiding principle is to count to 20 before interrupting a silent moment. The general idea is captured in the phrase "Don't just do something; stand there." However, there will likely be times when the silence indicates the group is stuck. Options for dealing with these moments include suggesting a group exercise, openly commenting that the group seems stuck, asking the group what would best help them at this time, and even the possibility that superficial discussion of a topic is appropriate.

Knowing what to do in these circumstances takes an experienced facilitator. I don't want to scare people off from offering support groups because they are worried about not being experienced enough. Good training can get novice facilitators prepared, and it is prudent to run groups with two facilitators—one with more experience and prepared to handle difficult situations. All colleges have people who know how to run groups well. Running groups with both an experienced and a novice facilitator also pays off in getting the novice needed mentoring and the ability to engage in reflective practice.

### Attendance Problems

Some group participants stop coming because they have gained all they wanted from the group. In many cases, attendance problems indicate other issues are at stake, for instance:

- the number of sessions is either too few or too many for some members;
- the group is making some persons face experiences that they would rather avoid;
- some persons do not find the group to be supportive or do not feel included;
- some persons have entered the group at the wrong time, such as too soon after a death over which their grief is much too intense.

The answer to these problems is to have open discussion and to be sure the facilitator team includes someone experienced in group dynamics. For a student whose pain is so intense that group participation conflicts with the need to maintain dignity in front of peers, one option is to suggest the student talk with a peer trained in helping skills until the group becomes a more inviting environment.

### Domination or Criticism by a Group Member or Giving Bad Advice

Group facilitators need to use group process skillfully to ensure that all persons get the opportunity to speak. One way to accomplish this group maintenance task[2] is to direct the flow of conversation, making sure that issues get addressed and offering persons the opportunity to speak. Guard against allowing group members to begin criticizing one another or turning a group member into a scapegoat. What facilitators can do to deflect criticism is to remind members that the purpose of the group is to be supportive of one another, offer suggestions on how to provide support, and emphasize that each person's grief is personal and normal. A danger is for the facilitator to take on the role of an expert who is there to counter bad advice. One way of avoiding this danger is by getting group members to consider the consequences of advice that has been given; group members typically identify corrections needed when given the opportunity to focus on consequences.

### Psychological Disorder in a Group Member

Facilitators need to determine if a group member's situation is more disturbed than the group can handle. At times, the disturbed individual will not recognize that the group cannot provide the support needed. A guiding principle is that unless a group can empathize with an individual, the person will not profit from being in the group, and the overall effect will be to make all the members uncomfortable.

Persons with difficulties beyond the group's ability to support need to be identified whenever possible in prescreening before the group begins and referred to individual counseling or therapy.[3] But when these individuals' problems become evident during the group, the facilitator has to discuss the matter privately with the person and indicate that individual sessions are more appropriate. Because the person will no longer be part of the group, the facilitator needs to let the group members know the person was offered an intervention that fit his/her needs. A difficult tension to manage is respecting confidentiality of the person whose troubles have led to a referral outside the group and encouraging open discussion about the difficulties that group members noticed the person was experiencing.

*Running Overtime*

From the beginning, the facilitator needs to establish rules about starting and ending on time. One strategy to use during a meeting is to provide a 10-minute warning prior to the meeting's end. The concern is to
let people wind up their conversations, quiet their emotions, and regain
composure for the world outside the group. Once the 10-minute warning
is given, new business cannot be introduced, and persons who wait for
this warning and then start talking about a difficult topic that will take
considerable time to process should be gently told to hold on to their discussion until the next meeting.

## Forming a Students of AMF Chapter on Your Campus[4]

The National Students of AMF Support Network (www.studentsofamf.
org/) has had a few years' experience in getting chapters functional
on college campuses. Chapters basically provide support groups for
bereaved students and organize community service projects open to
anyone on the campus. The organization has developed a guide to assist
persons wishing to start a chapter. The national organization holds an
annual conference in Raleigh, North Carolina. Experts on college student bereavement present talks. Students from around the country have
the chance to meet, share stories, and learn from one another. If interested in starting a chapter on your campus, contact the organization's
executive director to talk over options.

## FACULTY ACTIONS

Faculty members can focus efforts to assist the significant proportion of
students struggling with the pain of bereavement. Here are a few simple
actions easily carried out.

- Advisors can listen attentively and compassionately to what the student is dealing with.
- Advisors can write letters—or better yet, e-mail messages—to instructors asking them to give bereaved students support and understanding.
- Course instructors can allow students to make up exams and turn in
  work later than stated deadlines.
- Academic Affairs Committees can determine what percentage of
  bereaved students drop out of school and why they leave.

■ The Dean of Student Life can research the impact of bereavement on student academic performance and make an official report to the campus.

## PLANNED INTERVENTIONS

College programs developed to assist bereaved college students will almost assuredly attract females more than males. There are several indicators that support my assertion. Consider, for instance, the data we already know about the greater likelihood of females to make use of programs colleges design to assist students. Further, in the realm of bereavement, the evidence is clear that females in considerably higher numbers participate in bereavement support groups and in bereavement research.

People on many college campuses have been giving considerable thought on how to engage males in services the campus provides. Making programs available is important, but so is offering them in accessible formats. Perhaps failure of typical programs to engage males stems from failure to consider men's characteristic focus on instrumental values of achievement, work, problem solving, and success. Developmental theorists underscore what has been proposed about instrumental versus intuitive grieving patterns. One way being tried on some campuses is engaging males in physical activities, even video games, to promote use of college services. There is such widespread appeal of computer games to college students, particularly males, that devising an interactive game on bereavement for college students seems to me worth pursuing.

It may be that programs aimed to assist bereaved college students appeal more to intuitive grievers and attract fewer male grievers because males are more inclined to use instrumental than intuitive approaches. Insisting that instrumental grievers engage in practices that focus on expressing feelings is an exercise in futility. One issue, therefore, for planning and delivering college programs to help bereaved college students is whether to balance activities expecting self-disclosure about feelings with activities offering physical investment in doing things. The Students of AMF offer both support groups emphasizing self-disclosure and community involvement actions that emphasize doing things.

As an example, consider this idea taken from Will H. Courtenay, a member of the board for McLean Hospital Center for Men at Harvard Medical School. Courtenay suggests that asking a male "How do you feel?"—even in a physical exam—elicits common responses that are, in effect, not very informative. He suggests instead that the question be aimed at the man's experience, such as, "How do you experience that?" (see Courtenay, 2004, p. 66). Asked of a grieving male (or, indeed, of an instrumental griever), the question could bring in the holistic framework and be asked such as, "How does your bereavement impact you physically?" or "How does your bereavement impact you cognitively?" or "How does your bereavement impact you interpersonally?" and so on.

Courtenay has developed health programs for college men around such program aspects as Humanize, Educate, Locate Supports, and Highlight Strengths. These four ideas provide structural components for programs aimed at male college student bereavement: The campus would humanize grief, educate about bereavement, locate supports that allow men to seek help, and highlight strengths that promote adaptation. For instance,

- Humanizing grief would mean giving it a face, acknowledging its prevalence, bringing it into open awareness, and making clear that grief is the normal response to a dreadful, irreparable loss.
- Educating about bereavement would mean offering information about bereavement, grief, and mourning in a variety of venues that attract college student attention. One venue is workshops, and another venue is material placed on the Internet.
- Locating supportive resources has the underlying value of linking help seeking to problem solving, thereby allowing men to seek help while retaining a sense of self-sufficiency and efficacy. Such supportive resources could take the form of social support groups. It could mean simply having students identify who are the persons who do the following things for them (and, conversely, who are the persons for whom they do these things):
  - ☐ Who elicits the best out of you?
  - ☐ Who allows you to ask for help even though you value independence?
  - ☐ Who asks you difficult questions?
  - ☐ Who enjoys you for just who you are?
- Highlighting strengths, in Courtenay's scheme, is a clear endorsement of instrumental values. He writes about such highly adaptive coping attributes as setting goals and intellectualizing, working well in teams, and having a sense of control or mastery.

I will take one example of these four program components. Consider building on Courtenay's idea of educating. The college can offer workshops on bereavement. Topics can be as wide ranging as the presence of bereavement on the campus, what bereavement entails, and coping with bereavement. Let's take the coping idea as our example. Workshops grounded in coping theory can be offered. Substance for these workshops can be found in the ideas of the dual-process model, in Leighton's sociocultural model, and in the Moos and Schaefer model of coping with life crises. These workshops would likely have a support group aspect as well as an educational component. Such interventions would be designed and administered by faculty and/or staff, have a built-in program evaluation component, and likely offer clinical experience to graduate students in such fields as counseling psychology, school psychology, social work, and clinical psychology. As one example, here is the structure for a social support intervention grounded in the Moos and Schaefer coping model and aimed at bereaved college students.

## An Intervention Grounded in the Moos and Schaefer Model of Coping

I am going to present in overview a social support intervention designed and implemented at Kansas State University. My intent in this chapter is to give the structure and purpose of each meeting. The adaptive tasks and coping skills of the Moos and Schaefer model of coping formed the basis for the intervention.

### Facilitators

There was a group facilitator who ran each meeting. Each facilitator was a graduate student in training to be a marriage and family therapist. The point was emphasized that the meetings were not therapy sessions but rather a combination of education and social support. One function of the facilitator role was to provide a safe, nonjudgmental environment in which participants could discuss the death and express their feelings, reactions, and ideas. The facilitators modeled attentive listening, empathic communication, openness in talking directly about the death, acceptance of the expression of emotions, and recognition and affirmation of differences in coping styles. Each facilitator drew attention to adaptive tasks and coping skills being used by participants and ensured that all group members had the opportunity to participate actively. The facilitators and I met frequently to review the psychological status of each group member, to discuss what had occurred in the meetings, and to identify if any participants needed referral for clinical services. No one required clinical help due to participation in the support group meetings. We learned that some students sought therapy for reasons not connected with their bereavement.

### Session Structure

Each session lasted at least 2 hours, and some went longer. The goal of the sessions was to encourage participants to talk about their experiences and to analyze what was shared in terms of the Moos and Schaefer framework. Generalizations occurred as participants connected the framework to their experiences and those of other group members. Here are the objectives and procedures of the eight sessions.

- Session 1: Structure the first group meeting to promote participants' getting to know each other, to promote self-disclosure, to establish group norms about purpose and confidentiality and the necessity for peer participation, to introduce the Moos and Schaefer conceptual framework, and to generate personal understanding of the adaptive task of establishing meaning and understanding the significance of the crisis event.
- Session 2: Structure the second session to build on the experiences of the first. Continue the process of soliciting self-disclosure, listening attentively and providing empathic feedback, and promoting connections between personal experiences and the Moos coping model. Educational material for this session involves the adaptive task of confronting reality and responding to situational requirements.
- Session 3: The leader will continue group process and dynamics that promote sharing, self-disclosure, and applying personal experiences to the conceptual model. Educational material for this session involves the adaptive task of sustaining interpersonal relationships.
- Session 4: The format will be the same as in Sessions 1–3. The educational material in Session 4 involves the adaptive task of maintaining emotional balance.
- Session 5: The format will be the same as in earlier sessions. The educational material in Session 5 involves the adaptive task of preserving a satisfactory self-image and maintaining a sense of self-efficacy. At this session, the leader will remind the participants that after Session 5 only three sessions remain.
- Session 6: The format will be the same as in earlier sessions. The educational material in Session 6 involves appraisal-focused coping skills of logical analysis, cognitive redefinition, and cognitive avoidance or denial. One example of logical analysis is drawing on past experiences

when dealing with a crisis. Cognitive redefinition involves admitting the reality of an event but looking to find something favorable in the situation. Cognitive avoidance or denial involves denying or minimizing the severity of the life crisis. The leader will facilitate group discussion of how these coping skills have been present in the participants' experiences—and/or how they could have been put to use—and if they have worked well in some circumstances but not in others. Participants will be asked to recall group discussions when these coping resources were mentioned by participants. The leader will encourage the participants to consider how they would use the skills in the future, which skill is easiest to use, and which skill the most difficult.

- Session 7: The format will be the same as in Session 6. The educational material in Session 7 involves problem-focused coping skills of seeking information and support, taking action, and identifying alternative rewards. The leader will facilitate group discussion of how these coping skills have been present in the participants' experiences—and/or how they could have been put to use—and if they have worked well in some circumstances but not in others. Participants will be asked to recall group discussions when these coping resources were mentioned by participants. The leader will encourage the participants to consider how they would use the skills in the future, which skill is easiest to use, and which skill the most difficult.

- Session 8: The format will be the same as in Sessions 6 and 7. The educational material in Session 8 involves emotion-focused coping skills of affective regulation, emotional discharge, and resigned acceptance. The leader will facilitate group discussions of how these coping skills have been present in the participants' experiences—and/or how they could have been put to use—and have they worked well in some circumstances but not in others. Participants will be asked to recall group discussions when these coping resources were mentioned by participants. The leader will encourage the participants to consider how they would use the skills in the future, which is the easiest skill to use, and which is the most difficult.

In Session 8, the leader will facilitate discussion on plans, hopes, and fears now that the support group is coming to an end. A half hour will be added to provide for closure. Materials needed include sheets of paper, pens/pencils, an 8½ × 11 manila envelope that can be sealed, a filled helium balloon, and string with which to attach the manila envelope to the balloon. Participants (including the facilitators) will write two sets of statements: (a) statements of what he/she wants to take from the sessions and (b) statements expressed to the person who died and/or to other persons. Once these statements are written, the facilitators will ask the participants if they wish to share what they have written. After listening to statements that are read, the facilitators will gather the papers, seal them in the manila envelope, attach the envelope to the balloon, go outdoors if not there already, and release the balloon into the sky.[5]

## Education Programs

I am going to present two approaches that can be taken to promote skilled helping. One is a more conventional approach to teach helping skills to peer counselors via established methods known to counselor educators for years. The other is a less conventional approach that relies on use of the creative arts to teach persons more advanced in helping skills than beginning peer counselors. In addition, I am going to present an idea for a workshop based on the ideas of the dual-process model of coping with loss.

### Peer Counselor Training

Conversations with students have taught me that, while going to a counseling center for help is foreign to most of them, talking informally with an interested, informed peer is acceptable. The college can develop a curriculum to train students to become peer counselors. Peer counselors will get certificates upon completing the curriculum. The University can advertise the peer counseling program and make available a list of peer counselors for students to contact informally. The development and implementation of such a curriculum needs to be the job of interested, informed persons; perhaps they could be appointed by the Provost and be chaired by the Dean of Student Life (or the person with the concomitant duties on your campus). Here is an example of what such a program could look like.

Build these peer counseling training programs around the concept of enhancing skills in attentive, empathic listening. These are interpersonal skills that counselor educators have decades of experience in teaching. The basics of attentive listening need to be stressed first, and students need to be given opportunities to practice. These practice sessions can have simple vignettes for one person to enact and another person to respond to as the peer counselor. Feedback has to be built in so that participants learn what others saw and heard during practice sessions.

Students participating in the training should be placed in small groups of three persons who will rotate through these roles: client, counselor, observer. It needs to be stressed that the persons who played client and counselor never switch roles with one another. The reasons for this rule should be stressed explicitly: Boundaries need to be maintained, and it is never appropriate for a counselor to seek counseling help from a client. Not allowing persons in the practice session to switch roles will reinforce this rule about maintaining boundaries.

Another training tool that has been remarkably useful for building insight and enhancing empathy is to use the method called interpersonal process recall (IPR). This training approach records a session, and then it is played back for the parties involved. At times, there is a facilitator running the IPR session, and in the approach I am suggesting the facilitator would be the person in the role of observer. The procedure is for persons to watch the playback (or listen if only audio recording is possible). At any point anyone may stop the tape to offer reflections on what he or she was thinking and/or feeling at that moment in the session, or to ask what the other person was thinking and/or feeling at that point in the session. It is not to focus on what you are thinking and feeling currently. It is uncanny how persons can readily recall what they were thinking and feeling at specific moments reproduced on tape. The recall questions can also ask a person such things as "Is there something you wished you had said here?" or "What would you have liked the other person to have done at this point?" At times, stopping the tape is prompted by nonverbal cues one sees or hears in one of the persons who has been recorded. Getting both the counselor and client to notice the nonverbal behavior and reflect on it builds insight and also courage as persons learn they don't have to feign not having noticed what was plain to anyone who was attentive.

Another benefit of IPR is that it helps participants to know when they completely missed something in an exchange. I cannot count the number of times persons learning helping skills with the IPR method will stop the tape and say, "At that point in the session I didn't even hear what she was saying. I was so concerned about what I was going to say next." Seeing oneself not paying attention actually increases attentive listening as long as the training sessions are built on trust and everyone is allowed to make mistakes.

These peer counseling training sessions can address the main reasons people do not assist others in distress. The main reasons are (a) feeling overwhelmed with the other person's pain and becoming in effect paralyzed, (b) being unsure what to do or say, and (c) seeing no obligation to listen attentively or act compassionately. We will trust that persons who see no obligation to listen attentively or act compassionately will either not seek peer training or will be removed from the training once their lack of motivation is noticed. The two other main reasons—feeling overwhelmed and being unsure what to do or say—are dealt with directly by the training. With practice, reflection, and feedback, persons learn how to gain the confidence to be present to someone in distress and trust themselves in responding; they even learn that at times what is appropriate is to say nothing or do nothing, but just be present.

### Using the Creative Arts

The curricula of mental health counselors, student life professionals, and school psychologists (a) do not deal with assisting persons to cope with bereavement and grief and (b) do not focus on working with bereaved persons from varied cultures. A mandate for these professionals is to be sensitive to persons of various cultural backgrounds, to be attentive to the explicit and tacit messages they communicate, and to facilitate expression of what is difficult to put into words. Given the centrality of loss in the life experiences of children, adolescents, and adults, it is puzzling that counselors and psychologists and student life professionals are ill equipped to work productively with persons for whom loss forms a significant influence in their lives.

The creative arts provide a dynamic means to bridge the training gap concerning loss and to extend the repertoire for interacting well with persons of varied cultures. Creative arts promote physical and psychological wholeness, foster expression, allow persons to give voice to their inner worlds, and provide means to communicate across cultures. The proposed project (a) will teach mental health counselors, student life professionals, and school psychologists the essentials about human bereavement and grief across cultures; (b) will teach them how to use the creative arts when working with persons who are bereaved; (c) will provide a supervised opportunity to apply this knowledge with bereaved families and individuals from the surrounding community and from the student body; and (d) will enable faculty and students to develop long-term collaborative efforts aimed at cross-cultural competencies centered on bereavement, grief, coping, and resiliency. This intervention will provide as well an outreach from the campus to the wider community.

*Implementation Plan*

The four-part project will occur on the campus in this manner:

*Part 1.* Experts in thanatology and the creative arts will run a 1-day edu-cational workshop for campus professionals as well as mental health counseling, student life, and school psychology graduate students: (a) 2 hours on the basics known about human bereavement and grief across cultures, (b) 2 hours on the basics of using the creative arts in counseling and psychology venues, (c) 2 hours of practice with various media (drawing, painting, sculpting, writing, and music) to express expe-riences with loss, and (d) 1 hour reflecting on the practice component, looking at themes, examining obstacles, and roadblocks.

*Part 2.* The experts who conducted Part 1 will run a half-day refresher session for participants 1 week later, reviewing the objectives of Part 1.

*Part 3.* Faculty and the participants from Parts 1 and 2 will sponsor on the campus a 1-day session for bereaved students and for families recruited from the larger community. They will be invited to come to a day focused on coping with loss via creative arts. Following introductions and an overview of the day's expectations, the project leaders will sepa-rate participants into three groups: the college students, the children, and the adults. Each group will be facilitated by participants from Parts 1 and 2 who will work with them on using creative arts to express loss. All per-sons will be brought back together to share with each other their creative arts projects. In small groups, participants will discuss what people expe-rienced, what they learned, provide some links to what is known about human bereavement, and ask the participants for their observations.

*Part 4.* Provide a half-day evaluative reflection on the whole project. In this session, workshop leaders, participants in Parts 1, 2, and 3, and the creative arts therapists can examine strengths and areas needing atten-tion and discuss implications for the ongoing curricula in the programs.

*Anticipated Benefits*

Community residents and students will benefit from professionals who listen attentively to their narratives and who foster expression of their stories through the creative arts. The faculty and students will gain sen-sitivity and skill in communicating with people from diverse cultures, including listening attentively to one another. Lessons learned about multiculturalism and diversity will be taken back into the curriculum for further education of students on matters of bereavement, grief, coping, and resiliency.

### A Workshop Based on the Dual-Process Model

One venue to obtain instrumental grievers is a 2-hour educational workshop presenting material about bereavement and grief. Instrumental grievers are almost assuredly not going to take part in a social support group and, I suspect, not in peer counselor training or in creative arts training. The content of a workshop can be the dual-process model.

The emphasis of this workshop and the approach will be educational. Persons will not be asked to share their experiences of bereavement. The presenter(s) will discuss in brief overview the main explanatory models of bereavement—in particular the emphasis on grief work found in Freud, Lindemann, and Bowlby—and then present the modifications to these models introduced in the dual-process model by the notions of a restoration orientation, a loss orientation, and oscillation between these orientations. Some discussion can go into whether these two orientations are completely separate or whether a griever can be engaged in each simultaneously. Examples will help to illustrate the concepts. An example that can be used is one from my discussion in Chapter 5 of how my mother dealt with my father's favorite chair after his death. Of interest to me was that Tom Attig used a similar example about a chair in the introduction to the reprinting of his book *How We Grieve* (see pp. xlv–xlvi).

## Continuing Education Offerings

Although making referrals to a counseling center frequently is the first suggestion to address needs of bereaved students, there is widespread skepticism among grief counseling practitioners whom I know whether most campus counseling center professionals understand the issues presented in bereavement. When I asked some bereaved college students what they would recommend colleges do to assist bereaved students, one person responded, "Colleges should provide counselors who are experienced in dealing with grief for students to talk to." Counselors I have met have concurred that their graduate training gave little attention, if any at all, to bereavement, grief, and mourning.

A proactive stance will be to develop guidelines for campus counseling that require counselors be trained in the treatment of grief. Such training can come with continuing education workshops offered at the college or at workshops and webinars run by the Association for Death

Education and Counseling (ADEC). An excellent overview regarding such workshops can be found in the special issue of *New Directions for Student Services* aimed at assisting bereaved college students.

Part of preparing counseling center staff to deal with students' bereavement can be helping staff develop techniques for collecting loss histories from students. Experiences with loss form the backstory of many students' lives. Although the student's presenting problem may not focus on a current or past loss, such losses may have important ties or clues to the current issue facing the student, and thus it is worth the effort of ascertaining such connections. In taking a loss history, it is important to focus both on death-related and non–death-related losses that affect this population. Examples of non–death-related losses include divorce of parents, breakup of romantic relationships, inability to achieve academic dreams, loss of important possessions, and homesickness.

## POLICY DECISIONS

The prominent decision is to put in place bereavement policies for students. Workplaces have such policies for employees. Without such guidelines in place, students are left on their own to figure out what to do. They sometimes face the skeptical looks and even insensitive queries from faculty who figure the students are running a scam. The policy needs clearly to cover absences from class, deadlines for assignments, makeup work, and incomplete grades. The policy needs to be featured prominently in the student handbook, be published for all on the university to know, and be presented to faculty in a reminder from the Office of the Provost every semester. A simple sentence could be required in each syllabus directing students to the bereavement policy link on the college Web page.

One university has in place just such a policy. The Faculty Senate at the University of Wisconsin at Green Bay (UWGB), under the leadership of Illene Noppe, UWGB Faculty Senate President, passed unanimously in February 2011 a "Policy on College Student Bereavement." The policy gives direction to faculty, staff, and students in cases of a student's bereavement. Specifically, the UWGB student bereavement policy identifies who is eligible to use the policy and the steps to take.[6]

In the UWGB policy, *bereavement* refers to the death of a loved one, usually a family member, and the bereaved student is instructed to contact the Dean of Students. Options available through the Dean of Students are (a) an excused absence from the college for 1 week, with the possibility of negotiated extensions and (b) an extended leave of absence for up to a full semester. The policy identifies steps the Dean of Students will take on behalf of the bereaved student, such as notifying the student's teachers.

Responsiveness to ongoing circumstances is built into the policy. As an example, the policy allows the student to negotiate excused leaves beyond a week. There are provisions covering whether students excused for a semester need to apply for readmission: Students whose leave begins after a semester has begun will not have to apply for readmission; students whose semester leave commences before the start of the semester are required to apply for readmission. Such applications for readmission are administrative formalities, not roadblocks being placed in the student's path.

It is possible for excused students to withdraw from courses or to request instructors give them incompletes. Excused students in good academic standing, that is, not on academic probation, have the opportunity to complete course credits when they return. UWGB faculty are to include in their syllabi reference to the Student Bereavement Policy.

The passage of this UWGB policy is a watershed moment in the institutional response to college student bereavement. Although other colleges and universities can frame their own individualized responses, the complete policy statement from the UWGB Faculty Senate may serve as a guide to other institutions, and it is reproduced in the following. A clear and persuasive rationale assists in focusing the attention of decision makers on the need for a comprehensive approach. The UWGB policy statement drew heavily on the work of Purdue University Professor Heather Servaty-Seib, who has been campaigning for bereavement leave policies for college students.

---

### UNIVERSITY OF WISCONSIN AT GREEN BAY

#### Policy on College Student Bereavement

*University Committee—Spring 2011*

I.  Introduction and Rationale
The UW-Green Bay University Committee proposes that a university-wide policy regarding student bereavement be created for implementation as of Fall 2011. Please note that bereavement policies for faculty and staff already exist. Current policy may be

found at http://www.uwsa.edu/hr/upgs/upg10.pdf. In a white paper proposing the need for a summit on college student bereavement, Dr. Heather-Servaty-Seib (published researcher in this area) of Purdue University writes:

*Rationale for Policies to Support Bereaved Students*
*At any one point in time, 38–45% college students are grieving the death of a loved one who died in the previous 2-year period.*

- *As most other employers, colleges and universities include bereavement leave policies as standard course for employees.*
- *However, few colleges and universities have bereavement leave for students.*
- *Faculty members make individual decisions regarding the students' ability to "make-up" work missed as a result of bereavement-related situations.*

*Perception of Institution as Responsive to Students' Needs*
- *Having a policy communicates that the institution is aware of most recent scholarly literature and aligned with empirical evidence.*
- *Communicates respect of students as adults who have lives outside of the institution and experience difficult events that affect their academic functioning.*
- *Communicates sense of compassion with regard to difficult life events experienced by students.*

*Quality of Student Life*
- *Bereaved students exhibit significantly lower GPAs (in the semester of death loss) when compared those who are not bereaved (Servaty-Seib & Hamilton, 2006).*
- *Bereavement students report challenges in their interpersonal relationships with peers and faculty (Balk, 1997; Silverman, 1987).*
- *A policy would allow students structure for navigating academic challenges at a time when they are likely debilitated by their grief.*
   - *Although students generally have an option to speak with their professors individually or seek assistance from staff members (Dean of Students, for example, or similar office), lack of a policy requires excessive effort on student's part; effort at a time when emotional resources are low.*

*Resource/Economic*

- *Students who are bereaved appear to be at risk for higher attrition than their non-bereaved peers (Servaty-Seib & Hamilton, 2007).*
  - *Tinto, in his model of attrition and retention, includes clear foci on academic and interpersonal integration.*
  - *Bereaved students are at risk in both the academic and interpersonal domains.*
- *A policy would provide faculty and staff structure for navigating issues related to student bereavement.*
  - *Faculty would include the policy on their syllabi.*
  - *Faculty would not need to spend effort on generating an individual approach for their classes.*
  - *Faculty could refer students to policy and consistent procedures would be followed.*
  - *Reduction in clock hours spent by staff members (Dean of Students or similar office) that now handles each case individually.*
    - *Most cases would fall under policy and could be handled with little staff contact.*
    - *More complex cases could be allotted more appropriate amount of time and consideration.*
- *Students who feel positive about their institution and who perceive that they have been respected and supported will be more likely to stay connected as alums and be more likely to contribute to the institution.*

Quoted with permission from Dr. Heather-Servaty-Seib
December 2010

II. Student Bereavement Policy

1. Students who experience the death of a loved one must contact the Dean of Students (DOS) office if the student wishes to implement either the Standard Bereavement Procedure or the Leave of Absence Bereavement Procedure (Nos. 3 and 4 on next page). The DOS has the right to request a document that verifies the death (e.g., a funeral program or death notice).

2. Typically, this death involves that of a family member, in parallel to the bereavement policy for faculty and staff. However, it is up to the discretion of the DOS to determine if a death outside of

the immediate family warrants implementation of the student bereavement policy.

3. Standard Bereavement Procedure:
   - Upon approval from the DOS, the student is allowed 1 week, commencing from the day of notification to the DOS, of excused absence. Should the student feel that he/she needs additional days, these should be discussed with individual course instructors and/or the DOS.
   - The DOS will contact the student's advisor and faculty and academic staff of the student's courses.
   - Faculty and academic staff will be advised that extensions must be granted to the student for the period of 1 week of excused absence.
   - Further extensions may be negotiated with the student when he or she returns to campus. Students are encouraged to discuss options with their instructors.

4. Leave of Absence Bereavement Procedure:
   - Students may be allowed to withdraw from the semester in which the death occurs.
   - The Bereavement Leave of Absence is for one semester only.
   - Students who have opted to take the Bereavement Leave of Absence and have already attended classes for the semester of the leave will be allowed to re-enter the following semester without having to reapply to the university. Students who wish to take the leave of absence prior to the beginning of the semester will be required to reapply for the following semester.
   - For students who are in good academic standing, they will be given the opportunity to successfully complete the credits for the semester in which they return. Students will consult with the DOS, on a case-by-case basis, as to whether they should withdraw from their courses during this leave of absence or to request incompletes from the faculty member.
   - Given that there may be a potential impact on financial aid, students who receive financial aid and who take the Bereavement Leave of Absence, upon arrangement with the DOS, will meet with a financial aid advisor prior to taking this option.

5. As an option, and in consultation with the DOS, students may take the Bereavement Leave of Absence after the Standard Bereavement.

6. Reference to the Student Bereavement Policies will be noted on course syllabi.

## CONCLUDING COMMENTS

Application is the focus of this chapter. Encouraging students, faculty, and administrators to be proactive is explicit in what I present. The idea is to change the campus to be a place responsive to the needs of bereaved students. A variety of approaches has been presented, and I hope readers see prospects in adapting variations on these ideas to the specifics of their own campus.

Many outsiders to a distressing event seldom appreciate how intense and long-lasting are the responses to life crises. Such lack of appreciation extends from the individual level to the organizational. One should not be surprised that colleges' responses are basically "So what?" when learning that 25–30% of their student body is likely to be in the first 12 months of grieving a family member's or a friend's death.

This reaction comes for various reasons, and I think it cannot be simply cast as the mark of gross insensitivity. One reason for the response surely comes from persons who have been bereaved at some point in their lives, have recovered, and think the students obviously will too. Perhaps it is the sense that bereavement is a human misfortune, but persons recover without outside interference. Another reason for the skeptical response comes from doubting there is any place in the mission of a university to devise services or programs for bereaved students. But let's look at the matter this way:

- Student retention and graduation is a major motivating force for colleges.
- Bereavement imperils the academic achievement of a great proportion of bereaved students, particularly in their first semester of bereavement.
- Student retention and graduation will be enhanced by devising policies and practices pertinent to students struggling in school due to bereavement.

What better way to acquire loyal alumni than to provide needed help during their undergraduate years, help that will enable students to finish their degrees?

Bereaved students are in a special position to discuss what they wish were available to assist them in their time of need. We are talking here about a campus response that would be accessible, available, and sensitive to the issues presented when bereavement marks a student's life. Awareness that there are different bereavement trajectories suggests that a college needs to tailor various responses, and not assume one size fits all. Also, counseling programs need counselors who understand bereavement, grief, and mourning. It is clear that few counselor preparation programs spend much time on the topic of human responses to loss, and therefore college counseling programs may well be staffed with persons who are not familiar with the nuances and complexities about bereavement. There very likely need to be continuing education workshops run by qualified persons, such as persons who could be identified through contact with ADEC (www.adec.org). What we don't need is clinicians who are convinced that bereavement recovery occurs in stages and who attempt to push people along.

## NOTES

1. Portions of this chapter appeared in *Death Studies*, 1993, *17*, 427–450.
2. Group maintenance tasks refer to actions that promote communication, cohesion, and acceptance in a group. Examples would be pointing out that the group has not been listening to someone, encouraging someone to share with the rest of the group, and indicating you would like to hear what someone has to say.
3. There are alternative approaches that run groups open to anyone who wishes to join. No screening is done.
4. AMF stands for Ailing Mothers and Fathers. The group began at Georgetown University due to the initiative of David Fajgenbaum, whose mother was dying of brain cancer. I write more about Students of AMF elsewhere in the book.
5. An earlier version of this closing exercise involved a practice that my wife explained is more than likely forbidden today. That practice was each group member, including the facilitator, will be given a candle and some paper on which to write a statement of what he/she wants to take from these sessions. Once these statements are written, the leader will ask the participants if they wish to share what they have written. At the end of the

meeting, the participants will light their candles, and using their candle's flame each participant will set afire the written statement and place the burning paper into a fireproof container brought to the meeting by the facilitator. Some persons oppose releasing balloons into the environment due to concerns over pollution.

6. On March 21, 2011, the Purdue University Faculty Senate passed a college student bereavement policy, which may be accessed at this web address: http://www.purdue.edu/faculty/download.cfm?file=08101130-C521-927F-93787A20297BDF24.pdf&name=University%20Senate%20Document%2010-6%20GAPS-%20Revised.pdf

## FURTHER READING

Attig, T. (2011). *How we grieve: Relearning the world* (rev. ed.). New York: Oxford University Press.

Bales, R. F. (1976). *Interaction process analysis: A method for the study of small groups.* Chicago, IL: University of Chicago Press.

Balk, D. E. (1997). Death, bereavement, and college students: A descriptive analysis. *Mortality, 2*, 207–220.

Balk, D. E., Tyson-Rawson, K. J., & Colletti-Wetzel, J. (1993). Social support as an intervention with bereaved college students. *Death Studies, 17*, 427–450.

Barnett, M. A., & McCoy, S. J. (1989). The relation of distressful childhood experiences and empathy in college undergraduates. *Journal of Genetic Psychology, 150*, 417–426.

Barnett, M. A., Thompson, M. A., & Pfeiffer, J. R. (1985). Perceived competence to help and the arousal of empathy. *Journal of Social Psychology, 125*, 679–680.

Courtenay, W. H. (2004). Best practices for improving college men's health. In G. E. Kellam (Ed.), *Developing effective programs and services for college men. New Directions for Student Services* (No. 107, pp. 59–74). San Francisco, CA: Jossey-Bass.

Egan, G. (2007). *The skilled helper: A problem-management and opportunity-development approach to helping* (8th ed.). Belmont, CA: Thomson.

Kagan, N. (1969). Interpersonal process recall. *Journal of Nervous and Mental Disease, 148*, 365–374.

Kagan, N., Krathwohl, D. R., & Miller, R. (1963). Stimulated recall in therapy using video tape: A case study. *Journal of Counseling Psychology, 10*, 237–243.

Kagan, N. I., & Kagan, H. (1990). IPR: A validated model for the 1990s and beyond. *The Counseling Psychologist, 18*, 436–440.

Moos, R. H., & Schaefer, J. A. (1986). Life transitions and crises: A conceptual overview. *Coping with life crises: An integrated approach* (pp. 3–28). New York: Plenum.

Pelikan, J. (1992). *The idea of the university: A reexamination.* New Haven, CT: Yale University Press.

Rosenblatt, P. C. (2008). Grief across cultures: A review and research agenda. In M. S. Stroebe, R. O. Hansson, H. Schut, & W. Stroebe (Eds.), *Handbook of bereavement research and practice: Advances in theory and intervention* (pp. 207–222). Washington, DC: American Psychological Association.

Servaty-Seib, H. L., & Hamilton, L. A. (2006). Educational performance and persistence of bereaved college students. *Journal of College Student Development, 47,* 225–234.

Servaty-Seib, H. L., & Taub, D. J. (2008, Spring). *Assisting bereaved college students. New Directions for Student Services* (No. 121). San Francisco, CA: Jossey-Bass

Servaty-Seib, H. L., & Taub, D. J. (2010). Bereavement and college students: The role of counseling psychology. *The Counseling Psychologist, 38,* 947–975.

Silverman, P. R. (1987). The impact of parental death on college-age women. *Psychiatric Clinics of North America, 10,* 387–404.

Stroebe, M. S., & Schut, H. (1999). The dual process model of coping with bereavement: Rationale and description. *Death Studies, 23,* 197–224.

Stroebe, M. S., & Stroebe, W. (1989). Who participates in bereavement research? A review and empirical study. *Omega, 20,* 1–29.

Tedeschi, R. G. (1996). Support groups for bereaved adolescents. In C. A. Corr & D. E. Balk (Eds.), *Handbook of adolescent death and bereavement* (pp. 293–311). New York: Springer Publishing.

Wood, D. D., & Near, R. L. (2010) Using expressive arts when counseling bereaved children. In C. A. Corr & D. E. Balk (Eds.), *Children's encounters with death, bereavement, and coping* (pp. 373–393). New York: Springer Publishing.

# 10

# *Self-Disclosure, Bereavement, and College Students*

The topic of this chapter is self-disclosure in the life of college students, in particular, bereaved college students. I presented the substance of the chapter in somewhat different form at a national conference of the Students of AMF in August 2010. In this chapter, I have worked with some material presented in earlier chapters to provide a synthesis for readers. The argument I have set forth examines what research has to say about self-disclosure, and I make an effort to link the material to your own lives. In the process of presenting the material, I have examined such topics as

1. Bereavement research and the prospects of recovery;
2. What has been written about self-disclosure;
3. What has been written about empathy;
4. A story from my life;
5. An opportunity extended to readers to engage in self-disclosure.

## BEREAVEMENT RESEARCH AND THE PROSPECTS OF RECOVERY

As reviewed earlier, in the early 1940s a gifted psychiatrist in Boston, Dr. Erich Lindemann, was faced with the daunting task of providing clinical assistance to persons grieving the deaths of friends and family members who were killed in a conflagration at the Cocoanut Grove Restaurant. I have reprised that information here.

Licensed for a capacity crowd of 500 persons, on the night of the fire over 1,000 persons were crowded into the place.

> A young couple, wanting privacy, reached to a palm frond to unscrew a 7.5-watt bulb. Told by a bartender to restore the light, a 16-year-old busboy climbed upon a seat, and then struck a match to locate the socket. A moment later, someone noticed flame along the satin ceiling. At first, people were amused by the antics of waiters trying to douse the fire with seltzer water. Outside, meanwhile, the temperature was 28, the air dry. A few blocks away, firefighters were extinguishing flames in an automobile when they spotted smoke at the Cocoanut Grove. They were among the first to arrive at a fire that eventually involved 187 firefighters, 26 engine companies, five ladder companies, three rescue companies and one water tower.
>
> Jack Thomas, 1992, retrieved September 7, 2010, from
> www.boston.com/news/daily/21/archives_cocoanut_112292.htm

Within 15 minutes 492 persons had died.

The Cocoanut Grove fire occurred slightly less than 1 year following the United States' entrance to World War II, and Lindemann wrote his paper when American soldiers and sailors were being defeated in many arenas on two oceans and on three continents. Lindemann was interested to work with the bereaved survivors of the restaurant fire not only for their own sake, but also because he believed effective treatment would be needed for the massive numbers of persons bereaved over the deaths of American family members and friends killed in the war.

Lindemann had been deeply influenced by Sigmund Freud's ideas about bereavement, grief, and mourning. Remember that Freud had written that to deal with the profoundly distressing misfortune when someone loved dies, a person had a very difficult, draining struggle ahead. The struggle drained a person physically, emotionally, intellectually, and interpersonally. I don't find evidence that Freud talked about how bereavement drains a person spiritually: Freud dismissed any notion that connections to the sacred could be other than an illusion, and in Freud's view construing the meaning of a death amounted to accepting the reality that the person was gone forever. In short, Freud said, what the struggle entailed was:

1. The person had to confront the many instances that brought back distressing reminders of the person who had died.
2. The person had to emotionally detach from the person who died.

3. The person had to form a mental representation of this person, a memory not filled with emotional distress.

Freud said these three things were very hard to accomplish, and his bereavement recovery ideas have been named "the grief work theory." Freud's grief work theory has been very influential, and other than Bowlby's ideas about bereavement and attachment, until recently no other ideas about bereavement had such influence as did the grief work theory. Freud said bereavement is a profound human misfortune, is a normal response to the irreparable loss of someone loved, and takes time to manage. Freud said it would never occur to him that a person who is bereaved needs professional help. Freud said bereavement mimicked clinical depression, but there were major differences between clinical depression and bereavement:

- A clinically depressed person thinks there is something fundamentally wrong with him or her.
- A bereaved person thinks there is something fundamentally wrong with his or her world.

Lindemann designed his intervention around Freud's grief work theory. And Lindemann added that to engage in grief work it is essential to openly express the feelings that grief stirs up. He said self-disclosure is indispensable for persons to recover from bereavement.

There is considerable controversy in the bereavement research literature whether it is necessary for bereaved persons to engage in grief work. There is research evidence that some bereaved persons avoid any confrontation with the distress of grief and yet appear to be functioning well. There is growing evidence that many persons maintain an ongoing attachment to the person who died. There is a clear picture that persons who do engage in what the grief work theory maintains—namely, confronting the distress that bereavement causes—also spend other time in restoring their lives, in going on with life. They are said to oscillate between (a) confronting the distress of their bereavement and (b) engaging in living. There is skepticism that openly expressing one's feelings is necessary for everyone to recover from bereavement.

## INSTRUMENTAL AND INTUITIVE GRIEVERS

How some persons express their grief is not in talking to others but in other, often more private ways, such as, reflecting on their experience and engaging in activities to restore normalcy to a shattered life. Examples of such activities are found in Paul Newman's life. You may know that the Newmans's son Scott died of a drug overdose at the age of 28. Paul Newman said of his son's death, "It never gets better." You may know that Newman and his wife, Joanne Woodward, set up camps for terminally ill children—called Hole in the Wall camps—and you may know about the immensely successful charity fund raiser he established through his food products. It is my contention that Newman did these things, at least in part, as a means to restore normalcy to a shattered life. I think of him as a model of instrumental grieving. I also know that it is simplistic to attribute his actions to but one motive. After all, Newman said he engaged in philanthropy because his life had been so blessed that he had to give back.[1]

We call instrumental grievers persons who express their grief in private ways. Instrumental grievers would not have fit in well with Lindemann's expectation that talking about one's feelings is needed to cope with bereavement. And yet, we know that instrumental grievers do give expression to their experience while being hesitant to discuss their feelings. And they do cope in healthy ways, just as do persons whose primary orientation is to share their feelings openly and directly.

Persons who prefer to share their feelings with others we call intuitive grievers. Women typically are socialized more to share feelings with others than to keep feelings to themselves. It is becoming recognized that there are persons who do not fit neatly into the instrumental or the intuitive camp, but rather engage in both instrumental and intuitive grief.

I am going to make an assumption about persons reading this book. I assume that many of you are characterized by both an instrumental and an intuitive orientation to grieving. Some of you may be primarily, perhaps exclusively, intuitive grievers. Some of you may be primarily, even exclusively, instrumental grievers. I expect what is true is that one form of grieving dominates but the other is there. For instance, you may greatly appreciate the opportunity to share your feelings with an attentive listener, and at the same time you see the need to engage in actions that assist students who are bereaved.

An unreflective examination of the phenomenon would indicate that the bereaved persons who value self-disclosure are exclusively intuitive grievers. I contend that all human persons value being connected to others and value meaning making, and that given the right opportunity, instrumental grievers engage in self-disclosure.

I expect that persons reading this book tacitly, if not explicitly, endorse the value of disclosing the experience of bereavement. You want the college campus to know about the prevalence and impact of bereavement on the lives of a great proportion of students on campus. You want bereaved students to know they are not alone. However, it would be presumptuous of me to assume each of you is a no-holds-barred, self-disclosing individual: You are not going to open up to just anybody about your experience and what it has meant to you. You are not fools. Choosing to disclose does not mean being clueless.

From what students who are bereaved have disclosed to me, here is some of what I know about their experience.

1. Their college milieu does not give any sense it understands what bereavement entails, what bereaved students need, or how many students are grieving deaths of family members or of friends.
2. There are very few, perhaps no, peers on campus who feel comfortable talking with bereaved students about the deaths the students are grieving and how they have changed the students.
3. While there may have been some willingness to hear their story at first, persons become wary of being around persons who are bereaved, so students have learned it is prudent to camouflage their feelings in order to maintain associations with acquaintances, perhaps even with friends.
4. Students feel alone in their grief and want the opportunity to share with others their distress, but there are few, perhaps no peers who have the emotional maturity to let people mourn in their presence.
5. There is much bereaved students would share if there were attentive, empathic listeners.
6. There is much bereaved students would welcome hearing as attentive, empathic listeners.

## JOURARD AND SELF-DISCLOSURE

I am going to assume you value self-disclosure and you realize it is a treasure that comes along rarely. And I am going to write a bit about what we have learned about self-disclosure. Some of these ideas come from a pioneer in the study of self-disclosure, namely Sidney Jourard. Here are three important ideas that Jourard learned about self-disclosure and human persons:

1. *Jourard's idea*: "Physical and psychological health are profoundly affected by the degree to which (the person) has found meaning, direction, and purpose in his existence." (Jourard, 1971, p. ix)

Jourard believes that finding meaning, direction, and purpose are greatly influenced by having someone with whom one shares intimacy—that is, a person with whom one discloses things that are private and that matter. You may recall that a fundamental developmental task for adolescents and young adults is to enter into and maintain close friendships. Obviously, self-disclosure is essential to accomplishing the task.

When the person disclosing feels accepted, some lasting basic benefits of disclosure are growth of self-awareness and acceptance and insight, connection to another person, and a dampening of being afraid. It greatly helps when the person receiving the self-disclosure uses the discloser's frame of reference when making comments. Picking up on the client's frame of reference gets us into the realm of empathy, and I will discuss empathy soon. I'll start by referencing the impact bereavement can have on what a person takes for granted about reality.

We know that for some persons a major issue involved in bereavement recovery involves one's assumptions about the world. The very meaning of existence may be up for grabs. Having an attentive, empathic confidant with whom one can share thoughts and feelings provides an outlet for regaining a sense of the meaning of things. It provides a means to know you are not alone. You find you don't have to go through this experience on the margins of society. Someone else understands you. It affords a means to achieve such essential human sentiments as belonging to a moral order, securing and maintaining membership in a human group, and securing recognition.

## EMPATHY

An empathic person understands someone else's situation and has an emotional connection with this other individual. Frequently, sympathy is contrasted with empathy: Sympathy is feeling sorry for the other person's plight, whereas empathy is understanding the other person's experience and having an emotional connection with the person.

There are obstacles to engaging empathically with someone else.

▪ You may feel you have no obligation in the situation, even though you are aware of the distress going on. I suspect this response explains the dismissive reactions of many of us to the emotional appeals on TV to help persons or animals in distress.
▪ Then another obstacle to empathy occurs when the individual feels so overwhelmed by what is going on and is virtually paralyzed.
▪ A third obstacle occurs when the person feels clueless about what to do or say.

It would not surprise me that several persons on campus who do not engage attentively with bereaved students do so because of one or more of the obstacles to empathy. Remember the story in Chapter 1 about Sarah's first day at her new job.

Knowing these obstacles exist provides direction for efforts to promote a campus environment sensitive to persons in distress. Workshops and other educational efforts aimed at student growth present a major mechanism to consider. Other workshops can be aimed at staff development, particularly counselor understanding of bereavement. I presented some suggestions in Chapter 9.

> *2. Jourard's idea*: "Research evidence indicates women disclose more data about themselves to the significant people in their lives than men." (Jourard, 1971, p. 12)

This research finding about gender differences in self-disclosure probably shows itself in who takes part in bereavement research: 75–80% of persons who take part in bereavement research are women. Bereavement research typically asks participants to discuss the relationship they had with the person who died. Men seem more likely to go inward rather than to discuss relationships and share feelings outwardly. We looked at these ideas when discussing intuitive and instrumental patterns of grieving.

> *3. Jourard's idea*: "There's no way to force somebody to talk about himself. You can only invite." (Jourard, 1971, p. 14)

Harm occurs when persons, whether distressed or not, are coerced or manipulated into disclosing more about themselves than they wish to share. What is needed is for an attentive, empathic listener who understands and accepts someone else's fears and troubles and who offers the opportunity to open up. There is no guarantee that such an offer will be accepted. While you may be emotionally mature and able to listen empathically and attentively, while you may engage in self-disclosure and thereby model what you hope the other person will do in return, the other person is under no obligation to accept this invitation. A counseling psychology mentor during my graduate school days wisely told me that you should not expect someone to do what you are not willing to do yourself. It later struck me that there is something else to remember: Just because I am willing to do something does not mean others have to do it as well. Because no one should be pressured into self-disclosure, support groups typically have an explicit rule that a person's wish not to talk will be honored.

## THE ROLE OF ACCEPTANCE IN FOSTERING SELF-DISCLOSURE

There are risks to self-disclosure. We may share and be rejected. We may be made fun of or judged. We may feel ashamed. We may find the other person completely misunderstands what we shared. We may feel ignored or dismissed as of no importance. Have you ever had the awful experience of sharing with someone a topic of consequence to you, something that matters, only to have the other person change the subject? Empathic, attentive listeners stay focused on what the person is disclosing.

A fear that inhibits disclosing is the concern about being judged or rejected or dismissed. The concern is expressed in essence with such words as "If I tell her this information, she will be disappointed in me.... Or she will think less of me...Or I will be subject to ridicule or contempt." Another concern is that putting something into words makes it real. Putting something into words may lead a person to relive a dreadful experience. In short, concern over being vulnerable keeps people from engaging in self-disclosure. And I suspect that many college students have found that it is better to keep their story of grief private because others are not open to hearing it.

The great counseling psychologist Carl Rogers coined a phrase that has been treated rather shabbily over the years. The phrase is "unconditional positive regard." While one reason for people's skepticism about the phrase may be its very odd phrasing, another and more substantial reason is that the phrase's optimism seems to many persons patently beyond human reach. So, what did Rogers mean? He said that what people most wanted and what facilitated growth and development was unconditional positive regard. What does that unwieldy phrase mean? It means in short that acceptance of another person is not contingent upon the person saying or doing approved things. Unconditional positive regard means listening attentively and suspending judgment. In counseling sessions with clients, Rogers found persons grew and changed when they learned the counselor accepted them and did not pass judgment on them even though they had difficulties in living, even though they were not perfect.

I believe each of us has the means to offer one another unconditional positive regard, but I don't believe we do so consistently. Sometimes we are better at it than at others. I believe in many cases each of us offers and receives unconditional positive regard. For all of us, such moments are transitory.

Reception of self-disclosure with unconditional positive regard depends on two related phenomena:

1.  Someone has to be open and share information about self.
2.  Someone else has to listen attentively and empathically.

We have it in our interpersonal skill set to do those two things, and people who are inept with attentive listening can be taught those skills.[2]

I am going to offer you an opportunity to engage in self-disclosure with someone of your choice through an exercise I have placed at the end of this chapter. I realize you can only be invited to engage in such self-disclosure, not forced. So, if you decide not to participate, that must be accepted as your choice.

I will offer some self-disclosure of my own, at least to make it clear that I am not asking you to engage in something that I would never do. However, as I have said earlier, just because I am willing to do something does not place any obligation on you. I will tell you a brief story about me. In other chapters, I related some stories about my time with my dying father and mother. The exercise I am proposing you engage in involves writing about your best friend and about holistic aspects to your bereavement. My story this time is about how I met my best friend.

## STORY ABOUT MYSELF

Until I was in my early 30s I was emotionally and personally adrift. There was nothing I had sunk my teeth into to make my own. There was no other person in my life to whom I had made a lasting commitment. In terms of the major tasks we give adolescents and young adults, I was clearly a late bloomer, in danger actually of remaining diffuse and without direction.

I had gone from being a devout Catholic studying for the priesthood to a young man who was well aware that there are many competing demands on belief but who had made no new faith decision other than a commitment to relativism. I found implausible the faith story I had been brought up to believe. I had not found any other story compelling. I was afraid to commit myself when the answers were ambiguous. I wanted certainty, and I knew it did not exist. However, intimate, lasting friendships scared me too. What was required was personal commitment. That was more than I felt capable to give.

A man I greatly admire, whom I had known in my undergraduate days as a Catholic seminarian, had become the abbot of a Benedictine monastery in Missouri. He was interested in developing an outreach program from the monastery to the surrounding community, and he wanted the program to offer something that would help youth. He offered me the chance to come to his monastery, do the needed research, and come up with a plan. I accepted, and thus my life changed. I did not know it at the time.

What I began doing in my research is what I now realize is called "key informant research" and "snowball sampling." I started interviewing persons who had special knowledge of the needs of youth in this semirural area of Missouri. I talked with school counselors, with a newspaper reporter, with psychologists, with a probation officer, with a judge, and with a sheriff. In each interview, I would ask the person who else I could talk with. And one day, the sheriff of Festus, Missouri, recommended I talk with someone at a delinquency prevention program in St. Louis County called Project Youth Opportunity (PYO).

When I got to the PYO office, I was a little early. And I didn't have a clue who the person was other than her name. The PYO office was located in a two-story office building. Walking down the hall toward the PYO office, I passed the second floor restrooms, and out of the women's restroom stepped this attractive young woman tucking her shirt in her trousers. I found out her name was Mary Ann and learned she worked for PYO. She asked if she could help me; I told her who I was looking for at the PYO office, and she took me to meet that person. I do not remember the name of the person I interviewed that day.

Later that week or the following week I was back in the neighborhood to interview someone else. The day had been a bust. None of the persons I was supposed to interview kept their appointments. Finding myself in the vicinity of the PYO office, I decided to step in. The attractive young woman was there and asked me how my day was going. I said it was going lousy. She said why not go out for dinner. So we did. And then we began going out more, and then frightened by the commitment that she and I were edging into I abruptly broke off my relationship with her.

Two months later, we were back in touch because I had arranged for presentations of various youth programs to the decision makers at the monastery. Her program had agreed to make a presentation, and her program director called to see if the presentation was still on. I said it was and arranged to meet with Mary Ann to discuss preparations.

All I can say is that I had done some soul searching and had talked with a Benedictine monk I trust and like very much about my personal life and my concern over running away from love. Somehow Mary Ann was still interested in me, and she gave me another chance. We started going with one another again. And that was back in 1973, and she and I have been married since 1975. We have a daughter in her 30s with whom we are close and whom we think of as a neat kid. Mary Ann and I have had our experiences of "for better, for worse, in sickness and in health." As for the part about "for richer, for poorer," so far we have not had "richer." This year alone both Mary Ann's mother and my mother died; they were in their 90s. Mary Ann's mother had slipped deeply into Alzheimer's before she died, and my mother died of renal failure brought on by pancreatic cancer. Unlike Mary Ann's mother, my mom to the end had a clear mind and a very frail body. Mary Ann and I know even more the wisdom of the phrase "growing old isn't for sissies." And just last month one of our nephews, a man in his 40s, died in the early morning of a heart attack. He lived alone, and his body was not found until 2 days after he had died.

Mary Ann and I are together even when apart, and we love one another. She is my emotional anchor. One day a few years ago when I was visiting my mother in Phoenix, she said to me that meeting Mary Ann had been the best thing that had ever happened to me. My mother was very wise.[3]

## AN OPPORTUNITY TO ENGAGE IN SELF-DISCLOSURE

I want to offer you the opportunity to reflect on a couple of important aspects of your life and to share your reflections with another person of your choice. I hope what you share will be information the other person does not know about you already. I am also hoping you will see that this opportunity is one for your partner in the exercise to both listen attentively and share with you some important aspects of his/her life. Your partner need not be bereaved, and if not then it is likely the person can only write about the first topic I have posed.

Take some paper and write an answer of about 250 words to these questions:

1. Who is your best friend? Write about this person and your relationship.
2. What has bereavement been like for you physically, emotionally, behaviorally, cognitively, interpersonally, and spiritually?

I am going to ask you to read your answers to the other person, and I want the other person to listen and then tell you what she/he understands you disclosed about yourself. I want you to listen to what the other person will read to you, and then you tell that person what you have heard. I cannot compel you to engage in this exercise. I hope it is something you are willing to do.

## CONCLUDING COMMENTS

I embedded the value of self-disclosure for bereaved college students within what Lindemann wrote about bereavement recovery. For Lindemann, it was crucial that bereaved persons openly talk about their feelings. I make no claims that the only option for persons to manage their grief well is to talk openly about their experience. I understand that for some persons opening up to others about private matters is not their first choice. However, a singular intervention endorsed by bereaved students is finding someone who listens attentively. Another intervention bereaved students endorse is support group meetings with peers who are also bereaved. Self-disclosure is necessary for those two interventions to work. (It may be that we know about bereaved college students' preference for interventions that require self-disclosure because the persons who told us engage in self-disclosure.)

Self-disclosure is impeded when persons feel judged or when they are anxious about people's reactions to them. Another impediment comes from persons who do not listen attentively. Some people just don't pay attention to what the other person is saying. If you listen to many conversations, you will hear this pattern: The first person talks about herself, and when she is done the second person talks about herself; then when the first person talks again, she talks about herself, and then when the second person gets her chance, she talks about herself, and so on ad infinitum. Attentive listeners make it clear to the other person that they understand what the other person has said; attentive listeners also pick up on nonverbals in body gesture and in tone of voice. Persons who are not adept at attentive listening can learn these skills. It is a matter of great hope to me that we know how to teach attentive listening, and that many persons on campus either already possess attentive listening skills or are willing to learn.

## NOTES

1. Brook McClintic, Director of Research for Judi's House, a program supporting bereaved children and adolescents in Denver, noted that her husband Brian Griese, who founded Judi's House, is another example of an instrumental griever. He created the program and champions grieving children; his mother died when he was 12. Brook also mentioned that Candy Lightner, the woman who started Mothers Against Drunk Driving, offers another example of someone who transformed grief into social action.
2. The best book I have found on teaching helping skills is Gerard Egan's *The Skilled Helper*.
3. I have been asked, "What did you 'hear' in your own self-disclosure?" The story most of all expresses appreciation for persons who have graced my life with their acceptance of and belief in me, most particularly my wife, my mother, and two Benedictine monks. It must have been trying to see a young man with promise drifting and in danger of never becoming an adult. I find a search for meaning, one grounded in faith, hope, and love, not simply in reason. Between the lines one can infer the presence of losses brought on by my emotional immaturity. One can also sense my relief at accepting and returning the love Mary Ann offered me. And there is the value I place on my mother's insights about me and Mary Ann.

## FURTHER READING

Attig, T. (1995). *How we grieve: Relearning the world*. New York: Oxford University Press.

Berman, J. (2001). *Risky writing: Self-disclosure and self-transformation in the classroom*. Amherst, MA: University of Massachusetts Press.

Berman, J. (2010). *Death education in the writing classroom*. Amityville, NY: Baywood.

Bonanno, G. A. (2009). *The other side of sadness: What the new science of bereavement tells us about life after loss*. New York: Basic Books.

Egan, G. (2009). *The skilled helper: A problem-management and opportunity-development approach to helping*. Belmont, CA: Brooks Cole.

Jourard, S. (1964). *Transparent self: Self-disclosure and well-being*. Princeton, NJ: Von Nostrand.

Kauffman, J. (Ed.). (2002). *Loss of the assumptive world: A theory of traumatic loss*. New York: Brunner-Routledge.

Lindemann, E. (1944). The symptomatology and management of acute grief. *American Journal of Psychiatry, 101*, 141–148.

Martin, T. L., & Doka, K. J. (2000). *Men don't cry…women do: Transcending gender stereotypes of grief*. Philadelphia, PA: Brunner/Mazel.

Rogers, C. (1942). *Counseling and psychotherapy: Newer concepts in practice*. Boston, MA: Houghton Mifflin.

Stroebe, M. S. (1989–1990). Who takes part in bereavement research? A review and empirical study. *Omega, 20*(1), 1–29.

Thomas, J. (1992). The Cocoanut Grove inferno. *The Boston Globe Online*. Retrieved September 7, 2010, from www.boston.com/news/daily/21/archives_cocoanut_112292.htm

# Reflections About Recovery Following Bereavement[1]

## A MODEST PROPOSAL

One of the counterintuitive aspects of a life crisis is that it may lead to growth and transformation. We find this assertion in all the mainline views of coping with life crises developed in the past half century. We find this point of view eloquently presented in Erik Erikson's psychosocial model, in which he argues human development over the life-span centers on specific fundamental decisions that shape personality. Greater maturity is possible but so are other outcomes such as narcissism and timidity; in short, a beneficial outcome is not assured. There is the possibility of long-term harm, or the matter would not be a life crisis.

While a life crisis contains a serious threat to well-being and challenges a person's repertoire of coping skills, dealing well with a crisis produces greater self-confidence and a greater sense of self-efficacy. What can contribute more to one's own self-efficacy beliefs than the experience of mastering a difficult situation?

I am not pretending that life crises are only make-believe with no emotionally wrenching and anxiety-provoking features, nor that dealing with a life crisis is a simple matter and is resolved in no time at all. It is only persons unaffected by a life crisis, with no appreciation for the intensity and enduring quality of a crisis, who seem to underestimate the demands of a life crisis.

There are residual effects of life crises, and people who go through a life crisis are changed by the experience. Some are the worse for the experience, and some are stronger psychologically, emotionally, and spiritually. You are going to see me argue in this chapter that recovery following bereavement can lead to persons being stronger psychologically, emotionally, and spiritually. An Episcopal priest I know and admire is prone to say during a sermon "Hear me on this point," when there are particular ideas he wants people to notice. So, hear me on this point: I do not claim that recovery from bereavement leads all persons to be stronger nor do I claim that recovery from bereavement means everything returns to the way things were before the death.

Bereavement is the prototypical life crisis. Empirical data clearly show that most persons overcome the severe challenges that bereavement presents to living. Most persons do recover from being bereaved. I was surprised at how strong was the adverse reaction of many persons to my suggestion that recovery is the normal outcome following bereavement. With a bow to Jonathan Swift, I then offered this modest proposal:

> No one recovers following bereavement. Because no one recovers following bereavement, no one gets beyond bereavement. No one grows after being bereaved, and people learn nothing following bereavement. In short, the phrase "recovery following bereavement" is inappropriate, inaccurate, and insensitive.

I reject that modest proposal in its entirety. I contend it is nonsense to reject the term *recovery* from any serious consideration of the consequences following bereavement. I reject the sweeping claim that no one recovers following bereavement. I contend that the usual outcome following bereavement is recovery and that it is obvious that bereaved persons typically recover. I contend that it is utter hogwash to maintain that persons do not recover once bereaved.

## DISLIKE IN SOME CIRCLES FOR THE WORD *RECOVER*

There is nothing modest to the widespread resistance to using the term *recovery* when speaking of bereavement. There is distaste—at times visceral—for this term when bereavement is the topic. The bereaved have suffered an extraordinary misfortune, and to many the term recovery trivializes that misfortune. After all, the whole damned point of an irreparable loss is that what has been lost cannot be recovered, and the common understanding of the term recovery is to regain what had been lost, an outcome clearly beyond possibility when the bereavement is over a loved one's death. There is no returning to how things were before the loss. Better to use, I am told, more subtle and evocative terms than recovery: Some terms now in accepted usage are adaptation, reintegration, management, and resiliency. Resiliency in particular seems to be gaining adherents.

Is there any import to this debate over use of the word *recovery* when thinking about bereavement? Is all this discussion so much word-spinning with no implications for human experiences with struggle, growth, and change, and no implications for working with persons who are bereaved? In my mind, the issues converge on a matter of central importance, what happens once people are bereaved; in other words, the outcomes of bereavement.

Let's look at the term that many persons currently find acceptable, even preferable. That term is *resilience*. One of the more formidable advocates for this term, George Bonanno, argues that resilience characterizes the normal response of human beings to distress and misfortune. Now it is clear even from Bonanno, however, that many persons' responses to bereavement are not marked by resilience. As I have reflected on the matter, it struck me that an examination of the meaning and use of the term *resilience* was needed.

What I have uncovered has underscored for me the irony that endorses acceptance of *resilience* but rejection of *recovery* when bereavement outcomes are the topic. What does *resilience* mean? All of the English language dictionaries I have consulted, other than a specialized dictionary for psychology, define the basic meaning of resilience is to recover quickly from some challenge or adversity. In short, common usage and understanding of the term resilience is that it falls under the larger umbrella of recovery. For psychologists, however, recovery has nothing to do with resilience, except at best peripherally. Psychologists' understanding is that resilience denotes competency to withstand the problems to which others fall prey. Recovery, on the other hand, is defined by psychologists neither as a process nor an outcome but rather as the period of time in which a person manifests ongoing improvement in response to some adversity.

## PEOPLE DO RECOVER FOLLOWING BEREAVEMENT

The point of view that "persons do not and should not recover" is, I believe, the accepted understanding within bereavement research and practice. It is unseemly to suggest people recover. Perhaps the phrase "recovery following bereavement" is heard as a coarse, insensitive dismissal of the importance and salience of an excruciating, irreparable loss. Perhaps "recovery following bereavement" is rejected because there is no return to how things were prior to the loss. Perhaps "recovery following bereavement" is rebuffed because of the obvious evidence that on occasion acute grief reactions return in fury when the person has been "grief free" for some time. There may be other reasons the phrase is disallowed, all reinforcing the view that "persons do not and should not recover." It is a view that I question.

Is it that people do not recover once bereaved? I say no. I say that recovery following bereavement is the normal course of events. I contend that the term recovery depicts normal human experiences with being bereaved. And thus, my purpose to examine forms of the term recovery, and see if there are instances in which its use is appropriate in denoting human responses to being bereaved.

## DIFFERENT MEANINGS OF THE WORD *RECOVER*

The *Oxford English Dictionary* (*OED*) devoted nearly six pages of small print to the term recover and its derivatives (e.g., recoverability, recovering, and recovery; pp. 366–371). The term has both transitive and intransitive uses, as well as reflexive meanings.

1. As a transitive verb, the term recover means "to regain possession of something lost or taken away," "to regain territory by conquest," "to acquire again a quality, state, or condition...health or strength...(or) a faculty of the body or mind," "to bring back, recall to memory," "to restore to consciousness...(or) to health," "to make right again (or) to rescue or deliver someone (from harm)," and "to get over, get better from a sickness, misfortune, or affliction" (*OED*, 1989, pp. 367–368). As an example, consider the sentences, "The soldiers recovered the territory they had lost in the earlier battle" and "The lady took steps to recover her reputation."
2. As an intransitive verb, the word has many of the same meanings of recover in its transitive form. For instance, the verb means "to regain health after a wound or sickness," "to regain consciousness," "to rally...(and) to gain ground," "to regain one's footing," and "to make up a loss again" (OED, 1989, pp. 368–369). As an example, consider the sentences, "The tightrope walker stumbled and then recovered" and "It took the child time to recover after being teased."

3. Terms with reflexive meanings refer to action turned back upon the subject performing the action. Reflexive statements always contain words such as myself or itself. As an example, the *OED* (1989) referred to the Great Fire of London and noted, "London soon recovered itself" (p. 368). Feifel (1977, p. 9) denoted the reflexive properties of recovery from bereavement when he indicated bereaved persons "redefine and reintegrate ourselves into life."

Two distinct meanings of the notion of recovery occur in scientific circles. One is medical: Physicians and psychiatrists refer to ill persons returning to their "premorbid condition." Thus, when providing emergency services to a boy who ingested poison, the goal would be to stabilize his condition and enable him to recover his former strength. Another meaning is physiological. Exercise physiologists refer to the concept of recovery following a bout of exercise. In this regard, the body recovers from the physical exertion of a workout by returning to a state of equilibrium but not without some response to the exercise stimulus. Over time repeated bouts of exercise followed by recovery translate into significant increases in physiological parameters such as muscular strength and endurance: In this context, recovery means growth and transformation.

## INDICATORS OF RECOVERY FROM BEREAVEMENT BASED IN RESEARCH

As presented elsewhere in this book, the term *bereavement* denotes being in a state of loss. I have also noted the multidimensional aspects of bereavement, that is, its holistic impact. To recap, the holistic impact of bereavement manifests in persons' lives physically, emotionally, behaviorally, cognitively, interpersonally, and spiritually. Here are some examples to illustrate the point:

- Physically a bereaved person may experience fatigue, chills, and diarrhea.
- Emotionally a bereaved person may feel guilt, anxiety, loneliness, and fear.
- Behaviorally a bereaved person may experience bouts of crying and may have trouble sleeping and eating.
- Cognitively a bereaved person may have difficulty concentrating and remembering and may be flooded with intrusive images and thoughts.

- Interpersonally a bereaved person may remain isolated from others, find that others become uncomfortable when the bereaved person is present, and may lash out unpredictably at others.
- Spiritually a bereaved person may question the meaning of existence, lose hope, and feel adrift in the world.

Do persons never recover from any of these manifestations of bereavement? To answer affirmatively seems absurd. For many persons, physical manifestations abate, emotional issues fade, behavioral troubles extinguish, cognitive difficulties end, interpersonal relationships are renewed, and spiritual questions are answered as hope is restored. But there is a sense that the very resolution of these manifestations of bereavement indicates the bereaved person's life does not return as it was before the death. The fundamental core that is grieving a loss is the human person, not parts of the person. With a bow to my systems theory colleagues, the meaning of this discussion is that the whole (in this case, the person) is greater than the sum of its parts (for instance, the physical or the emotional or the behavioral).

Recovering oneself (the reflexive use of the term) may be the more difficult challenge than dealing with discrete manifestations of bereavement, but is recovering oneself an impossibility once bereavement touches one's life? A glimmer of an answer suggests itself from the life crises literature. You will see I am returning to and recapping ideas expressed in the chapter about bereavement as a stressful life event.

## Recovery Examined From the Point of View of Life Crises Literature

A life crisis is considered to be an event that defies a person's normal abilities to cope, presents a threat to well-being, and offers both the prospects of growth and development as well as the possibility of harm and dissolution. As such, crises are seen to be "dangerous opportunities." Much of life-span human development scholarship is founded on the notion of change in response to normative and nonnormative transitions, and one of the most influential models of psychological development sees normative crises as presenting necessary transitions for human growth and development. Without the impetus from life crises, growth and development would not occur.

Life crises and transitions come in a variety of guises but two types predominate: sudden and unexpected events (such as being in a car wreck, winning the lottery, or finding out you have cancer) and anticipated and predicted events (such as graduating from high school, retiring, or dying from cystic fibrosis). Bereavement is the prototypical life crisis, and much of the work of crisis intervention started with and has been modeled on efforts to work with the bereaved. Coping with bereavement involves psychosocial transitions integral to resolving life crises and to achieving growth and development.

In an elegant, extended essay examining the links between community integration and human psychological development, Alexander Leighton noted that life crises, which he called cross-sections of the moment, have more than momentary duration and possess "temporal thickness," reaching back into one's history, defining one's present, and extending into one's future. Contemporary scholars have noted that outcomes to life crises are integrally linked to various background and personal factors (one's history), to assessment of the importance of the crisis (one's present), and to anticipation of how things will turn out (one's future). Leighton asserted that all human beings continually and dynamically strive to achieve fundamental objectives he called essential human sentiments. Although Leighton said no list of such sentiments could apply to all persons in all cultures, he did identify sentiments whose fulfillment he considered critical to healthy human functioning. An abbreviated list of these sentiments includes (a) to possess physical security, (b) to express love, (c) to secure love, (d) to secure and maintain membership in a human group, and (e) to belong to a moral order. See Chapter 5 for a discussion of all the sentiments in Leighton's sociocultural model.

One way to understand recovery following bereavement in terms of redefining and reintegrating oneself into life would be to see the sentiments as markers for bereavement resolution.[2] Bereavement presents a significant obstacle to achieving most of the sentiments. It is as though the anticipation of the future stretching from the griever's cross-section of the moment holds forth no successful striving after the sentiments. If we can find means of assessing the presence, absence, and importance of the essential human sentiments in the lives of persons, we would have a powerful mechanism to infer the extent to which recovery following bereavement has occurred. On another count, Leighton gave us direction in teasing out the prospects that recovery has meaning when applied to bereavement. In regard to the "temporal thickness" involving bereavement, time following a death is never the same as time prior; and grieving individuals discuss how their lives have changed and what they have learned in the midst of oscillating between focusing on their grief and focusing on reintegrating into the world. Can the term recovery denote the fundamental changes that have taken place over time in the bereaved person as a whole, not simply in parts of human experience?

The links between recovery and bereavement are multifold. There are several conceptual links found in the analysis of critical life events, particularly in the sense that these events present transitions for the whole person, involve striving after essential human sentiments that have been blocked by unresolved bereavement, and extend in temporal thickness. Another link comes from analyses of responses to critical life events, specifically (a) the phenomenological analysis of how we grieve and (b) empirical analyses of life following bereavement. I have examined the conceptual links and turn attention now to the phenomenological and empirical research links.

## Phenomenological Analysis of Bereavement and Recovery

Rejection of the notion that recovery can denote outcomes following bereavement may reside in an intuitive judgment that, even though life goes on, it does not do so unaltered. In short, there is no return to the premorbid condition. What one recovers is not life as it was before the death. In this light, I have noted that resiliency following bereavement is a notion more acceptable to many persons than the term recovery. I am maintaining that recovery encompasses resiliency.

Tom Attig distinguished between bereavement, which happens to someone and over which a person has no control, and grieving, in which a person actively relearns relationships to self, to other persons, and to the external world. This phenomenological analysis maintains that, at the core, bereavement sunders not only our relationship with someone who has died but fundamentally challenges our very humanity. We recover our humanity as a function of both reframing and relearning our place in the world, our relationships with others, and our relationship with ourselves. The continuum of humanity following bereavement thus encompasses at one extreme individuals who withdraw completely from all engagement with others and the world, and at the other extreme, individuals who give themselves over to larger goals and causes; examples of the latter individuals would be Elie Wiesel and, I believe, Paul Newman.

Wiesel is a survivor of the Nazi Holocaust and winner of the Nobel Peace Prize who has worked tirelessly for the spiritual renewal of humanity. Newman was a consummate actor who, following the deaths of his son and members of his larger family, devoted considerable time and fortune to charitable efforts, saying he had been fortunate in life and had to give back. It seems apparent to me that these men have forged out of the crucible of their own losses renewed understandings of self, others, and the world. To extend the kinesiological use of the term recover, these men exerted themselves in grieving and recovered.

## Empirical Research Into Bereavement and Recovery

Empirical studies of bereaved individuals demonstrate that the road following bereavement is mixed with loss and gain, mixed with an enduring sadness, and a new appreciation for life and other persons. The message here is thus not a naive assertion that recovery means insulation from pain, but rather that positive growth and development may often emerge over time. Studies of bereaved adolescents continually have uncovered both sets of outcomes, namely, loss and gain.

Daniel Offer's longitudinal study of high school boys faced with such family tragedies as the death of a father or permanent injury to a sibling indicated they responded initially with fear and eventually with maturity greater than that of their same-aged, nonaffected peers; they used the crisis as a means to grow. Kevin Oltjenbruns noted that bereavement led some adolescents to lose support from friends (what Oltjenbruns labeled "secondary loss and incremental grief"), but Oltjenbruns also detailed the positive outcomes adolescents ascribed to having grieved a death; for instance, deepened appreciation for being alive, enhanced empathic skills, strengthened emotional bonds, and improved problem-solving skills. Bereaved adolescents develop empathy for and a courage to be present to people who are suffering. Mark Barnett and Sandra McCoy noted that distressing experiences in childhood correlated strongly with college students' empathy for others experiencing troubles. Once they have engaged in grief work, bereaved adolescents are no longer afraid to be in the same room with someone else who is bereaved; they don't literally or figuratively flee, change the subject, or pretend the other person's pain is nonexistent

## CONCLUDING COMMENTS

It is obvious that recovery is an absurd term to apply to bereavement if by that is meant the grieving person regains what has been lost, namely, the person who died, or that the grieving person will return to being the same as before the death. Freud worked out elegantly in his examination of grief and depression that accepting such a loss was at the heart of the difficulty facing the person bereaved over a death. We have seen some refinements to Freud's incisive analysis, but the issue that Freud identified cannot plausibly be meaningless for the bereaved. We may or may not stay connected with the deceased, but bereavement is not resolved by efforts to deny that death happened. As Feifel (1997) said, "The dead must die before we are able to redefine and reintegrate ourselves into life" (p. 9).

A means to operationally define recovery following bereavement as "redefining and reintegrating ourselves into life" is to apply Leighton's essential human sentiments and Attig's existential phenomenological constructs about fundamental human relationships. In short, we can define relationships with self, the world, and others as indicated by the presence of striving after specific human sentiments. As an example, relearning our relationship to others will contain sentiments of giving and receiving love. Striving after the essential human sentiments provides a mechanism to examine the multidimensionality of bereavement. For instance, how the person understands belonging to a moral order provides a link to spiritual aspects of seeking meaning and having hope in the face of loss. Thus, we would systematically examine Feifel's notion of bereavement resolution by seeing the extent to which the essential human sentiments are being achieved, and striving after the sentiments would indicate the work toward relearning the relationships that Attig has written mark the essence of how we resolve grief. Such examinations of bereavement resolution would inspect the various types and levels of recovery, assume that recovery is not an all-or-nothing phenomenon but rather an ongoing process of integration and reintegration, and expect there to be both qualitative and quantitative opportunities to understand recovery following bereavement.

Recovery following bereavement is the outcome of an active engagement with the central disruptions to one's own existence. We can mature, become more attuned and empathetic to the sufferings of others, and reach out to do what we can in framing new relationships with others, the world, and ourselves. In this complex, but paradoxically simple sense, we recover following bereavement, and thus I believe in this sense it is correct to say the term recovery can be applied meaningfully to one's responses to the death of a loved one. In this sense, I believe the concept *recovery following bereavement* has meaning and that its most profound meaning is in its reflexive properties: Recovery from bereavement means we recover ourselves; we redefine and reintegrate ourselves into life.

While I have argued for the term recovery, I admit the term has baggage that burdens its usage. I acknowledge the subtleties of the multiform positive outcomes following bereavement don't immediately come to mind when persons hear recovery being applied to bereavement. While there is a reflexive meaning to the term recovery, such that to recover from bereavement means to recover oneself, to recover one's humanity, when I mentioned this fact to a workshop filled with practitioners, one person's rebuttal was that it seemed unlikely bereaved people would turn to the *OED* to understand their response to their loss. Of course they wouldn't. That doesn't mean the term recovery has no relevance, however, or that the reflexive meaning does not aptly convey the sense of growth, or transforming change, not just diminishment, following bereavement.

Corr and his colleagues as well as Tedeschi and Calhoun have argued that the term recovery takes us to the conceptual web of disease and pathology. Tedeschi and Calhoun are strong, compelling advocates that transforming growth occurs in some persons' lives following major life crises. Irwin Sandler and his colleagues, who are concerned over the problems attendant on a term that conjures for the typical person detestable meanings, offered the term resilience as preferable to recovery. Robin Paletti has written about the value of an educational model that (a) addresses the vital role culture plays in responding to bereavement and (b) accounts for the self-transformation that can occur in response to bereavement. Paul Rosenblatt has argued that the term recovery is embedded in a positivistic, modernist view of reality, and he noted the multiplicity and diversity to reality advocated by a constructivist and postmodern view calls for openness to accepting recovery as one of many possible understandings of the reality of outcomes to bereavement—as one of many possible realities that are bereavement outcomes. And, in a similar vein with deep ties to postmodernist philosophical reflections, Jeffrey Kauffman has considered the value of and societal implications of what it means to prefer the assertion that there is no recovery once bereaved. Ester Shapiro has made a singularly compelling case to place bereavement within individual, familial, and cultural boundaries.

All of these arguments from my colleagues have led me to acknowledge there may be a better word than recovery to unambiguously designate when the human person, the human spirit, rises from the ashes following bereavement and enacts significant emotional, behavioral, spiritual, interpersonal, and cognitive changes. Resilience, understood as quickly returning to baseline functioning, does not denote these positive outcomes. If the term to be used is some form of resilience as understood in most dictionaries, then the idea of recovery is being admitted through the back door, but I think without the roots for transforming growth. In Sandler and his colleagues' use of the term *resilient adaptation*, there may be room for growth and transformation. I have to think about the implications of the arguments from Richard Tedeschi and Lawrence Calhoun, from Paul Rosenblatt, from Robin Paletti, and from Jeffrey Kauffman that there is no one word to denote positive outcomes following bereavement.

In the end, I think our task is to examine rigorously, in collaboration with researchers and practitioners, what are the sequelae following bereavement. There is no single way to study outcomes following bereavement, but absent practitioner–researcher collaboration, I think the information will be missing important contextual aspects. If ever there were a project with strong potential for practitioner–researcher collaboration, what more than an examination of what occurs following bereavement and of what to name those outcomes? That is a modest proposal about bereavement, outcomes, and recovery I heartily endorse. Such collaborative work would afford one prospect for bridging the gap that separates researchers and practitioners, and it would focus on a matter of interest to all of us in thanatology.

## NOTES

1. Portions of this chapter appeared in *Death Studies*, 2004, 28, 361–374 and in *Death Studies*, 2008, 32, 84–93. Some persons who read earlier versions of the chapter expressed concern that as presented here, the chapter steps outside the scope and focus of the book. The issue of recovering from bereavement is at the heart of this book. In fact, I think recovering from bereavement lies at the heart of each person's experience of bereavement. We need discussion of what are the outcomes of bereavement. But more to the point of this book, we need a framework for thinking about what it means for college students to manage constructively their grief over the death of someone who matters to them. I hope readers will trust that the chapter is worth reading, thinking about, and applying to their understanding of the process of grieving a death and applying to their understanding of the bereavement experiences of college students.
2. Brook McClintic commented that some thanatologists do not like the term "resolution" because a person is bereaved for the rest of his/her live and thus grief is never resolved.

## FURTHER READING

Attig, T. (1995). *How we grieve: Relearning the world.* New York: Oxford University Press.

Balk, D. E. (2007). Bridging the practice-research gap. *The Forum, 33,* 1–4.

Bonanno, G. A. (2009). *The other side of sadness: What the new science of bereavement tells us about life after loss.* New York: Basic Books.

Feifel, H. (Ed.). (1959). *The meaning of death.* New York: McGraw-Hill.

Feifel, H. (1977). *New meanings of death.* New York: McGraw-Hill.

Freud, S. (1957). Mourning and melancholia. In J. Strachey (Ed. & Trans.), *The standard edition of the complete psychological works of Sigmund Freud* (Vol. 14, pp. 243–258). London: Hogarth Press. (Original work published 1917)

Kauffman, J. (2008). What is "no recovery?" *Death Studies, 32,* 74–83.

Leighton, A. H. (1959). *My name is Legion: Foundations for a theory of man in relation to culture.* New York: Basic Books.

Lindemann, E. (1944). The symptomatology and management of acute grief. *American Journal of Psychiatry, 101,* 141–148.

*Oxford English Dictionary* (2nd ed.). (1989). Volume XIII. Oxford, England: Clarendon Press.

Paletti, R. (2008). Recovery in context: Bereavement, culture, and the transformation of the therapeutic self. *Death Studies, 32,* 17–26.

Rosenblatt, P. C. (2008). Recovery following bereavement: Metaphor, phenomenology, and culture. *Death Studies, 32,* 6–16.

Sandler, I. N., Wolchik, S. A., & Ayers, T. S. (2008). Resilience rather than recovery: A cultural framework on adaptation following bereavement. *Death Studies, 32,* 59–73.

Shapiro, E. R. (2008). Whose recovery, of what? Relationships and environments promoting grief and growth. *Death Studies, 32,* 40–58.

Strack, S. (Ed.). (1997). *Death and the quest for meaning: Essays in honor of Herman Feifel.* Northvale, NJ: Jason Aronson.

Tedeschi, R. G., & Calhoun, L. G. (2008). Beyond the concept of recovery: Growth and the experience of loss. *Death Studies, 32,* 27–39.

# Spirituality and College Student Bereavement[1]

Chapter 11 posed the prospect that recovery can include radical changes to a grieving person's belief system. Bereavement serves as a precipitating event for such radical changes when the loss a person has experienced seriously challenges the person's assumptive world.

## ASSUMPTIVE WORLDS

What is meant by the phrase "assumptive world?" The phrase refers to what a person takes for granted about human existence and the wider reality in which the person lives. Some of these expectations are self-evident truths on the order of statements such as "No one can be in two places at the same time," "A person cannot be both alive and dead," "Things in the past occurred prior to things that will occur in the future," and "If something is true, it is not also false." Some science fiction writers love to play with self-evident truths and develop imaginary worlds where self-evident truths are false. I have read that quantum physics denies self-evident truths about causality (namely, the self-evident truth that causes precede effects), but I find such thinking fantastic and clearly beyond my ability to comprehend.

Some components of assumptive worlds are actually beliefs, not self-evident truths. Here we are getting into the arena of philosophy and religion. Assumptive worlds in this arena take on less universal properties than are found in self-evident truths, and reflect the multiplism and pluralism of human beliefs. For instance, many persons believe that there is a divine purpose to existence and that, therefore, all things happen for a providential reason. A belief held by some persons is that there is no divine purpose to existence, and also that events occur without any reference to an all-powerful, transcendent being. Some persons believe that God rewards the good, punishes the evil, and will not let bad things happen to good people. Some people believe that suffering is redemptive, and God purifies the human soul through suffering. Some persons believe that human existence is fundamentally tragic and dispute the assertion that meaning for this world depends ultimately on something transcendent to this life. Well, you get the picture.

Empirical evidence suggests the plurality of bereaved persons, possibly the majority, do not experience bereavement as a challenge to their assumptive worlds. I am referring to persons whose bereavement forms a resiliency trajectory. These individuals do experience distress over the death of a loved one, but they return fairly quickly to productive, functional lives. By the very definition of a resilient griever, challenges to assumptive worlds are ruled out. I am open to altering my views should someone complete longitudinal research that demonstrates resilient grievers do struggle with challenges to their assumptive worlds.

Recovery following bereavement requires some persons to alter their assumptive worlds. To recover from the wrenching reality of their loss, they find they must adopt a new belief system. The life crisis of bereavement has sundered not only their relationship with the person who died but also it has torn asunder what they took for granted about reality. I have two students to present to you, one who reframed her assumptive world after the death of her mother and one who remained stuck in grief, having given up on his ideals and dreams. First, we will turn to a student whose bereavement experience formed the recovery trajectory that Bonanno has identified, and then to a student in the enduring grief trajectory.

## A Student Slogging Through Grief to Eventual Recovery

I want you to meet Rachel, a college student who was raised a fundamentalist Christian. Her trust in a benevolent God was shattered as her mother died in excruciating pain from pancreatic cancer. Her religious faith got tested, and ultimately she cast it aside in response to comments from members of her church and comments from her pastor. Members of her church said such things as "God must have wanted your mother so much to have taken her from you" and "Be glad that your mother got to participate in our Savior's suffering." When Rachel was in the midst of acute grief over her mother's death, she confided in her pastor. He told her that her grief indicated her faith was weak, and in fact that her grief was a betrayal of God.

Rachel's grief eventually abated, and in the process she examined her religious beliefs. What she had been raised to believe no longer made sense to her. She looked for new ways to understand this profound experience that started with the illness, suffering, and death of her mother. To her surprise, she found meaning in accepting the very ambiguity that marked human existence. Rachel, a Christian raised to believe in God's redemption of humanity, found solace and meaning in the story of Jesus accepting his agonizing death and continuing to trust in God despite feeling he had been fundamentally mistaken about God's promise to him.

Rachel is but one case. Not all persons respond as she did. Obviously not all persons who grieve are Christians, let alone fundamentalist Christians. Other persons face the existential questions Rachel faced and make very different choices. The specificity of the choice is not what I am focusing on. The matter of having to make a choice that produces meaning is the point of this chapter on spirituality and college student bereavement. It is the need to reconstruct meaning when what a person took for granted can no longer be believed.

## A Student Stuck in His Grief

For some persons, the discrepancy between what has happened and their global beliefs overwhelms normal efforts at construing meaning. For these individuals, there is not only cognitive dissonance between their beliefs and their experience but also a challenge to the cardinal virtue of hope. The future looks bleak, there is nothing worthwhile to anticipate, and all one held to be true is up for grabs. These are persons who, in Leighton's sociocultural model, have experienced a devastating cross-section of the moment and find not only achieving their human sentiments blocked but also their expectations of the future drastically foreshortened. In Bonanno's scheme, these are persons in either the recovery trajectory or the enduring grief trajectory. You met Rachel, a student in the recovery trajectory. Now you will meet Daniel, a student whose grief simply did not lessen over time. This vignette does not have a happy ending.

Daniel had been a 20-year-old college junior at a large land-grant university 100 miles from his home. He had liked school, and the persons he had met there. He was in a pre-med program and felt confident about his desire to become a physician. Already he had arranged for a summer placement in a rural medical clinic. He knew once he became a physician that he would make a difference in people's lives. He had met Jenna at the university, and they liked each other a lot and had been dating seriously for several months. Actually, Daniel loved Jenna and looked to the day they would be married.

In short, Daniel had been doing well in school and felt good about being alive. Then everything changed 10 months ago when on a rainy night he lost control of the car he was driving and hit a bridge abutment. He was hardly scratched, but Jenna was severely injured, and eventually died. The police report said it looked to them that the car had hydroplaned and that what happened could not possibly be Daniel's fault.

Daniel took no comfort in what the police concluded. He had been responsible for keeping Jenna safe. He felt desolate and had recurring panic attacks. He had trouble sleeping, had constant thoughts about Jenna and the accident, could not concentrate on school work or remember things, and was very restless. Several persons at the university knew about the accident, but only one person, Jenna's roommate, made any effort to offer condolences. When he approached his organic chemistry teacher to see about getting an extension on course assignments, the teacher told him there would be no exceptions made about when assignments were due, and he would have to take the midterm with everyone else. It was clear to Daniel that other students became uncomfortable when Daniel was in the same room.

He made some efforts to study, but his course work seemed without meaning, and 5 weeks following the accident he simply packed up his things and came home. He had not considered contacting the Dean of Students or finding out if it was possible to take a leave of absence. Following the rules of the university for taking an official leave of absence was not a priority; getting away from school seemed a good idea. Getting away from all reminders of the accident seemed a good idea. The idea was to get away.

Daniel told himself over and over he was guilty and deserved to be punished. When his parents heard these comments, they became very concerned and arranged for Daniel to see a mental health counselor. The counselor had little understanding of bereavement and grief. He was concerned about suicidal risks and did ascertain that Daniel had no plan to take his life. After listening to Daniel's story, he explained to Daniel about Kübler-Ross's stages of grief and told Daniel it seemed clear he was in the anger stage. Daniel stopped seeing the counselor after the third session, thinking he did not deserve to get better.

Months passed. Daniel's grief remained relentless. To stop feeling bad about Jenna's death seemed to Daniel an utter betrayal of her. It would be like he didn't care. He constantly thought about Jenna and missed her intensely. Images of her bloody body came to him when asleep and when awake. He no longer had any plans about his life and did not take part in the internship with the rural clinic. It all seemed meaningless.

He had thought he could make a difference in people's lives. But now he realized life was a series of random events with no meaning. He had invested deeply, unreservedly in his school work and in Jenna. It had been a mistake. But there was one thing he was sure of: He was guilty of having killed her. And no one, not even his parents, seemed to appreciate the extent to which he had loved Jenna and how her death shattered him. He mostly stayed in his room at his parents' house, staring into space and now and then crying uncontrollably.

## MEANING MAKING, SPIRITUALITY, AND RELIGION

Various human properties or capabilities are said to be what set human beings apart from the rest of the natural world. Human beings are said to be dreamers, planners, or story tellers. We are persons. We are said to be rational beings. We are capable of wonder and awe. We are said to be tool makers. We hope. We are said to be organic machines with minds. We know we are going to die. We are said to be spiritual essences trapped in material bodies. We are the animals who ask questions about the ultimate meaning of existence. And so on.

In all these varied efforts to determine what makes human existence unique, the constant thread is the human preoccupation with establishing meaning. Human beings are makers of meaning. And meaning making is at the heart of what it means to be spiritual. In my assumptive world, spirituality is a fundamental dimension of human existence, and imposing meaning on reality is what human beings inherently do. Meaning making indicates that human beings exercise spirituality.

A key marker of meaning making is establishing purpose. We know from surveys done with college students across the United States that searching for meaning and establishing purpose are quests of crucial importance in their lives, but quests they frequently keep to themselves because they do not find the campus, particularly the faculty, open to discussing such concerns.

There are connections between religion and spirituality. A function of religion is to provide answers about the ultimate meaning and purpose of human existence. Religion grounds its answers about ultimate meaning and purpose in a transcendent holy being who somehow, inexplicably addresses us in our world. Religion makes it clear that the proper human response to the impinging of this holy being is faith and trust.

I think that persons who are religious are also spiritual, and I have had first-hand personal experience knowing such persons, particularly some Benedictine monks I met in an earlier part of my life. However, I believe all human beings are inherently spiritual but are not inherently religious. Albert Camus strikes me as the prime example of a person who was not religious but was searching for meaning and purpose. There are persons I know who have as much religious belief as does a table and yet who are clearly striving for and making meaning. One indicator of spirituality is the human response of wonder, appreciation, and awe, such as when a person is struck by the beauty of the night sky, the grandeur of the Grand Canyon, the delicacy of a hummingbird, the magnificence of a piece of music, or an intimate conversation shared with a friend; many persons I know have such experiences. In short, I am of the opinion that spirituality is inherent to being human, but religious belief is not. People could not be religious without being spiritual, for religion is only one form whereby humans construct meaning out of chaos and confusion, but people's spirituality does not mean they are religious.

Dennis Klass, a profound contributor to scholarship about making meaning out of bereavement and a thinker who has greatly influenced my views about bereavement, was educated primarily to be a scholar of religious studies. He takes strong exception to the assertion that a person can be spiritual without being religious. He notes that the assertion separating spirituality and religion arrived fairly recently in human consciousness (around 1985) and has led to a proliferation of definitions of spirituality (as many as 95). Klass writes that we have become less clear and more fuzzy-headed about spirituality, and he claims that spirituality is in itself a new religion. Klass notes that the distinction between spirituality and religion is one not shared by bereaved parents he knows, and observes as well that surveys of hospice patients and hospice personnel show that patients describe themselves as religious but the hospice personnel describe themselves as spiritual. I understand practical issues involved in this disconnect between bereaved persons and practitioners. I don't understand the options Klass holds out for people who are not religious if the point is all spirituality is a form of religion. Maybe the answer can be found in what Klass identifies religion provides and that prospect takes us to definitions of religion and of spirituality.

Scholars of the psychology of religion differentiate between substantive and functional definitions. Substantive definitions of religion and of spirituality focus on the sacred. A functional definition of religion denotes the purposes religion fulfills, such as religious beliefs and practices, and a functional definition of spirituality denotes the efforts in which people engage to establish meaning, find purpose, establish connectedness beyond oneself, and forge a set of core beliefs to live by. It is understood that religion serves this purpose of establishing meaning for some people. Spirituality may have practices such as meditation or other rituals. So the interconnectedness between religion and spirituality for psychologists of religion is plain.

For theologians as well there is an interconnectedness between spirituality and religion, and they consider religion to arise from humans' quest for the sacred; such a quest is seen as the core of spirituality. Theologians note that religion possesses three fundamental characteristics.

- First, religion expressly refers to a transcendent reality that human beings can experience, even if only momentarily. Note: This first point does not assert there is a God or a pantheon of Gods; it does not deny belief in God either. Thus, this aspect of religion holds for Hindus, Roman Catholics, Buddhists, and Muslims, to consider some examples. Can this aspect hold for an atheist?
- Second, religion posits there is a purpose or order of intelligence beyond ours that imposes meaning on events in the world. Again, this second point does not insist in belief in a deity, but does not rule out such belief.
- Third, religion finds expression in a community in which rituals and human interaction validate that there is a transcendent reality and there is a purpose to human existence that comes from the transcendent reality.

These constitutive features of religion are simply beyond plausibility for many persons I know. They do not believe there is a reality transcendent to our own, they do not believe there is an order to existence guaranteed by a reality outside this universe, and they do not belong to a community that celebrates and validates a religious worldview endorsing transcendence. These persons are not religious in any sense; all belong to secular communities that validate the efforts of human beings to determine meaning within the boundaries of this universe. I believe these persons are spiritual: They still work to make meaning and construct purpose and establish connectedness beyond themselves and forge a set of core beliefs to live by. They are engaged in an existential quest to establish meaning. But to repeat myself, these persons are not religious.

Not all persons agree that spirituality is at its core an existential quest to establish meaning or is the basis for core beliefs. The argument is that removing the sacred from the center of spirituality eviscerates it; spirituality for these persons becomes fuzzy if not meaningless when defined as the human search for meaning. Religion and spirituality are seen as integrally interconnected, and they are seen as fundamentally centered on a sacred, transcendent reality.

Because these viewpoints about religion and spirituality differ so fundamentally from what I am proposing in this chapter, I have had to ponder whether I am wearing blinders or am desensitized to realities not endorsed by secular society. Am I proposing basically a point of view not only lifeless but so general as to be without any power? I realize my point of view may be endemic to a small proportion of persons living in a secular culture focused on individualism, disenchanted with superstition associated with religious practices (for instance, praying for divine intervention), and convinced that the narratives taught by their religious traditions are implausible. We are persons who have discarded religion but who are committed to making a difference for others and to establishing meaning within this world, and outside religious traditions that assert ultimate meaning rely completely and solely on a transcendent reality.

I don't have an answer whether my view of spirituality is diminished due to my assumptive world that says religious interpretations of existence are implausible. I do know that I believe persons not only can but do reach beyond self and establish meaning and purpose that transcend the immediate moment. An example of such a spiritual endeavor is the effort to make sense of the bereavement experiences of college students.

College students are enmeshed in their own efforts to address fundamental questions. These questions are part and parcel of the identity formation going on in later adolescence and young adulthood. What some don't grasp is that the questions remain with us as we age. Some answer these questions with reference to religion, and some answer without any such reference. In all efforts to address these questions, students are engaging their spirituality. They are manifesting that they are spiritual.

As briefly touched on earlier in this chapter, surveys of college students have uncovered an explicit—if sometimes camouflaged—interest in spirituality. The assumption had been that college had a deadening effect on students' spiritual aspirations and on their religious practices.

What turned up was that religious practices do decline for many students once they are at college, but their interests in meaning and purpose intensify. Jennifer Lindholm, a national expert on spirituality in higher education, noted about college students that there is "a personal engagement with spiritual issues, including consideration of important life questions: 'Who am I?' 'What's important in my life?' 'How can I contribute?' 'How can I better serve others?' 'How can I understand the world around me?'" (see Bryant, 2009). The conclusion reached was that while some students are religious, for those interested in spirituality, the expression their quest takes involves developing core beliefs about self-identity, about relationships to others, and relationships to the wider world.

The connection between these fundamental inclinations toward spiritual development and Tom Attig's phenomenological analysis of the demands of bereavement is striking. You may recall from an earlier chapter that Attig noted that the challenge bereavement poses for persons is to reconstruct three principal relationships: with the external world, with other people, and with oneself. When bereavement results in an assault on one's assumptive world, I am contending that at heart the issue is spiritual and challenges what a person accepts about self, others, and/or the external world.

## PROGRAMS TO PROMOTE SPIRITUAL DEVELOPMENT IN COLLEGE STUDENTS

Empirical data are clear: Spiritual development is an important personal matter for many college students. In the chapter on college students (see Chapter 2), some time was spent looking at the growth of faith consciousness in the development of college students. Another term for growth of faith consciousness is spiritual development. Efforts are underway in various colleges and universities (for instance, St. John's University in Collegeville, Wellesley College, the University of Pennsylvania, Brown University, New York University, and Fisk University) to promote students' spiritual growth and development. I touch on some aspects of these programs next in this chapter and have drawn attention to issues separating college men and women in these matters.

These college programs to promote spiritual development vary in the extent to which they explicitly link spirituality and religion and vary in the linkage they make between God and spirituality. Many programs celebrate the religious pluralism and diversity that characterize the typical campus. At their core, these programs promote self-awareness, interconnectedness, and community involvement. While some programs express belief in God, they are tolerant of different understandings of God, including agnosticism and atheism.

These college programs represent responses to the student press for spiritual development, and they portray spirituality as holistic. These programs promote

- connecting deeply with oneself and with others;
- searching for the ultimate purpose and meaning of existence;
- experiencing life as an interconnected whole;
- detaching from blanket investment in materialism;
- opening oneself to creativity;
- appreciating life's mystery.

While spiritual development programs start with the premise that holism marks spirituality, they promote models of human development that run counter to, if not in opposition to, traditional views of masculinity. These traditional views of masculinity extol emotional separation and autonomy, downplay interrelationships, and raise suspicions about intuition and expression of feelings. The impetus seems to be to design some programs specifically for college men and design other programs specifically for college women. In my way of thinking, holism would benefit from mixed-gender spiritual development groups allowing sharing from both females and males. Perhaps the first hurdle, however, is for these programs to attract participants and ensure all participants get a chance to voice their ideas.

Suspicion of traditional views of masculinity presents an issue that has gnawed at me ever since I read the arguments from the developers of spiritual development programs for college men. There is ideologically influenced thinking in this distrust of traditional views of masculinity endorsing independence, self-reliance, rationality, and control of emotions. A corollary matter that also has me concerned is whether the spiritual development of men is seen to require a standpoint that basically undercuts and disenfranchises instrumental approaches to grieving. I admit that I am very interested in programs to foster college men's spiritual development, and indeed would have welcomed being part of such intentional growth when an undergraduate, but I have reservations about what strikes me as ideological blinders.

Historical Black colleges and universities (such as Fisk) pursue character formation of college men and women, understand that spirituality is integrally part of this formation, and amalgamate community service into the educational programs students follow. Spiritual development is at the core of the historically Black colleges and universities, and from all I can determine, establishing special programs at these schools to promote spiritual development is unnecessary: These colleges and universities locate spiritual development within the center of their educational mission.

## College Men

When examining the help-seeking behavior of college students (see Chapter 2), I learned about the pervasive repudiation male college students express for college programs designed to help them when these programs challenge the males' views of masculinity. These views of masculinity primarily emphasize individual control and autonomy. College males' attitudes toward programs designed to explore spirituality mirror their unease with values that they see attack what it means to be masculine.

College men are caught in a tension, captured well in these words from a paper focused on one university's efforts to include males in programs focused on spiritual development.

> The standards of American masculinity thus make it difficult for college men to acknowledge their spiritual natures to others, especially to other men. Yet research clearly indicates that spirituality is vitally important to the great majority of them. Compounding the situation is the fact that most colleges and universities, as bastions of secularity, do little to acknowledge and nurture the spiritualities of young people.
>
> (Longwood, Muesse, & Schipper, 2004, p. 88)

The intentional program at St. John's University (Collegeville, MN) begins with the value of personal choice: Students are invited to participate in a 4-year, small-group exploration of their spirituality. The groups are limited to 10 students, are facilitated by two adults, meet every 2–3 weeks for around an hour, and stress the utter expectation of confidentiality. Each meeting centers on one student's story about his personal spiritual journey. Time is set aside to allow other group members the opportunity to ask questions and share what the person's story has elicited in them. Themes shape the process through the 4 years. For instance, in the first year the theme is to reflect on the statement "Who I am and what I believe." In the second year, the groups examine the theme of relationships, beliefs, and self-understanding. The third year theme is left to the group to pick; some themes that have been examined are authenticity and beauty. The fourth year involves reflecting on what the group experience has produced. External evaluators report very favorably on the effectiveness of this program in the growth and development of the participants and on how the groups are an integral part of the educational mission of St. John's.

## College Women

The University of Pennsylvania developed a group format for women to share and explore their spirituality. Unlike the St. John's University 4-year program, which is offered to all students from their arrival on campus, the University of Pennsylvania screened applicants to ensure that participants' intents met the objectives of the group to

> explore the ways in which women develop spiritually, the links between mental, physical, emotional, and spiritual health, creating space for spiritual exploration in our lives, and sharing of our experiences as we seek to find our own unique paths
>
> (Soet & Martin, 2007, p. 91)

The group met four times over one semester with eight women students and two facilitators, and then due to demand another group met over the summer. The meetings ran about 90 minutes each session. Exercises were used in each session to kindle thinking about and discussions of what spirituality meant to each participant. There was also interest in what role ritual played in persons' lives, as well as interest in exploring and sharing each participant's "unique perspective on spirituality, community, and one's spiritual journey or path" (p. 92). Themes examined in the groups included the place of loss and grief to stimulate spiritual quests, as well as the need to accept ambiguity when on a spiritual quest. An indication of satisfaction with the group was that members remained in touch with one another and saw one another as integral members of their support system.

Wellesley College developed a program to foster spiritual growth and campus acceptance of diversity. This program intentionally drew on literature differentiating women's growth in self-identity from men's growth. The focus for female self-identity was seen to be relational and affective, and growth in spirituality was seen as part of growth in self-identity. (I wonder if the program participants at St. John's University in Collegeville would disagree with these statements; their student body is all male). Crucial to the acceptance of this program on the Wellesley campus was the explicit understanding that the program's *raison d'être* was embedded in the educational mission of Wellesley College.

One aspect of the program struck me. It was the question asked of the college women to share personal moments of meaning that occurred in classes. The women told stories of being transformed, of being "awakened to a deeper understanding of themselves, of others around them, and of the world" (Kazanjian & Laurence, 2007, p. 4). I want to call your attention once again to Attig's existential phenomenological template in which he says bereavement requires us to reconstruct our relationships with ourselves, with others, and with the world. There is clearly precedent to see that this process of being transformed through bereavement is integrally a spiritual endeavor.

## COLLEGE STUDENT BEREAVEMENT AND SPIRITUALITY

I believe that bereavement triggers spiritual change in some persons. This thesis stems from the notion that bereavement is a life crisis and returns us to the topic of assumptive worlds. Crises trigger spiritual change, but only those crises (a) that allow time for reflection, (b) whose aftermath is forever colored by the experience of the crisis, (c) that integrally challenge a person's assumptive world, and in conjunction with point "c", (d) that induce a psychological disequilibrium that resists readily being stabilized.

Bereavement affects our spirituality when it challenges our very assumptions about the meaning of human existence, that is, challenges our assumptive worlds. Empirical evidence has made it plain that bereavement does not shatter the assumptive worlds of the plurality, even the majority, of grieving individuals. But there are many, perhaps up to 40% in what Bonanno calls a recovery trajectory and maybe 10% in an enduring grief trajectory, whose intense and continuing distress over the death that has happened provides the catalyst for rethinking what they believe, for reshaping their assumptive worlds, and, in short, for transforming their spiritual identities. We need to allow grieving students the opportunity to explore and share with others how bereavement has stimulated them to a new understanding of human existence. We can take a possible lead from the programs developed at colleges to help students explore their spirituality, such as asking them to share their stories about moments of meaning in their grief.

## An Exercise for Reflecting on One's Interpersonal Connectedness

One aspect of spiritual identity has to do with interpersonal relationships. We see this aspect in functional definitions of spirituality that underscore interconnectedness, and we see it regarding bereavement theory in Attig's phenomenological analysis that calls attention to grieving as a matter of relearning our relationship with others. It is possible to combine these two points of view and engage bereaved students in an exercise asking them to examine their interconnectedness to others.

The inspiration for this exercise comes from work done to understand and overcome burnout. Persons who have burned out suffer from a holistic calamity that affects them in the same dimensions of human existence identified earlier when talking of the pervasive effects of bereavement. One consequence of burnout is an altered assumptive world. Note that I am not claiming that burnout and bereavement are identical, but am pointing out that each impacts the human person multidimensionally. Burnout affects persons physically (fatigue), behaviorally (inordinate effort to accomplish simple tasks), emotionally (frustration and anger), cognitively (self-deprecating thoughts), interpersonally (increasing isolation from others), and spiritually (cynicism, hopelessness, and helplessness).

One process of preventing burnout and of recovering from burnout involves interpersonal relationships. You may recall from the chapter in which bereavement is considered a stressful life event, that models of coping with life crises emphasize the importance of remaining in contact with other persons. Here is a simple exercise, taken from burnout literature produced by the Alban Institute, to enable bereaved college students (a) to reflect on their support systems and (b) to identify gaps in those systems.

The student takes a sheet of paper and fills it out twice: once to identify persons in the student's life who provide the actions identified on the paper, and then to identify persons for whom the student provides these actions. See Figure 12.1 for a suggested template. Once completed, the templates offer opportunities for discussion and for review of gaps in one's interconnectedness.

## Religion and Spirituality as Means of Coping

We know that spirituality and religion help some people cope with bereavement by providing a plausible way to accept what has happened. Spirituality and religion help grievers to place the loss in a larger context

Ask yourself: Whose names would I put into the various cells of the chart as the persons who do these things for me?

| Actions of Persons Who Support Me | Names of Persons Who Support Me in These Ways | | |
|---|---|---|---|
| Level with me | | | |
| Care enough to hold me accountable | | | |
| Ask me difficult questions | | | |
| Enjoy me | | | |
| Give me a sense of my own worth | | | |
| Affirm that I am competent while also allowing me to ask for help | | | |
| Evoke the best in me | | | |

Ask yourself: For whom do I do these things? Whose names would I put into the various cells of the chart as the persons for whom I do these things?

| Actions Whereby I Support Other People | Names of Persons I Support in These Ways | | |
|---|---|---|---|
| Level with the person | | | |
| Care enough to hold the person accountable | | | |
| Ask difficult questions | | | |
| Enjoy the person | | | |
| Give the person a sense of their own worth | | | |
| Affirm that he/she is competent while also allowing the person to ask for help | | | |
| Evoke the best in that person | | | |

**FIGURE 12.1**   An exercise to reflect on one's interpersonal connectedness.

that says all is well, even if persons find it difficult to understand what could be the purpose behind the death that so distresses them. However, it is not simply a straightforward matter that religion proves a helpful coping mechanism. For some persons religion is not helpful, and for some others it produces distress. One can imagine scenarios in which religion would prove distressing rather than helpful: people who believe the person they love is now in hell; someone whose fervent and devout trust that God would protect a loved one was shattered when the person died; a person who cannot fathom how a good God allows people to endure excruciating agony or to drift into dementia; a person who finds religion judges them rather than gives solace.

In my longitudinal study of college student bereavement at Kansas State University, the participants clustered into one of three groups regarding how helpful religion was as a means of coping with their loss: Nearly half said religion proved helpful, about one-third said it was not helpful, and not quite one-fifth said it was distressing. Students who found religion helpful trusted that their loved one was safe with God and discounted the notion that the death had been meaningless; they were willing to wait for the ultimate answer about the meaning to be shown them. They believed in God's plan, and no one was lost to God's goodness. They were part of a cohort of believers with whom they shared their views.

The bereaved students for whom religion did not prove helpful were much more likely than other bereaved students to be bothered by (a) keeping their grief to themselves, (b) working through their grief by themselves, (c) trying not to think about the death, and (d) keeping busy. Bereaved students for whom religion was distressing (a) had difficulty accepting the death, (b) expressed they felt apart from their friends, (c) felt different from their friends, (d) felt uncomfortable around their friends, and (e) remained concerned that something bad was going to happen.

You can see that the portrait of bereaved students for whom religion was not helpful depicts intuitive grievers. I am not saying that no intuitive grievers find religion helpful, but these college students who did not find religion helpful in dealing with grief were persons for whom grief becomes meaningful when it is shared. Quite apparently they did not find meaningful sharing their grief in a venue imposing a religious interpretation on their experience of loss.

Bereaved college students who found religion distressing may well have been in the midst not only of bereavement over a death but in the crux of another profound loss, the loss of their religious faith. Students like them present vulnerable individuals amenable to guidance and support, hopefully from persons who are informed, tolerant, and accepting. There are opportunities embedded in these crises with religion for intentional programs attentive to the students' needs.

One fundamental way that spirituality and religion provide effective help is by enabling the person to enact one of the primary adaptive tasks of coping, namely, to establish the meaning and personal significance of a life crisis. Spiritual and religious beliefs can enable the person to weather the discrepancy that emerges when a life event (in this case, someone's death) does not match one's global beliefs. Being able to find meaning, that is, establishing the meaning and personal significance, of the death and of one's grief means fundamentally resolving the discrepancy and means keeping one's assumptive world intact, even when that means constructing a new assumptive world.

## CONCLUDING COMMENTS

College students desire spiritual growth, primarily in areas of establishing purpose and developing a core set of beliefs about what makes life ultimately meaningful. For some students, their growth as persons is mirrored in spiritual development. Key indicators of such changes in spirituality over time center on self-understanding, connectedness to others, and active involvement in the world. The correspondence is striking between these key indicators of spirituality and the markers of recovery from bereavement identified by existential phenomenologists. A person's spirituality is manifested in fundamental beliefs the person takes for granted about being human. A name for such beliefs is the assumptive world.

Functioning productively and harmoniously seems contingent on accepting one's assumptive world. At their core, assumptive worlds embrace what gives meaning and purpose to people's lives. Life crises can place assumptive worlds at risk, and when this upheaval happens a person undergoes a spiritual crisis. Such events are by no means assured of working out well.

The prototypical crisis of bereavement can lead to a shattered assumptive world, especially when the death seems unfair, horrifying, and meaningless. Growth and transformation in spiritual identity may be prompted when an assumptive world no longer can be held with any integrity. Religion provides beliefs and rituals that some persons find helpful when coping with bereavement. Clearly, such is not the case for everyone, particularly for persons distressed by the harsh judgments that emanate from some religious understandings.

College programs focused on students' spiritual development have sprung up across many campuses. These programs vary in the extent to which they link religion and spirituality, but common to all the programs are objectives to promote self-understanding, interpersonal connections, and community involvement. A fundamentally important intervention in these programs is to ask students to relate moments of meaning experienced in the classroom and in other venues.

A link between this campus orientation toward spiritual development and the prevalence of college student bereavement is the elegant analysis of grieving found in existential phenomenological analysis: Recovering from bereavement requires grievers to relearn their relationship to self, to others, and to the world. In addition, part of bereavement is building a new narrative about one's life. Asking persons to reflect on and share moments of meaning in dealing with their grief is one way to build these new narratives. In short, recovery from bereavement is a holistic process, as is spiritual growth and development, and for some persons recovery from bereavement involves spiritual growth and development, a shifting in their assumptive worlds.

## NOTE

1. Portions of this chapter appeared in *Death Studies*, 1999, *23*, 485–493.

## FURTHER READING

Attig, T. (1995). *How we grieve: Relearning the world*. New York: Oxford University Press.

Balk, D. E. (1999). Bereavement and spiritual change. *Death Studies, 23*, 485–493.

Balk, D. E., & Hogan, N. S. (1995). Religion, spirituality, and bereaved adolescents. In D. W. Adams & E. J. Deveau (Eds.), *Helping children and adolescents cope with death and bereavement* (pp. 61–88). Amityville, NY: Baywood.

Bonanno, G. A. (2009). *The other side of sadness: What the new science of bereavement tells us about life after loss*. New York: Basic Books.

Bryant, A. N. (2007). Gender differences in spiritual development during the college years. *Sex Roles, 56*, 835–846.

Bryant, A. N. (2009). College experiences and spiritual outcomes: An interview with UCLA Spirituality in Higher Education project director Jennifer Lindholm. *Journal of College and Character, 10*(3), 1–6.

Cook, S. W., Borman, P. D., Moore, M. A., & Kunkel, M. A. (2000). College students' perceptions of spiritual people and religious people. *Journal of Psychology and Theology, 28*, 125–137.

Frankl, V. E. (1984). *Man's search for meaning: An introduction to logotherapy* (3rd ed.). New York: Simon & Schuster.

Freedman, J., & Combs, G. (1996). *Narrative therapy: The social construction of preferred realities.* New York: W. W. Norton.

Hays, J. C., & Hendrix, C. C. (2008). The role of religion in bereavement. In M. S. Stroebe, R. O. Hannson, H. Schut, & W. Stroebe (Eds.), *Handbook of bereavement research and practice: Advances in theory and intervention* (pp. 327–348). Washington, DC: American Psychological Association.

Kauffman, J. (Ed.). (2001). *Loss of the assumptive world: A theory of traumatic loss.* New York: Routledge.

Kazanjian, V., & Laurence. P. (2007). The journey toward multi-faith community on campus: The religious and spiritual life program at Wellesley College. *Journal of College and Character, 9*(2), 1–12.

Klass, D. (2007). Religion and spirituality in loss, grief, and mourning. In D. E. Balk, C. Wogrin, G. Thornton, & D. Meagher (Eds.), *Handbook of thanatology: The essential body of knowledge for the study of death, dying, and bereavement* (pp. 121–129). Northbrook, IL: The Association for Death Education and Counseling.

Lindholm, J. A. (2007). Spirituality in the academy: Reintegrating our lives and the lives of our students. *About Campus, 12*(4), 10–17. Retrieved October 12, 2010, from www.interscience.wiley.com

Longwood, W. M., Muesse, M. W., & Schipper, W. C. (2004). Men, spirituality, and the collegiate experience. In G. E. Kellom (Ed.), *Developing effective programs and services for college men. New Directions for Student Services, 107*, 87–95.

Macquarrie, J. (1966). *Principles of Christian theology.* New York: Scribners.

Maslach, C. (1982). *Burnout: The cost of caring.* Englewood Cliffs, NJ: Prentice-Hall.

McDermond, M. V., Jackson, A. R., & Curtis, J. A. (2001). Religion, spirituality, and historically black colleges and universities. In V. M. Miller & M. M. Ryan (Eds.), *Transforming campus life: Reflections on spirituality and religious pluralism* (pp. 89–95). New York: Peter Lang.

Miller, V. M., & Ryan, M. M. (Eds.). (2001). *Transforming campus life: Reflections on spirituality and religious pluralism.* New York: Peter Lang.

Neimeyer, R. A. (Ed.). (2001). *Meaning reconstruction and the experience of loss.* Washington, DC: American Psychological Association.

Oswald, R. M. (1991). *Clergy self-care: Finding a balance for effective ministry.* Washington, DC: The Alban Institute.

Soet, J., & Martin, H. (2007). Women and spirituality: An experiential group for female graduate students. *Journal of College Counseling, 10*, 90–96.

Wortmann, J. H., & Park, C. L. (2008). Religion and spirituality in adjustment following bereavement: An integrative review. *Death Studies, 32,* 703–736.

Yihong, F. (2001). Creating a learning community and the core values of spirituality. In V. M. Miller & M. M. Ryan (Eds.), *Transforming campus life: Reflections on spirituality and religious pluralism* (pp. 231–243). New York: Peter Lang.

Zinnbauer, B. J., & Pargament, K. J. (2005). Religiousness and spirituality. In R. F. Paloutzian & C. L. Park (Eds.), *Handbook of the psychology of religion and spirituality* (pp. 21–42). New York: Guilford.

# *Conclusion*

The pragmatic intent behind writing this book comes to a close in the book's final chapter. I review the plan I followed, and I discuss the place of hope in the overall reason for writing the book. It is important to keep in mind that hope is a finite human virtue and that it is realized when intelligent, pragmatic persons of good will and vision collaborate to make something specific happen.

# *Hope*

One of the teachers I liked a great deal during my doctoral days at the University of Illinois at Urbana-Champaign introduced me to the philosophy of science. Among his articulate presentations about this complex field of scholarship, I particularly remember two statements: "writing is an extension of thinking" and "we build our ships while already at sea." I have taken the former statement and run with it as I have developed college curricula and taught college courses; students in my courses will attest they write a lot. This book is an extension of my thinking about many of my professional interests over the past quarter of a century, not only about student bereavement but also about responding to life crises in general and about life on a campus to promote growth, development, and transformation.

The second statement, "we build our ships while already at sea," richly captures the situation facing us as we endeavor to act responsively to help the bereaved college student. We must start with where we are and build from there. There is no unencumbered point where we can begin. We have to start with the buzzing, booming confusion swirling around us. We don't have to accept the status quo, and we can take heart from the student initiatives to address bereavement that sprang up at Georgetown University and led to the National Students of AMF and its chapters on several campuses.

It is useful to learn how official things get done on a campus. Some of the actions I am calling for, such as campus-wide policies addressing needs of bereaved college students, require using official protocol. It is clear that on some campuses there are administrators inclined to help.

This book emerged from the awareness that helping bereaved college students is both an opportunity for colleges and universities and a pragmatic necessity. I now realize that writing the book was informed throughout by what theologians and philosophers call the virtue of hope. In particular, writing this book comes from what the French existential philosopher Gabriel Marcel termed a human disposition to overcome life crises with care for what is in the best interests of the other: In the case of this book, the other refers to the bereaved college student and, secondarily, to the college/university. So, you may want to ask me, "What are you hoping for?"

I hope this book leads to widespread understanding about the prevalence of college student bereavement and the risks bereavement poses for doing well in college. I hope that colleges and universities make intelligent decisions to help students who are bereaved, that professionals on college campuses enact roles responsive to bereaved students, and that bereaved college students realize how much they are not alone. I hope persons step forward at particular campuses to do something of import that will help the bereaved college student.

We need more thinking about college student bereavement. I hope my book stimulates such activity. There is much yet to learn, and I hope people become so engaged. So rather than some suggestion about closure, I chose the title "Hope."

I have not found any book on bereavement and college students. Students who are bereaved told me they looked in vain as well. I hope that bereaved college students will read this book, say it speaks to them, and say they recognize themselves in what the book offers. Campus counselors, mental health practitioners, campus ministers, and student affairs professionals have told me a book on college student bereavement would fill a void. I hope they read this book, find it useful, and identify ways to help bereaved college students.

## THE CRUX OF THE MATTER

The point of this book is to set forth a reasoned set of arguments for assisting bereaved college students. To make this point I constructed statements on three broad matters that I consider of primary importance:

- To make college student bereavement intelligible by presenting information on how college impacts students, by reviewing the epidemiology of such stress in the lives of college students, by discussing the substance and process of human responses to irreplaceable loss, and by looking at college student responses to bereavement.

- To offer a reasonable basis for implementing policies and practices in the best interests of bereaved college students and in the best interests of the university.
- To provide conceptual scaffolding for persons in student affairs, college counseling, and campus ministry to reach out and help bereaved college students.

## MAKING COLLEGE STUDENT BEREAVEMENT INTELLIGIBLE

Individuality characterizes bereaved college students. However, there are regularities to bereavement; otherwise, we would have no basis for even discussing grieving following a death. Who would understand references that bore absolutely no resemblance to experiences anyone else had shared? Yet, while acknowledging there are patterns to bereavement's impact—even as I intend to present some of these patterns—I want to underscore the importance of appreciating and accepting the individuality of every bereaved college student's story. So, what have we learned about the impact of bereavement on college students?

The most telling piece of information is that a considerable proportion of college students is in the first year of grieving the death of a family member or of a friend. Research data confirm that the prevalence rate ranges from 22% to 30%, and some recent research places the rate at closer to 30%.

Bereavement impacts a college student holistically. Much of what Lindemann uncovered about an acute grief syndrome is manifested in the holistic impact of bereavement on college students. As examples:

- Physical impacts are seen in students' fatigue, vulnerability to illness, sleep problems, chills, and diarrhea.
- Cognitive impacts are seen in students' trouble concentrating on school work, difficulty remembering things, plummeting grades, and problems with intrusive thoughts and images about the death.
- Emotional impacts are seen in students' confusion, guilt, anxiety, sadness, anger, and, in some cases, relief.
- Interpersonal impacts are seen in students' difficulties being around other people, camouflaging their grief lest friends and acquaintances become uncomfortable, and their overall sense of isolation in a life event no one else appreciates.
- Behavioral impacts are seen in students' restless agitation, failure to meet deadlines, problems sticking to a routine, daydreaming, crying, and in some cases lashing out at others for no apparent reason.

■ Spiritual impacts are seen in students' struggles with hopelessness, lack of confidence, disruptions to assumptive worlds, and, in some cases, a growing conviction that human existence has no ultimate meaning.

Not all students experience each of these holistic impacts. Some students' assumptive worlds have not been challenged, and issues of confusion or absurdity don't have any play in their lives. While upset over the death, some bereaved students move rather quickly into getting on with life and remain productive and functional. The array of impacts I described are going to be seen (a) in students whose bereavement forms what is termed a recovery trajectory and (b) in students in an enduring grief trajectory.

Persons in a recovery trajectory struggle with the distress their loss imposes. The distress spreads out holistically. Their process of grieving is engaging in grief work and engaging in living, and they show increasing signs of recovery over a 2-year span. Persons in an enduring grief trajectory remain stuck in the devastation of their loss and recover when given expert help.

## OFFERING A REASONABLE BASIS FOR CAMPUS POLICIES AND PROCEDURES

It is in the best interests of a college or university to reach out responsively to bereaved students. Bereavement can jeopardize a student's success in school. In some cases bereaved students' grades will crater, resulting in leaving school. So, to promote retention and graduation rates, it is in the primary interest of colleges and universities to assist bereaved students. Looked at pragmatically, assisting this significant proportion of the student body that is in distress affords an opportunity to build loyal alumni.

Jaroslav Pelikan has argued that the idea of a university calls for compassion and care to members in need. I believe this sense of a university can be realized as long as persons on campus have a clear sense of what responses make sense. As has been demonstrated, some persons who are empathic do nothing because they are at a loss over what will help. Several suggestions were given, particularly in Chapter 9, but spread as well throughout the book. Chief goals are to raise the consciousness about college student bereavement, to make the campus a safe place for grieving students (a place where they feel accepted, not disenfranchised, as they oscillate between grieving and living), and to enact policies that allow bereaved students the benefit of the doubt when it comes to such matters as making up course assignments, extending deadlines for course work, and permitting leaves that do not jeopardize matriculation.

## PROVIDING CONCEPTUAL SCAFFOLDING FOR INTERVENTIONS

Several major theorists have been instrumental in the growing awareness we have of bereavement. Ideas from these theorists include grief work; instrumental and intuitive approaches to grieving; relearning the world; the dual-process model of coping with loss; continuing bonds; Leighton's sociocultural framework; and cognitive models of coping with stressful life events. Any of these ideas provide the means for designing intelligently informed interventions.

Examples of interventions were offered, including social support groups, peer counselor training, and educational workshops focused on phenomena of bereavement. In all such interventions guiding principles should be practicality, clarity, and responsiveness to student need.

- Practicality in the sense that interventions must attract participants and be cost effective. The interventions must be shown to be effective, desired, available, and accessible.
- Clarity in the sense that interventions must be grounded in a firm comprehension of bereavement and of college students. The interventions must have a strong theoretical base and be grounded in conceptual frameworks describing what bereavement does.
- Responsiveness to student need in the sense that interventions are developed and recalibrated on the basis of analyses of empirical data gained from the participants. The interventions must have a clear feedback loop that examines objectives in light of program outcomes and unanticipated effects.

## SOME SUGGESTED NEXT STEPS

We will be all the richer when more research examines the phenomenology of college student bereavement, describes the impact of efforts college students employ to deal with bereavement, and evaluates the efficacy of diverse interventions to assist bereaved college students. We will be all the richer when practitioners share with researchers' questions about college student bereavement they want examined; when researchers listen attentively; and when practitioners and researchers collaborate on studies to address the questions important to practitioners.

There is a growing call for bridging the gap separating practitioners and researchers. Collaboration between practitioners and researchers regarding college student bereavement could answer this call. The phenomena of college student bereavement provide an arena abundant in practical and conceptual prospects to bridge the practice–research gap. Here are some prospects that come to mind.

- Longitudinal research to identify the trajectories of college student bereavement. We know from Bonanno's work about resiliency, recovery, and enduring grief trajectories. Do these trajectories encompass college students' experiences of bereavement? What proportion of bereaved students comprises each trajectory?
- Program evaluation to examine the efficacy of interventions aimed at assisting bereaved college students. These evaluation efforts can take the form of randomized clinical trials as well as the form of qualitative studies, such as program evaluations along the lines of responsive evaluation approaches.
- Research programs to examine the impacts of bereavement on college students' cognitive maturation (for instance, movement through William Perry's scheme), spiritual development (for instance, movement through James Fowler's scheme), identity formation (for instance, changes in ego development as portrayed in James Marcia's research and in Ruthellen Josselson's research), and growth in self-efficacy to manage life crises (for instance, self-efficacy development as offered in an amalgamation of Bandura's social learning theory and Moos and Schaefer's cognitive model of coping).
- Case studies to provide rich descriptions of college programs and policies aimed at assisting bereaved college students. Such case studies can look for issues that divide people, strengths such programs have, and areas for needed improvement. A singular goal can be to determine the extent to which particular programs enhance retention and graduation, and, if they exist, programs that have no appreciable impact.
- Assessments to appraise the power of programs to educate campus professionals about bereavement. These educational programs ought to build on the wisdom and practice of identifying cognitive and affective objectives. Program assessments can be focused to determine how well the objectives are achieved, with the proviso of looking for unanticipated and unintended outcomes.

■ Focus groups of bereaved students to identify practical issues they see important to address in terms of dealing with the demands of college and in terms of dealing with the grief that bereavement produces. A template for framing such focus groups comes from the dual-process model with its restoration orientation, its loss orientation, and its notion of oscillation.

■ Qualitative and quantitative procedures to learn more about bereaved college students' uses of the Internet. This generation of traditional-aged college students is tied to digital information and stays connected by means of Facebook and e-mail and text messages. We have a new phrase describing this generation's experience of bereavement: "the Google stage of grief." It is imperative to learn more about how these students cope with bereavement digitally.

## BRINGING THIS BOOK TO A CLOSE

Alexander Leighton noted that cross-sections of the moment possess temporal thickness. One aspect of this temporal thickness is anticipation of the future, that is, what one hopes for and expects. Critical focus on college student bereavement is at its own cross-section of the moment. Several things of positive impact can happen. Some are discussed in Chapter 9. There is no guarantee that the responses of colleges to the data about the prevalence of college student bereavement will lead to the actions posed in Chapter 9. I hope a plethora of actions responsive to bereaved college students do happen.

On our side is the fact that greater awareness of and understanding about issues central to bereavement and college students is taking hold. Several persons see that campus responses to college student bereavement are embedded within the university mission. That awareness provides some hope for leverage. I hope that bereavement on the college campus becomes a matter of serious discussion and planning by the various stakeholders involved. These stakeholders include student affairs professionals, college counselors, campus ministers, and academic officers. Not the least, these stakeholders include the bereaved college students.

I hope decision makers on college campuses see that college student bereavement presents an opportunity for universities to offer care and compassion. In an earlier draft of this chapter, I used the term *obligation* to denote college responses to student bereavement. Offering care and compassion toward bereaved college students won't happen because some of us think it is the right thing to do. It won't happen because some of us maintain it is in the best interests of the university. One of the next steps is to energize some pragmatic persons who know how to get things done on a campus. I hope this book has some influence in leading persons to promote such changes.

## FURTHER READING

Balk, D. E. (2007). Bridging the practice-research gap. *The Forum, 33*(1), 1, 3–4.

Bandura, A. (1997). *Self-efficacy: The exercise of control.* New York: W. H. Freeman.

Bloom, B. S., Madaus, G. F., & Hasting, J. T. (1981). *Evaluation to improve learning.* New York: McGraw-Hill.

Bonanno, G. A. (2009). *The other side of sadness: What the new science of bereavement tells us about life after loss.* New York: Basic Books.

Fowler, J. W. (1981). *Stages of faith: The psychology of human development and the quest for meaning.* San Francisco, CA: Harper & Row.

Josselson, R. (1987). *Finding herself: Pathways to identity development in women.* San Francisco, CA: Jossey-Bass.

Kerstiens, F. (1968). Hope. In K. Rahner (Ed.), *Sacramentum mundi: An encyclopedia of theology* (Vol. 3, pp. 650–655). New York: Herder and Herder.

Lynch, W. (1965). *Images of hope: Imagination as healer of the hopeless.* Baltimore, MD: Helicon.

Marcel, G. (1951). Sketch of a phenomenology and a metaphysic of hope. In G. Marcel, *Homo viator: Introduction to a metaphysic of hope* (pp. 29–69). Translated by E. Craufurd. Chicago, IL: Henry Regnery Company.

Marcia, J. E. (1980). Identity in adolescence. In J. Adelson (Ed.), *Handbook of adolescent psychology* (pp. 159–187). New York: Wiley.

Marcia, J. E., & Friedman, M. L. (1970). Ego identity status in college women. *Journal of Personality, 38,* 249–263.

Moos, R. H., & Schaefer, J. A. (1986). Life transitions and crises: A conceptual overview. In R. H. Moos (Ed.), *Coping with life crises: An integrated approach* (pp. 3–28). New York: Plenum.

Neimeyer, R. A., Winokuer, H., Harris, D., & Thornton, G. (Eds.). (2011). *Grief and bereavement in contemporary society: Bridging research and practice.* New York: Routledge.

Pelikan, J. (1992). *The idea of the university: A reexamination.* New Haven, CT: Yale University Press.

Perry, W. G. (1970). *Forms of intellectual and ethical development during the college years.* New York: Holt, Rinehart, & Winston.

Sofka, C. J. (2009). Adolescents, technology, and the Internet: Coping with loss in the digital world. In D. E. Balk & C. A. Corr (Eds.), *Adolescent encounters with death, bereavement, and coping* (pp. 155–173). New York: Springer Publishing.

Stake, R. E. (1967). The countenance of educational evaluation. *Teachers College Record, 68,* 523–540.

Stake, R. E. (1975). *Program evaluation, particularly responsive evaluation.* Paper No. 5 in occasional paper series (Reports-Research/Technical No. ED 163060). Kalamazoo, MI: Kalamazoo School of Education, Western Michigan University.

Stake, R. E. (2004). *Standards-based & responsive evaluation.* Thousand Oaks, CA: Sage.

Stake, R. E. (1995). *The art of case study research.* Thousand Oaks, CA: Sage.

Stratton-Lake, P. (1998). Hope. In E. Craig (Ed.), *Routledge encyclopedia of philosophy* (Vol. 4, pp. 507–510). New York: Routledge.

Stroebe, M., & Schut, H. (1999). The dual process model of coping with bereavement: Rationale and description. *Death Studies, 23,* 197–224.

# Afterword

## A Letter to Bereaved College Students

Hello, my name is David Balk. I thought it best to let you know a little about the person who wrote this book on bereavement, grief, and college students.

I have worked in two community mental health centers in Arizona and taught college students for over 20 years. I received my PhD in Counseling Psychology from the University of Illinois at Urbana-Champaign. My research interests have focused primarily on bereavement and adolescents, and for many years I have been interested in bereavement among college students. Some of the courses I have taught are Death and the Family, Bereavement, Adolescent Development, Coping with Life Crises, and Helping Skills. I am a member of the Association for Death Education and Counseling and a member of the Mental Health Advisory Board for National Students of AMF, an organization started by bereaved college students for bereaved college students. I am a Professor in the Department of Health and Nutrition Sciences at Brooklyn College.

But, to quote my daughter, all work and no play make for a rather dull existence. I also enjoy seeing movies, reading books on a wide variety of topics, and watching sporting events such as baseball and football. My favorite music is jazz, but I also like a variety of other music as well, including classical and rock from the '60s and '70s. My wife is an expert in many things, including computers, and it is rumored that she can fix anything. You will have read some more about her and her importance in my life in some of the chapters of the book. My daughter is a very gifted teacher, and I find I miss her a lot now that she has moved out and is living on her own. She married 4 years ago. We both enjoy many types of movies and often watch movies when we get together.

If you are a student and reading this book, it is likely someone you care for has died. You are dealing with some very difficult times, and you possibly feel you are alone. Grief over someone's death often is intense and lasts longer than you would have anticipated. Persons not touched by bereavement have no comprehension of how intense and long-lasting grief can be.

Bereavement is the word that identifies being in a state of loss, and grief is the word we use to name our responses to bereavement. You meet all the criteria for being bereaved if

1. You care deeply for someone;
2. Death has taken this person from you forever;
3. Now you are left to grieve.

There are many more bereaved students on your campus than you or other persons realize. Research has shown again and again that between 22% and 30% of college students are in the first 12 months of grieving the death of a family member or a friend. It is clear that there are many students coping with grief, and thus you are not alone. Linking up with persons who understand your sorrow and anger and confusion—and who understand the many other aspects that make up the impacts of bereavement—is more possible than grieving college students realize.

Bereavement can be scary because of the intensity of the feelings. For awhile, for instance in the first 4–6 months following the death, these intense reactions reveal themselves in many ways.

1. Bereavement affects a person physically. The bereaved person often experiences fatigue, chills, shortness of breath, problems sleeping, and diarrhea. Illnesses are more possible because the distress of bereavement noticeably weakens the immune system. Bereaved persons sigh a lot.
2. Bereavement affects a person emotionally. The bereaved person may feel angry, lonely, afraid, confused, anxious, guilty, and deeply sad. The world seems an empty place.
3. Bereavement affects a person cognitively. The bereaved person has difficulty keeping focused, is flooded with thoughts about the person who died, has trouble remembering things, and finds it difficult to concentrate.
4. Bereavement affects a person interpersonally. The bereaved person may find it difficult to be around other people. Other people become uncomfortable when bereaved persons reveal their grief. Many

bereaved students have said it is better to camouflage their grief rather than lose friends. The death of a mother or father can prompt students—particularly females—to think they should leave school and be with their families.

5. Bereavement affects a person behaviorally. The bereaved person may be agitated and restless, unable to stick to a routine. Daydreaming is common. Crying is not unusual, and there are some students who have told me they sobbed uncontrollably at times; they wanted to stop but could not.

6. Bereavement affects a person spiritually. The bereaved person may question God's goodness or God's existence. The purpose and meaning of life may become questionable. Hope may be thin, and self-doubt may dominate the person.

It is important to know what bereavement does and what grief reactions are like. There are various ideas that have been applied to explain bereavement. A very powerful explanation is that human beings become bereaved over someone's death because we first became emotionally attached to that person. If we did not have this bond, it would not matter to us if the person was not in our lives.

Looking to understand what coping with your loss means, you may turn to the notion that grieving develops in five stages. While I think there are much better understandings of grief beyond that it occurs in five stages, I am not going to argue you should not use it. If it helps you make sense of what otherwise is chaotic and confusing, then it serves a useful purpose.

In this book, I present some other explanations about the process of grieving that you may find meaningful. What matters above all is (a) to find a way of coping that allows you to mourn your loss and (b) to remain engaged in the world of the living. You don't have to feel distressed always, but at some times it may be important to be in touch with memories that are painful. People who are grieving also find moments of laughter and joy when they remember the person and the times they had together. It is common for there to be laughter even in the midst of grieving. What happens naturally is for grievers to feel the sorrow of their loss, to remain engaged with living, and even to have a good time now and then.

Some persons deal with bereavement by letting other persons know how they feel. They find persons with whom they can talk about their grief. For these persons grief is real when shared. These persons want to talk about their feelings and to listen to other persons sharing their experiences.

For other persons coping with bereavement is a private matter, and open expression of feelings is definitely not appealing. These persons prefer activity over talking. They may become involved in exercise, in community projects, or in building a memorial to the person who died. They will think about the loss and what it means to them, but they have no desire to join others and talk about grief.

These two approaches to grieving are normal. Women often prefer sharing their grief with others, and men often prefer keeping grief private. But there are exceptions. There are women who prefer to keep their grief to themselves, and men who want to talk with others. It can be a strain on a relationship when two persons are grieving the same loss but each with a different approach to grieving. This strain can be found in families when people do not accept that there are different approaches to grieving.

We know that most persons recover from bereavement. Recovery does not occur quickly, and it occurs in stops and starts. Sometimes the intensity of grief goes away, only later to return in frenzy. When a person has had a whole week without the distress of grief and feels confident that grief is finally over, it can be scary and disheartening when the feelings return. I will share a story told by a woman whom I met when I was a student at the University of Illinois.

> Think of all of human existence taking place on a vast beach. There is an enormous body of water ebbing and flowing into the beach. The water is death. There are persons everywhere on the beach, some in small groups, some in larger groups, and some by themselves. Some persons are right down at the water's edge. Some are on high ground where the water seldom reaches. Every now and then the water rushes in and grabs someone or a group of persons and drags them out to sea. Eventually, the water throws the persons back up on the beach, where they gasp and struggle. They have been touched by death, but are not dead. They are dripping wet, and eventually they are mostly dried off. But from then on they will never be completely dry again, even if it is only the soles of their feet that are slightly damp. Now and then, high tide returns to engulf the person, but these moments occur less and less often. But when they happen, it is like the whole experience has returned in fury. It is the people on high ground who have never been in the water who ask, "Are you still talking about being wet?"

To be honest, some bereaved persons do not experience the long, drawn-out distress considered the typical reaction to the death of a loved one. The death bothers them, but they are able fairly quickly to resume a functioning life, little different than it was before the death. These persons are not buffeted around by intense feelings of grief. If this description fits you and you wonder if there is something wrong with you, know that it is how many persons respond to bereavement. It does not mean you are uncaring.

I had many reasons for writing this book. I wrote this book because growth and development of college students matter to me. I wrote the book because I know that bereavement can interfere dramatically with a student's growth and development. I wrote the book because there was nothing available about college student bereavement. I wrote the book to overcome the perception of many bereaved students that they are alone in their grief.

While I aimed the book primarily to reach professionals on campus who are in positions to help grieving students, I hope students will find the book useful. I welcome learning from you your reactions to the book, what works for you, and what needs to be fixed.

David E. Balk
Brooklyn College
dbalk@brooklyn.cuny.edu

# Index

*Note*: Page references followed by "*f*" and "*t*" denote figures and tables, respectively.

Academic confidence, gender differences in, 11
Acceptance, of the reality of loss, 56, 74, 150
Accidents, as cause of death, 92, 96–97
Accommodation, meaning of, 51
Acute grief syndrome, 32, 43, 58, 101, 122, 124, 245
Adaptation, by family, 134–137
Adolescents
  and coping with death, 135
  homicides, 97–98
  identity formation in, 14–15
  suicide risk, 99, 100
Alban Institute, 234
Alcoholics Anonymous, 156
American Psychiatric Association, 103
Anticipated deaths, bereavement and, 87–89, 93–95
Anticipatory grief and mourning, 93–94, 95
Appraisal-focused coping, 72–73
  avoidance or denial, 73
  cognitive redefinition, 72–73
Asian American students, help-seeking behavior, 26
Assimilation, meaning of, 51
Association for Death Education and Counseling (ADEC), 183–184
"Assumptive worlds," 221–225, 233, 237, 246

Attachment to deceased loved one, 40–41, 44–46
Attendance problems, in support groups, 171–172
Attentive listening, 137, 156, 179, 205
Attig, Tom, 183, 214, 216, 229, 233, 234
Axen, Kathleen, xii, 7
Axen, Kenneth, xii

Balk, Janet, 87, 88, 91
Balk, Mary Ann, xii, 87, 202–203, 205
Bandura, Albert, 248
Barnett, Mark, 215
Baugher, Bob, 100–104
Behavioral impact of bereavement, 34, 124, 245
Bereavement and causes of death, 87–105
Bereavement resolution. *See* Recovery following bereavement
  biochemical stress and, 66
Berman, Jeffrey, xii, 60
Body, viewing of, 101
Boland, Chris, 88
Boland, Jeanne, 87, 88, 89
Bonanno, George, 54–55, 59, 147, 148, 209, 222, 223, 233, 248
Bowlby, John, 40–42, 60, 147, 183

Calhoun, Lawrence, 217, 218
Campus policies on bereavement, 167
  basis for change, 246–247
  changing, 168
  faculty actions, 173–174
  interventions, 174–184
    education programs, 179–184
    Moos and Schaefer model of
      coping, 176–179
    National Students of AMF Support
      Network, 173
    policy decisions, 184–189
    "safe place" on, 154–155
    support groups, 170–173
Camus, Albert, 3, 20, 226
Child abuse, and adolescent
  homicides, 98
Clinical depression, and bereavement,
  comparison, 39, 195
Cognitive impacts of bereavement,
  33, 126–127, 245
  avoidance and denial, 73, 178
Cognitive redefinition, 72–73, 178
Communication, 137, 138
Community, sense of, in college, 13
Community service, 157
Compassionate Friends, 73,
  92, 139, 156
Computer games, as bereavement
  aid, 24, 174
Conceptual complexity, handling
  of, 17–18
Concurrent life stressors, 132–133
Connectedness, spiritual identity
  and, 234, 235f, 245–246
Continuing bonds with deceased,
  44, 45–46, 58, 65, 94
Coping with bereavement,
  4, 42–58, 147
  acceptance of reality of loss, 150
  benefit finding, 53
  Bonanno, George, 54–55
  comfortable situations, 155–157
  discrepant coping styles, 135

disenfranchised grief, 48–50
dual process model of loss, 46, 47f
  emotion focused, 74–75
  expression of grief, encouraging,
    149–150
  family and, 137–139
  holistic impact, 149
  identity change, 53–54
  and instrumental grieving,
    47–48, 49t
  Kübler-Ross, Elisabeth, 55–58
  Lindemann, Erich, 42–43
  meaning, restoration of, 50–52
  permission to grieve, 149
  safe places, creation of, 153–155
  Worden, J. William, 43–46
Coping with stress, model for, 68–77
Coping styles, 135–136
Corr, Charles, xii, 152, 217
Creative arts therapy, 181–183
Crisis management theory, 94
Cross-section of the moment, 79–80
Cultural diversity, and gender
  differences in, 11

Darwin, Charles, 20, 60
Daugherty, Elaine, 88, 89
Daugherty, Jeanne, 88
Daugherty, Roy, 88
Death, anticipated, 93–95
Death, bereavement over, 31,
  215–216
  Bowlby's theory, 40–42
  coping with, 42–58
    benefit finding, 53
    Bonanno, George, 54–55
    disenfranchised grief, 48–50
    identity change, 53–54
    intuitive and instrumental
      grieving, 47–48, 49t
    Kübler-Ross, Elisabeth, 55–58
    Lindemann, Erich, 42–43
    meaning, restoration of, 50–52

sense making, 52–53
Worden, J. William, 43–45
Freud's theory, 39–40
holistic impact of, 31–35
phases of, 41–42
resiliency, 36
spiritual impacts, 34–35
timespan of, 35
trajectories of, 35–38
Death, causes of and bereavement, 87–105
accidents, 96–97
homicides, 97–99
natural causes vs. human action, 93
suicides, 99–104
Death, on-time vs. off-time events, 92–93
Death, preventability, 90–91
Delayed grief, 54, 55, 60
Depression, 56, 103, 215–216
and bereavement, 33, 37, 103
medications for, 102
Development, individual markers of. *See* Individual development, markers of
Digital generation, 21–24
Digital immigrants, 21, 22
Digital natives, 22–24
Disenfranchised grief, 48–50
Doka, Kenneth, 48
Dual process model of coping with loss, 46, 47*f*, 55, 58, 73, 148, 183
Dying, stages of, 55–56

Education programs, 179–183
benefits, 182–183
creative arts, 181–183
dual-process model, workshop based on, 183
implementation plan, 182
peer counselor training, 179–181
Egan, Gerard, 205
Emotional impact of bereavement, 32–33, 125–126, 245

Emotional support, 134, 156
Emotion-focused coping, 74–75
Empathy, and self-disclosure, 198–200
Enduring grief trajectory of bereavement, 37–38, 162, 223–225, 246
Erikson, Erik, 14, 207
Even-related death factors, 90–93
extent of suffering, 92
intentionality, 91–92
natural causes vs. human action, 93
on-time vs. off-time events, 92–93
persons affected, 92
preventability, 90–91

Facilitators, to coping with grief, 176–177
Faculty and student grief, 173–174
Fajgenbaum, David, 74
Faith consciousness, 20–21. *See also* Spiritual development programs
self-identity and, 20, 232–233
Family dynamics, 131–139
communication, 137
concurrent life stressors, 132–133
coping tasks, 137–139
family roles, reassigning, 137–138
perception of the event, 134–137
positive outcomes, 134–135
resources for, 132–133
support, providing, 138–139
Family grief, 132
Family members, death of
causes, 112, 113*t*, 116–117
communication pattern, 112, 114*t*
prevalence of, 111–112, 116
Family, resources for, 132–133
Family roles, reassigning, 137–138
Feifel, H., 216
Fleming, Stephen, xi
Fowler, James, 248
Frankl, Victor, 51

Freud, Sigmund, 39–40, 60, 147, 183, 194–195, 215–216
Friends, death of
  causes, 113, 113*t*, 117
  communication pattern, 113–114, 114*t*
  prevalence, 112–114, 116


Games, computer, as bereavement aid, 24, 174
Gender differences
  in academic engagement, 10–12
  in bereavement, 47
  in completed suicide, 100
  in emotional separation from parents, 10–11
    well-being, sense of, 11
  in help-seeking behavior, 24–25
  in homicides, 98
  in moral reasoning, 18–19
General adaptation syndrome, 66–68, 84
Genogram, 139–143, 140*f*
Gilligan, Carol, 18
Grief, phases of, 41–42
Grief, types of, 215–216
  anticipatory grief, 93–94, 95
  delayed grief, 54, 55, 60
  disenfranchised grief, 48–50
  dyssynchrony, 136
  family grief, 132
  incremental grief, 135
Grief work theory, 46, 55, 58, 60, 65, 93, 147–148, 194–195
Griese, Brian, 205
Guilt
  and acute grief syndrome, 43
  and death preventability, 91
  and suicides, 102


Help-seeking behavior, 24–26, 231
  gender differences in, 24–25
Hogan, Nancy, xi, 45

Holistic impact of bereavement, 31–35, 122–130, 149
  behavioral impacts, 34, 124
  cognitive impacts, 33, 126–127
  emotional impacts, 32–33, 125–126
  interpersonal impacts, 34, 127–129
  physical impacts, 32, 122–123
  spiritual impacts, 34–35, 129–130
Home, as safe place, 153
Homicides, 97–99
  adolescent, 98
  child abuse and, 98
  gender differences in, 98
  prevalence, 97
Hope, 51, 72, 243–251


Identity change/confusion, 14–15, 53–54
Identity formation, 14–15, 27, 228
Immune system, affects of grief, 32, 66
Incremental grief, 135
Individual development, markers of, 14–21
  career choice, 19
  faith consciousness, 20–21
  identity formation, 14–15
  intellectual growth, 15–18
  interpersonal relationships, 21
  moral reasoning, 18–19
Information technology (IT), in digital generation, 23, 24
Insecure attachments, 40–41, 46
Instrumental grieving, 47–48, 49*t*, 69, 174, 183, 195–197
Intellectual growth, 15–18
Intentionality of death, 91–92, 104
Internet, as safe place, 153–154
Interpersonal connectedness, spiritual identity and, 234, 235*f*, 245–246
Interpersonal impact of bereavement, 34, 127–129, 245
Interpersonal process recall (IPR), 180

Interpersonal relationships, 21, 40, 43, 138, 151, 234
  sustaining, 71
Interventions, 39, 204, 247
  education programs, 179–184
  Moos and Schaefer model of coping, 176–179
  planned, 174–184
Intuitive grieving, 47–48, 49t, 69, 135, 174, 195–197, 236

Jordan, Jack, xi, xii, 100–104
Josselson, Ruthellen, 248
Jourard, Sidney, 197–200
  and self-disclosure, 197–198
Judi's House, 205

Kauffman, Jeffrey, 217, 218
Kelly, George, 51, 54
Kennedy, Jacqueline, 69
Klass, Dennis, xi, 44, 45, 226
Kübler-Ross, Elisabeth, 55–58

Leighton, Alexander, 77–82, 149, 213, 216
Lewis, C. S., 152
Life arc, 79, 79f
Life crises literature, bereavement and recovery, 212–214
Lightner, Candy, 205
Lindemann, Erich, 42–43, 47, 58, 93–94, 147, 150, 183, 193–194, 204
Lindholm, Jennifer, 229

Marcia, James, 248
McClintic, Brook, xii, 205, 218
McCoy, Sandra, 215
McNeil, Joan, xi
Meaning making, 50–54, 129, 197, 225–229

Medications for suicide-related anxiety/depression, 102
Mental health problems, and suicide, 99–100
Mental preparation, for loved one's death, 72
Millennials. *See* Digital generation
Moos, Rudolf, 68, 75, 84, 176–179, 248
Moral reasoning, 18–19
Mothers Against Drunk Driving (MADD), 91, 98, 139, 156, 205
Mother Theresa, 20
Multiplier effect. *See* Pile up

National Institute of Mental Health, 155
National Students of AMF Support Network, 73, 74, 92, 156, 157, 173, 174
Neimeyer, Robert, 52
Net generation. *See* Digital generation
Newman, Paul, 196, 214
Nickman, Steven, 40, 45
Noppe, Illene, xii, 184

Offer, Daniel, 215
Oltjenbruns, Kevin, 215
On-time vs. off-time events, 92–93

Paletti, Robin, xii, 217, 218
Parents, gender differences in emotional separation from, 10–11
Parents of Murdered Children, 92
Parents Without Partners, 73, 156
Parkes, Colin Murray, 41, 96
Peer counselor training, 179–181
Pelikan, Jaroslav, 169, 246
Perry, William, 248
Personal construct theory, 51
Personality formation, human, 78–79, 85

Phenomenological analysis, of
  bereavement recovery,
  214–215, 229, 234
Physical impacts of bereavement, 32,
  122–123
"Pile up," 133
Planned interventions, 174–184
  education programs, 179–184
    benefits, 182–183
    creative arts, 181
    dual-process model, workshop
      based on, 183
    implementation plan, creative
      arts, 182
    peer counselor training, 179–181
  Moos and Schaefer model of
    coping, 176–179
Policy decisions of university, 184–189
Posttraumatic stress disorder
  (PTSD), 91, 96
Prevalence of college student
  bereavement, 4, 110, 114–117
  family member's death,
    111–114, 116
  friend's death, 112–114, 116
Project Youth Opportunity (PYO),
  202–203
Prolonged grief disorder. *See*
  Enduring grief trajectory of
  bereavement
Psychological decompensation, 67
Psychological disorder, in support
  group member, 172
Psychological exhaustion, 67–68
Psychological moratorium, in identity
  formation, 15
Psychological stress, 65–66
Purdue University, policy on student
  bereavement, 191


Rabin, Laura, xii, 46, 59
Reality, confronting, 71
Reality, constructing, 51–52

Recovery following bereavement,
  36–37, 158, 162, 222–223, 246.
  *See also* Coping
  empirical research, 215
  indicators of, 211–215
  in life crises literature, 212–214
  meaning of, 210–211, 217
  phenomenological analysis of,
    214–215, 229, 234
  psychosocial model of, 207–208
  research, 193–195
  resistance to, 208–209
Recovery trajectory of bereavement,
  36–37, 158, 162, 246
Reflective judgment, 16–17
"Reframing," 53
Religion
  bereavement and, 234–237
  definition of, 227
  and spirituality, interconnectedness
    between, 225–229
Religious beliefs, 134
Research on bereavement
  recovery, 215
Resiliency, 36, 55, 209, 214, 217–218, 222
Resiliency trajectory of bereavement,
  35, 36, 222
Rogers, Carl, 200, 201
Rosenblatt, Paul, 217, 218


Safe place(s), 153–155
  on campus, 154–155
  Internet as, 153–154
Sandler, Irwin, 217, 218
Schaefer, Jeanne, 68, 75, 84,
  176–179, 248
Schut, Henk, 46
"Scope," definition of, 92
Secure attachment, 40–42, 45–46
Self-concept, 71
Self-confidence, 72
Self-disclosure, 193–205
  empathy, 198–200

fostering, 200–201
instrumental and intuitive
    grievers, 195–197
Jourard, Sidney, 197–198
opportunity to engage in,
    203–204
risks to, 200
Self-discovery, 14–15
Self-efficacy, 71–72
Self-forgiveness, 103
Self-identity, and faith
    consciousness, 20, 232–233
Selye, Hans, 66–68
Sentiments, in bereavement
    resolution, 80, 98, 213
Servaty-Seib, Heather, 185, 186
Shapiro, Ester, 217
Sharing of grief, 5–6, 43, 71, 151, 196,
    200, 203–204, 233, 236
Sibling, death of, 120–121
    holistic impacts in, 121–122
Silences, during support groups, 171
Silverman, Phyllis, 40, 44–45
Social networks/relationships, 139,
    155–156
Social support, 139, 155–156, 176
Sociocultural model for dealing
    with stress, 77–83
    exercise for, 81–82
Somatic responses to bereavement,
    122–123
Spiritual development programs,
    229–233
    for college men, 231–232
    for college women, 232–233
Spiritual impact of bereavement,
    34–35, 129–130, 246
Spirituality, 20–21, 221–238
    "assumptive worlds," 221–225
    identity of, 234, 235f
    and religion, interconnectedness
        between, 225–228, 234–237
    spiritual development programs,
        229–233

for college men, 231–232
for college women, 232–233
St. John's University, spiritual
    development programs at,
    231–232
Stress, 65–66
    human body's reaction to, 66–68
    model for coping with, 68–77
    sociocultural model for dealing
        with, 77–83
Stressful situation, establishing
    personal significance of, 70–71
Stroebe, Margaret, 46
Student engagement, fostering, 12–14
Substance abuse, and suicides, 100
Sudden deaths. *See* Unexpected
    deaths
Suicide(s), 91–92, 99–104
    causes of, 99–100
    completed, gender differences in, 100
    reaction to
        first few days after, 100–101
        first few months after, 102–103
        first few weeks after, 101–102
        first year after, 103–104
    incidence in, 109
    medications for anxiety/
        depression, 102
Support groups, 6, 73, 92, 96, 104,
    155–156, 170–173
    attendance problems, 171–172
    bad advice, 172
    group member domination or
        criticism, 172
    nonproductive silences, 171
    psychological disorder in a group
        member, 172
    running overtime, 173
    superficial discussions, 171
Survivors Network of Those Abused
    by Priests (SNAP), 156
Survivors of Suicide, 156
Sussman, Sheri, xii
Swift, Jonathan, 208

Tedeschi, Richard, 217, 218
Temporal thickness, 79–80, 213, 249
Thinking critically, 16
Toray, Tamina, xii
Tragedy Assistance Program for
 Survivors (TAPS), 92, 98

Unconditional positive regard,
 self-disclosure, 201
Undergraduate experience, 9–14
 gender differences, 10–12
 student engagement, fostering, 12–14
Unexpected deaths, 95–104
 accidents, 96–97
 homicides, 97–99
 suicides, 99–104
University of Pennsylvania, spiritual
 development programs at, 232
University of Wisconsin at Green Bay
 (UWGB), 184–185
 policy on student bereavement,
 185–189

Vehicular accidents, 91, 96–97
Vision of college, 13

Walker, Andrea, 115, 116
Wefald, Jon, 4
Well-being, gender differences in
 sense of, 11
Wellesley College, spiritual
 development programs at,
 232–233
Wiesel, Elie, 214
Winfrey, Oprah, 69
Worden, J. William, 40,
 43–46, 58, 147
Workshops
 about bereavement, 148,
 176, 183, 199
 about coping with bereavement,
 176–179, 183, 199
 using creative arts, 181–183